EXPOSITORY STUDIES IN 1 JOHN

Titles by Ray C. Stedman in the "Discovery Books" Series:

Authentic Christianity (2 Corinthians 2:14–6:13)
Behind History (Parables of Matthew 13)
Death of a Nation (Book of Jeremiah)
Jesus Teaches on Prayer
The Queen and I (Book of Esther)
Riches in Christ (Ephesians 1–3)
The Ruler Who Serves (Mark 1–8)
The Servant Who Rules (Mark 9–16)
Spiritual Warfare (Ephesians 6:10–18)
Understanding Man (Genesis 2–3)
From Guilt to Glory (Romans) Vols. 1 and 2

A DISCOVERY BIBLE STUDY Book

EXPOSITORY STUDIES IN 1 JOHN

LIFE BY THE SON

RAY C. STEDMAN

WORD BOOKS
PUBLISHER
4800 WEST WACO DRIVE
WACO, TEXAS
76703

Scripture quotations, unless otherwise noted, are from the Revised Standard Version of the Bible, copyright 1946 (renewed 1973), 1956, and © 1971 by the Division of Christian Education of the National Council of the Churches of Christ in the USA, and are used by permission. Those marked TLB are from The Living Bible, Paraphrased (Wheaton: Tyndale House Publishers, 1971) and are used by permission. Those marked Phillips are from The New Testament in Modern English (rev. ed.), copyright © 1958, 1960, 1972 by J. B. Phillips. Those marked ASV are from the American Standard Version of the Bible. Those marked TEV are from the Today's English Version of the Bible (Copyright © American Bible Society 1976).

Discovery Books are published by Word Books, Publisher in cooperation with Discovery Foundation, Palo Alto, California.

ISBN 0-8499-2918-0
Library of Congress Catalog Card Number: 80-51449
Printed in the United States of America

Contents

Preface   **7**

Book One: Maintaining Fellowship
  1. Life with Father (1 John 1:1–4)   **11**
  2. God Is Light (1 John 1:5)   **23**
  3. The Man Who Ignores Light (1 John 1:3–7)   **31**
  4. The Man Who Denies Sin (1 John 1:8, 9)   **41**
  5. The Man Who Rationalizes Sin
     (1 John 1:10–2:2)   **51**
  6. Counterfeits and Reflectors (1 John 2:3–6)   **61**
  7. Visible Christianity (1 John 2:7–11)   **72**
  8. Growing and Maturing in Grace
     (1 John 2:12–14)   **84**
  9. The Enemy Around Us (1 John 2:15–17)   **101**

Book Two: Maintaining Truth
 10. The Nature of Heresy (1 John 2:18, 19)   **113**
 11. The Hard Core of Truth (1 John 2:20, 21)   **124**
 12. No Son, No Father (1 John 2:22, 23)   **134**
 13. The Living Word (1 John 2:24, 25)   **146**
 14. The Teaching Spirit (1 John 2:26, 27)   **159**
 15. The Coming Day (1 John 2:28)   **169**

Book Three: Maintaining Righteousness
 16. Recognizing the Unrecognized
     (1 John 2:29–3:1)   **185**

17. What Shall We Be? (1 John 3:2, 3) **195**
18. The Greatest Revolution (1 John 3:4, 5) **206**
19. The Mystery of Righteousness (1 John 3:6, 7) **215**
20. The Mystery of Evil (1 John 3:8) **224**
21. When the Spirit Says No (1 John 3:9) **233**
22. One or the Other (1 John 3:10) **243**

Book Four: Maintaining Love
23. The Path of Love (1 John 3:11–18) **255**
24. The Course of Hate (1 John 3:11–18) **266**
25. The Christian's Tranquilizer (1 John 3:19, 20) **276**
26. Power in Prayer (1 John 3:21–24) **285**
27. When Unbelief Is Right (1 John 4:1–6) **295**
28. God Is Greater (1 John 4:4–6) **305**
29. Love Made Visible (1 John 4:7–12) **314**
30. Love's Accomplishments (1 John 4:13–21) **324**

Book Five: Maintaining Assurance
31. We Shall Overcome (1 John 5:1–5) **337**
32. Why Do We Believe? (1 John 5:6–13) **346**
33. Praying Boldly (1 John 5:14–17) **358**
34. Christian Certainty (1 John 5:18–21) **372**

Preface

Watchman Nee, in his book *What Shall This Man Do?*, calls the apostle John "John the Mender," the Apostle whose special mission it is to call believers back to the strong foundational faith which they had from the beginning. In such a role John writes this first epistle to believers who were struggling with their relationships—both with God and with other Christians. They were finding it difficult to love one another, and they were plagued by false teachers who subtly fed their disaffections by implying that they could be both doctrinally sound and unloving. They could be "right with God" and ignore the tiresome clamor of brothers in need around them. This is an old problem among believers. Isaiah, in chapter 58 of his prophecy, attempted to snap the Israelites to attention, calling them away from empty religious forms which served only to bolster their own egos toward the reality of true worship; that of loosening the bonds of the oppressed. Worship of God, true worship, has to begin with a relationship with God—and this John's readers had. But if that relationship does not issue in fellowship with others who have the same relationship, then something is wrong. This is the issue John addresses in this letter. What are the obstacles to fellowship, and how can we deal with them effectively?

Book One

Maintaining Fellowship

1

Life with Father

The apostle John lived during the reign of the Roman emperor Domitian, whose cruelties exceeded all those before him, including even the infamous Nero. The Church was under great attack at the time John was writing this letter, not only from the direct and frontal violence of the Roman empire, but also from the subtle and much more dangerous attacks of various false ideas which had arisen from within.

We live in the same kind of situation; today much of the Christian church around the world is under direct and frontal attack. Here in America we are free from that, (for which we ought to give thanks every day), but we are daily exposed to a powerful barrage of devious errors. The Christian faith is threatened with a subtle undermining that removes all vestige of vitality, leaving us dull, dead, and useless. Therefore this letter of John's has tremendous significance for us today.

As you may know, it was the task of the apostles to lay the true foundation of the church, the only foundation which men can lay, which is Jesus Christ. But each of the apostles had a specific function in laying this foundation. Paul did not do the same thing as John; Peter had a different task than either Paul or John, and Jude was called to yet another ministry. God committed something original to each of these men to be passed along to us.

Watchman Nee, in his very helpful book, *What Shall This Man Do?*, suggests that the ministries of John, Peter, and Paul can be distinguished and characterized by the tasks each was performing when he was called of God. Peter, for instance, was a fisherman, and we are told in the Gospels that the Lord found him casting a net into the sea. That work of fishing for men is characteristic of the apostle Peter. He is always beginning things, initiating new programs. To him were committed the keys of the Kingdom by which he could open the door to the new things God was introducing. On the day of Pentecost he used one of those keys and led 3000 new believers into the kingdom of God.

To the apostle Paul, however, a different task was committed. When Paul was called he was a tentmaker. He made things. The ministry committed to the apostle Paul, then, was to build. Not only did he lay the foundation, he built upon it. He called himself "a wise master-builder" and to this mighty apostle was committed the task of building the great doctrinal foundation upon which the Christian faith rests.

To Call People Back

But John is different from both of these. When John was called, he was found mending his nets. John is a mender. His written ministry comes when the church has been in existence for several decades and at a time when apostasy had begun to creep in. A voice was needed to call people back to the original foundations. The ministry of the apostle John was to call men back to truth. When we begin to drift, when some false concept creeps into our thinking or our actions, it is John who is ordained of the Lord to call us back, to mend the nets, and to set things straight.

The first four verses constitute his introduction to this first letter.

> That which was from the beginning, which we have heard,
> which we have seen with our eyes, which we have looked
> upon and touched with our hands, concerning the word of
> life—the life was made manifest, and we saw it, and testify
> to it, and proclaim to you the eternal life which was with
> the Father and was made manifest to us—that which we
> have seen and heard we proclaim also to you, so that you
> may have fellowship with us; and our fellowship is with the
> Father and with his Son Jesus Christ. And we are writing
> this that our joy [or your joy] may be complete (1 John
> 1:1–4).

Three things are highlighted for us in this introduction:
a relationship, a fellowship, and a joy. But all must begin
with this matter of relationship, for John is concerned
first about the family of God. It was Peter's task to talk
about the kingdom of God and Paul about the church of
God, but John is concerned with the family of God.
(These are all the same thing, viewed from three different
angles.) It is into the intimacy of the family circle, now,
that the apostle John takes us. Thus this letter can be
properly described as introducing us to life with the
Father, the intimacy of the family circle of God.

Read through the letter and you will find that John
gives four different reasons for writing it. One is in verse
4: "And we are writing this *that your joy may be
complete.*" Then in chapter 2, verse 1, he says, "My little
children, I am writing this to you *so that you may not
sin.*" And in chapter 2, verse 26, he gives us the third
reason: "I write this to you *about those who would
deceive you.*" In chapter 5, verse 13, he gives us the
fourth reason: "I write this to you who believe in the
name of the Son of God, *that you may know that you
have eternal life*" (italics mine).

If you think about these four reasons for a moment you
will find something remarkable about them. He is first
concerned about the joy of companionship which is, of
course, the solution to the problem of loneliness. Nothing
is more helpful in curing loneliness than a family circle.
When you get lonely, where do you want to go? Home,

to the family! So John writes, "I write this that your joy may be full" (KJV), answering the fear and problem of loneliness.

Then he says, "I am writing this . . . so that you may not sin." Here he is dealing with another great threat to human happiness, the problem of guilt.

Again he says, "I write this to you about those who would deceive you." In other words he is writing to protect us, in order that we might be free from deception. Here is another great problem area of life. Where do we get answers? How do we know what is true? This letter is written so that we might be free from deception.

Finally he says, "I am writing this to assure you"—that you might find security, freedom from fear. Who of us is not concerned with that? How do you find your way through life successfully? How do we know we are not going to fail? John says, "I write this in order that you might have assurance," be secure, free from the fear of failure.

Beginnings

Now let us go back to these opening verses and see what he has to say. First, he is talking about a relationship.

> That which was from the beginning, which we have heard, which we have seen with our eyes, which we have looked upon and touched with our hands, concerning the word of life—

It is evident he is talking about a person, whom, he says, is "from the beginning." This is one of the favorite phrases of the apostle John. There are at least three "beginnings" in the Bible. The Bible opens with the phrase, "In the beginning God created the heavens and the earth" (Gen. 1:1). That is the beginning of the material creation, and how far back it goes no one knows. That verse speaks of the very dawn of creation and it is impossible for us to tell how far back it is. Neither science nor Scripture answers us. Science suggests it was millions of years ago, and Scripture is quite ready to accommodate that. However long ago it was, there was a time of beginning. That first beginning is the beginning of creation.

In the first verse of the Gospel of John, there is another "beginning": "In the beginning was the Word, and the Word was with God, and the Word was God." That beginning goes back *before* creation. That is the unbeginning beginning, the beginning that is eternal. That simply means the starting point, the farthest point backward that we can go. We humans have to start somewhere in our thinking. We are finite creatures and we have to start with A in order, eventually, to arrive at Z, and it is that A which John is describing in his gospel. Before there was anything at all there was the Word. That Word was a Person and he was with God, and he was God.

But now, in this letter, there is still a third beginning, "that which was from the beginning." Here John does not mean either the time of creation or the unbeginning beginning, the timeless beginning. He is referring to a definite time here. Note a few places where he uses this phrase and you will see what he means by it. In chapter 2, verse 7, he says, "Beloved, I am writing you no new commandment, but an old commandment which you had *from the beginning.*" In verse 14 he says, "I write to you, fathers, because you know him who is *from the beginning.*" In verse 24 he says, "Let what you heard *from the beginning* abide in you. If what you heard *from the beginning* abides in you, then you will abide in the Son and in the Father." Chapter 3, verse 11: "For this is the message which you have heard *from the beginning,* that we should love one another" (italics mine throughout).

It is difficult to locate this beginning, is it not? It seems to shift around from one time to another. It is what we might call the "contemporary beginning," or the "existential beginning"—the beginning I am experiencing right now. John is really referring to the continuous experience of the Christian life, which is contemporary all the time, new and fresh and vital, a continuous "beginning." It has been available for all time but *you* only began it when you came to know Jesus Christ. The writers of the New Testament began it when they came to know him, and John began it when he first knew him. It thus relates to him who is from the beginning. It is a timeless beginning that is right now, an eternal now.

Although it may be difficult to grasp the concept, it is important, for John warns all through this letter that we must cling only to that which is "from the beginning." If someone comes to you with something new, he says do not believe it. The cults today say, "Look, we have something different, something that has come along much later in history than the Bible. We have an additional revelation to give you." Say to them, "Keep it. I want that which is from the beginning."

Shared Life

Now John says, this one who was from the beginning is a Person and he has been seen and heard and handled. In other words, Christian faith rests upon great facts, the acts of a human being in history. Our Christian faith does not rest simply on ideas, or creedal statements. That is why becoming a Christian is not simply a matter of joining a church or believing a certain creed or signing a doctrinal statement. That has nothing to do with becoming a Christian. John points out that becoming a Christian is to be related to a Person.

All of us are related to someone. We live in families. God delights to "setteth the solitary in families" (Ps. 68:6, KJV). Children are related to their parents and parents to their children. Why? Because they share the same life. In the same way a Christian is one who shares the life of God by relationship to a Person, the only

Person who has that life, the Lord Jesus Christ, the Son of God. At the close of this letter John tell us, "He who has the Son has life; he who has not the Son of God has not life" (5:12). It is that simple. No matter how religious you may be, you do not have life if you do not have the Son: that is, you are not a true Christian.

That which was from the beginning, John says, is a real Person. "We looked at him, we heard him, we touched him, he actually appeared in history. He is a historical being. We knew him, fellowshiped with him, lived with him, ate with him, slept with him, heard his words, and have never forgotten them." This is the point to which all objections to Christianity are ultimately directed. The forces which seek to overthrow Christian faith today try to undermine our confidence in the facts of Scripture, these great historical truths about a Person who appeared in time. That is why it is not at all unimportant that we should believe the story as it is recorded in the Gospels. We must see these as facts, the acts of God in history. That is where John begins; he tells us what he himself experienced. We touched him, he says, we felt his warm, human flesh, we looked into his human eyes, we felt the beating of his human heart. And yet, as we did, we became aware that we were listening to the heartbeat of God. In some amazing way we were looking into the eyes of God and feeling the heartbeat of God and coming into contact with the life of God. He took that life and laid it down so that we might have it. He gave it to us through the cross, and that life is what makes us part of the family.

Now he goes on to say, in verse 2, that this life was made manifest, made visible. Twice he says it. What does he mean by it? He means that this eternal life was visible in the relationship of the Father and the Son. Jesus did not come to show us God, but man related to God. As you look at the life of Jesus you will see this relationship, this lost secret of humanity, by which man is intended to live—a continual dependence upon the life of the Father. Look at the earthly life of Jesus and this is exactly what you see. He keeps saying, "It is not I who accomplishes these works, it is the Father who dwells in me." He is continually reminding people that he says only what the Father is saying through him. The words are not his words; he simply looks to God and trusts God to be working through him, leading him to think the thoughts and to say the things God wants him to say. In doing this he expresses exactly the mind of God. It is that life that John is talking about, a new way of living, a new way of reacting to situations in dependence upon God.

A Christian man once came up to me at a conference where I was speaking and said, "I've been a professional baseball player all my life. I learned early that in order to be a success I had to have self-confidence. I became one of the top players in my league, and I did it by being self-confident. Now you tell me that this is not the way, that I'm not to have confidence in myself but to have confidence in God *in* me. How do I do this?"

I replied, "It's very simple. You must renounce your confidence in yourself and recognize that God, working through you, can do far more than you could ever do. When you are confident in yourself, all that you accomplish is what you can do. But when God is at work in you, you not only accomplish what you can do but far more that you can't see. You change lives. People are affected permanently and you leave an impression behind that is not forgotten."

He said, "I think I see what you mean, but I have a great deal of difficulty with this."

I told him, "I know; this is one of the hardest things to learn because it is a wholly different way of life than the way we were brought up. But it is the way that was manifest in the Lord Jesus himself. He lived this way. The explanation of that one unforgettable life is that he demonstrated what it means to walk in continual dependence upon a God who dwelt within him."

Something in Common

Then John says that this life will result in two wonderful things: First, fellowship, the most beautiful thing about family life.

—that which we have seen and heard we proclaim also to you, so that you may have fellowship with us— (1:3a).

What is fellowship? In the Navy we used to say it was two fellows on the same ship, and that is partly true. They do have something in common—the same ship. Essentially this word means "to have things in common." When you have something in common with another you can have fellowship with him. If you have nothing in common, you have no fellowship. We all have things in common— human life, American citizenship, many other matters. But John is talking about that unique fellowship which is the possession only of those who share life in Jesus Christ, who have this different kind of life, this new relationship that makes them one. The basis for the appeal of Scripture to live together in tenderness and love toward one another is not that we are inherently wonderful people, or remarkable personalities, or that we are naturally gracious, kind, loving, and tender all the time. For at times we are grouchy, scratchy, and irritating to others. But we are still to love one another. That is his point. Why? Because we share the Lord Jesus, his life, and, therefore, we have fellowship with one another.

Ah, but that is not all, and it cannot be all. The horizontal relationship depends upon a vertical one. He goes on, "and our fellowship is with the Father and with his Son Jesus Christ" (1:3b). We shall discover, as we go on as Christians, that the horizontal relationship is directly related to the vertical one. If the vertical is not right, the horizontal one will be wrong, and if it is wrong it is because something is wrong between us and the Father. If we want to straighten out the horizontal relationship, that of getting along with our fellow Christians and fellow men, we must be sure that the vertical connection is straight. Our fellowship is with the Father and with his Son, Jesus Christ, our Lord.

Communion with Christ

Now *fellowship* here means exactly the same thing it means elsewhere. It means having things in common. Here we come to the most remarkable thing about Christian life, communion, or fellowship with Christ. It takes two English words—partnership and friendship—to bring out what this really means. There is, first of all, a partnership, a sharing of mutual interests, mutual resources, mutual labor. God and I, working together, are a partnership. All that I have is placed at his disposal. Well, what do I have? I have me—my mind, my body. True, these are gifts of God, but they are put at my disposal to do with as I please. That is what I have. And now I put them at his disposal. When I do, I discover something most remarkable. Everything that he is, is put at my disposal. Is that not marvelous? The greatness of God, the wisdom, the power, the glory of his might: all is made available to me, when I make myself available to him. This is the great secret of fellowship.

This means that he makes available to me that which I desperately lack—wisdom and power, the ability to do. There are things I know I want to do, things I would like to do because it is what he wants. But I can only do them as I make myself available to him, depending upon him to come through from his side, making himself available to me. Then I discover that I can do what I want to do, as Paul says: "I can do all things in him who strengthens me" (Phil. 4:13).

But there is also friendship. Friendship and partnership together spell fellowship. Have you ever thought of this, that God desires you to be his friend? What do you do with a friend? You tell him secrets. That is what friends are for. You tell a friend intimate things, secrets. You are to tell your secrets to God (see 1 John 1:9). And God wants to tell us secrets. Jesus said to his disciples, "No longer do I call you servants, for the servant does not know what his master is doing; but I have called you friends, for all that I have heard from my Father I have made known to you" (John 15:15). He said this in a context in which he was attempting to impart to them the secrets of life. Now God will do this—he wants to do it. This is what that wonder word *fellowship* means. But it will be as you are able to bear these secrets. As you grow along with him you will discover that your eyes are continually being opened to things you never saw before. God will tell you secrets about yourself, about life, about others around you, about everything, imparting these to you because that is part of fellowship. That is what we are called to. The fellowship is based upon the relationship. You cannot have the fellowship until you first come to Christ and receive him. When you have the Son you are related to the Father, and when you are related to him, you can have fellowship with him.

When you have fellowship, you also have the third thing that John mentions: joy. Perhaps it will be more helpful for us to understand what John means if we use the word excitement—"that your excitement may be complete." Joy is a kind of quiet inner excitement which results when we really experience the fellowship John is writing about.

When we discover that God is actually using us, it is the most exciting experience possible to men. I have seen young people become so excited over this that they literally jump up and down. A dear girl I know cannot relate what the Lord does without bouncing as she tells it. I have seen men, familiar with the world of high finance, get so excited over the fact that God was using them in some simple way that they trembled as they told about it. I have known women who have discovered how exciting it is to have God at work in their neighborhood, using their home, their kitchen, and their coffee pot, that they have not been able to sleep at night. John is talking about life, as life was intended to be lived, filled with joy. Oh yes, with many pressures! Do not make the mistake of thinking that the only way to have joy is to be free from pressures or problems. No, you will have all of these, but along with them that wonderful feeling down inside that God is at work, and he is at work in you. God is using you to do his eternal work.

2

God Is Light

This life which Christians share, John goes on to say, is also a message. We know how a man's life can become a single message. The life of Adolf Hitler, for instance, has become a message to the world of how pride, pursued to the full, opens the door to demonic powers, and terrible, frightening things can follow. But there are other kinds of messages men can communicate by their lives. A few years ago, I read the biography of that amazing American, George Washington Carver, the dedicated black scientist who, though born into slavery, became one of the greatest scientists this nation has ever produced and whose discoveries have blessed the whole world. The message of his life is that true humility is the open door to learning. It is exactly the opposite of the message of Hitler.

The whole life of Jesus Christ is also a message given to us here in one verse:

This is the message we have heard from him and proclaim to you, that God is light and in him is no darkness at all (1 John 1:5).

That is the message of the life of Jesus. That is what he came to tell us, and what he imparts to us as we learn to know him. It is put both positively and negatively: "God is light and in him is no darkness at all." It is easy to see how that message was incorporated and fulfilled in the life of Jesus. John opens his Gospel with the words, "In him was life, and the life was the light of men. The light shines in the darkness, and the darkness has never put it out" (John 1:4, 5, TEV). That is the glory of this life. Our Lord himself said, "I am the light of the world; he who follows me will not walk in darkness, but will have the light of life" (John 8:12). There it is again, a life that is light. Again, he said, "This is the judgment, that the light has come into the world, and men loved darkness rather than light, because their deeds were evil" (John 3:19).

What, exactly does this message mean, "God is light"? Obviously the apostle John expects us to think about this a bit, for he says this is the sum, this is the meaning, of all that Jesus came to do and to be, whether we are considering his life lived in history, or the life he will live in us right now. It will all come out here, "God is light and in him is no darkness at all" (1:15). Notice something else. John does not say, "Light is God." It is, "God is light." You cannot reverse that. If it were, "Light is God," then, of course, the Indians who greet the rising sun with outstretched arms and burn incense to it are truer worshipers of God than we. No, it does not say "Light is God," but "God is light."

All about Light

That means that what light is, on a physical plane, God is on every level of human experience. If you want to understand the character of God, then observe what light is. What light does, God does. What light accomplishes, God can accomplish in your life. Well, then, what does light do? In this enlightened twentieth century we feel we have learned a great deal about light, much more than men knew fifty or a hundred years ago. We have analyzed it, broken it down into its spectrum; we can take fractions of it and use them for various purposes. We have timed it, measured its speed; we know that it is the fastest thing known in the universe. We have managed to produce x-rays and laser beams which do amazing things. But after all this we have really learned nothing essentially new about light. That is the humiliating thing about it. The great functions of light are universally known and have been known ever since the beginning of history. In the earliest dawn of humanity men experienced what light could do as fully as modern men do today.

The function of light, basically, is threefold. First, the most characteristic thing about light, and probably the first discoverable fact about light, is that light reveals.

A number of years ago, I visited the Grand Canyon for the first time. I was driving alone from Texas to Southern California and on the way I picked up two high school boys who were hitchhiking. On the spur of the moment the three of us decided to leave highway 66 and drive up to see the Grand Canyon. It was about ten-thirty at night when we made our decision, and we knew we would have to spend the night somewhere. Since we had sleeping bags with us, we decided to drive up inside the park, find a place to sleep, and see the Canyon in the morning. We arrived in the park long after midnight and not knowing where the Canyon was, we drove on until we found a wide spot in the road and pulled over. Taking out our sleeping bags we walked a few feet into the trees and went to sleep. When I awoke in the morning, the sun was high. To my astonishment I found that I had been sleeping within arm's length of the edge of the Canyon. If I had rolled over in my sleep, I would have fallen off the edge of a 500-foot precipice. In the darkness, we had not seen it but the light made it clear. We were grateful that we had not tried to go further from the car that night.

Life in Focus

The first function of light, then, is to enable us to see things that have been there all the time. That is exactly what John means; God reveals reality. God, through

Christ, opens the eyes of the heart and brings life into focus so that we see clearly, without distortion. It does not all happen in one amazing transformation. Often, it is a gradual process, for we would not be able to take the full revelation all at once. But God's purpose in entering human hearts is to show us reality. Light reveals, and so does God. The enigmas of life will gradually unfold, the great mysteries will become clear, illusions will be seen for what they are—deceiving phantasmas that disappear as the light shines upon them.

Entering college for the first time, I was not at all sure about what I was getting into. I displayed an outward appearance of confidence and the ability to handle anything, but within I had a deep sense of uncertainty. I felt as though I were trying to play a game without knowing the rules, but trying to guess them as I went along. It was rough. I was baffled, as all young people are baffled, by the great questions of life. What am I here for? What is it really all about? What is worthwhile about life, and how do you tell? How do you fit death into this whole picture? The more I learned about life the more baffled I became, until I met Jesus Christ and began to understand the message of his life, the message revealed in his Word. Bit by bit things began to come clear. First came the answers to some of the greater issues, like what life is all about, and what happens after death. Then details began to filter through the fog and little by little matters became much clearer. Much remains, but I am no longer confused. The road ahead is clear.

Out of my darkness one fact became increasingly clearer to me. A great mystery that impinged upon every other question of my life was resolved. I discovered that it was the key to many things. It was the fact that the solution to most of my troubles lay within me. The problems were not outside of me, as I once thought; I was the big problem. As I began to see that, I saw what it was in me that was creating the problems. Little by little I began to understand myself. The mystery of self was revealed by the light as it shone upon me from the word of the only One who knows what is in man. I began, then, to see the answers to the problems of life. God is light and light reveals.

Measuring Stick

But that is not light's only quality. It also measures. Did you ever watch a man pick up a stick and sight along it? What is he doing? He is trying to see whether it is crooked. What reveals that? A beam of light. Light is straight and anything that does not correspond to it is crooked. Surveyors use light to measure distances and angles, to see whether they are up or down, high or low, right or left. They have an instrument with a small telescope on it which uses light as a measurement. Also, in the vast, illimitable reaches of space today the only adequate measuring stick is light-years, the distance measured by the speed of light.

That is what light does, and that is what God does. God is a measuring stick, a point of reference. You can use God to measure everything else. In economic life, political life, social life, scientific life, psychological life, whatever it may be, we are confronted with mysteries and puzzles wherever we turn. As men seek to ferret out the solutions to these puzzles they come up with many proposed solutions. Some are contradictory, some are supplementary to each other, some are absurd, some are stupid, some are very appealing and practical. Every one of us, facing this welter of advice, is constantly asking, how do I know which one is right? How do I know who has the real answers? Where do I get a measuring stick that can be applied to these voices I hear? That is where God comes in.

I read recently a very interesting book on the great economic philosophers of the past. These men have analyzed the social and economic structures of life and have tried to explain what happens to the market to make it rise and fall so that men go broke or become rich overnight. It discusses the theories of men like Adam

Smith, Karl Marx, John Keynes, and others. It is an interesting book because it reveals that no one knows the full answers. All the guesses have fallen short; no one can really put his finger on the secret of economic management in society. The reason is that none of the thinkers sees man as God sees him. None of them sees man as he really is, and therefore they miss the point. But God sees man according to the truth, according to the light. All the conflicting voices we hear today can be sorted out and measured by his revelation of what man is.

Now that is very practical. Is your marriage working out? Do you get all kinds of advice on how to make it work? Well, the light that shines from God's Word about marriage is the full truth about what makes marriages work. If you measure the advice you get by God's Word, you can tell what to believe. It is the only measure there is when you fall in love with another woman or another man, and your own home looks dull and hopeless, and you are drawn by the temptation to forget it all and run off with the other person and start all over again. It all looks so lusciously attractive. But then you measure it against God's Word and there you learn the unpleasant truth—which may be quite unpalatable to you at the moment—that your dream will not work: it will only increase your misery, and hurt and destroy everyone involved. Because you see that and have learned to trust the light a bit, you say, "All right, even though I want to do this I won't." Later on the blindness passes and you are so grateful, so eternally thankful, that God's light stopped you from going on into darkness. "The light shines in the darkness," John says, "and the darkness has never put it out" (John 1:5, TEV).

Electric Invitation

Light not only reveals and measures, but light energizes as well. That is the most dramatic quality about light. It imparts life, it activates and quickens. Some years ago I ran across a most eloquent description in one of the sermons of Phillips Brooks along this line. He says,

> When the sun rose this morning it found the world in darkness, torpid and heavy and asleep, with powers all wrapped up in sluggishness; with life that was hardly better or more alive than death.
>
> The sun found this great sleeping world and woke it. It bade it to be itself. It quickened every slow and sluggish faculty. It called to the dull streams and said, "Be quick"; to the dull birds and bade them sing; to the dull fields and made them grow; to dull men and bade them think and talk and work.
>
> It flashed electric invitation to the whole mass of sleeping power which really was the world and summoned it to action. It did not make the world. It did not start another set of processes unlike those which had been sluggishly moving in the darkness. It poured strength into the essential processes which belonged to the very nature of the earth. It glorified, intensified, fulfilled the earth.

That is what God does. God is light and God intensifies, fulfills, and glorifies our essential humanity. He does not destroy it. He takes it and leads it on through the darkness into an ever-growing experience of life and vitality and productivity.

Right at this point comes the often unspoken question, "All right, I grant you this happens to a few, but why only to a few? What's the matter with the rest of the Christians? Why is it that all Christians are not this way? Why are they not alert and informed, stable and dependable, alive and attractive? Why is it that the Christians I meet are so untrustworthy, so critical, so harsh, repelling, and negative? If God is light and he can do this, why does it seem to happen to only a few?"

These are the questions the world is asking, are they not? And that is exactly the question John takes up next. He goes on to point out three reasons why the light does not help, even though it is shining. There are three conditions that are like umbrellas that we Christians erect to shut out the healing, cleansing, glorifying, fulfilling light. God is light and he does reveal truth; he does measure life and give us a reference point by which the false can be separated from the true. Best of all, he fulfills, he glorifies, he energizes, he vitalizes. But he does so only as we learn to take down the umbrellas that hide the light from us.

3

The Man Who Ignores Light

Why is it that some Christians seem to be transformed by contact with Jesus Christ—their lives are perceptibly different—but others are not? Some Christians, even Christians of long standing, seem still to be very much conformed to the world around them, even deformed in their views and outlooks. Yet all of them stoutly assert that they are Christians, that they, too, have been born again by faith in Jesus Christ. Is is not strange that the world asks, what is wrong?

The secret, John says, is fellowship, that is, experiencing Christ. Relationship is accepting Christ; fellowship is experiencing him. You can never have fellowship until you have established relationship, but you can certainly have relationship without fellowship. Relationship puts us into the family of God, but fellowship permits the life of the family to shine out through us. That is what marks the difference between Christians. Relationship is to be "in the Lord" but fellowship is to "be strong in the Lord, and in the power of his might" (Eph. 6:10, KJV), as Paul so beautifully expresses it in his letter to the Ephesians.

Relationship means that all God has is potentially yours, but fellowship means you are actually drawing upon his resources. Relationship is you possessing God;

fellowship is God possessing you. Fellowship, then, is the key to vital Christianity.

John sees three ways by which Christians miss out on fellowship. In the first chapter we will see that he uses the phrase, "if we say," three times: verse 6, "*If we say* we have fellowship"; verse 8, "*If we say* we have no sin"; and verse 10, "*If we say* we have not sinned." Three times a profession is indicated, but the condition or action that follows belies the profession. In this first instance, John says,

> If we say we have fellowship with him while we walk in darkness, we lie and do not live according to the truth; but if we walk in the light, as he is in the light, we have fellowship with one another, and the blood of Jesus his Son cleanses us from all sin (1 John 1:6, 7).

What is the problem here? This is a very common condition. Here is a Christian, John says, who has established a relationship with God, he has come into the family of God by faith in Christ. Perhaps that relationship has actually been established for years. The man has been a Christian a long time, and he *says* that he has fellowship with God. That means he claims to be experiencing the full flow of the life in the Spirit, the life of God. He claims that the life of Jesus Christ is his in experience as well as in potential. But, John says, there is no sign of it in his life. He lies. He does not live in accord with his claim. He does not live according to the truth. His life is harsh, perhaps, and loveless; critical and demanding of others. Or perhaps it is intemperate, frivolous and flippant, shallow and superficial. Or perhaps it is gossipy and sharp-tongued, or resentful and filled with bitterness.

A Great Misunderstanding

Well, what is wrong? Nothing is wrong with the relationship. It does no good to talk to this person about becoming a Christian: he is a Christian. He understands what it means to know Jesus Christ. Well, what is wrong? John analyzes it: such a person, he says, is "walking in darkness." Do we not greatly misunderstand this phrase? It is often thought to refer to having fallen into sin, what was once called "a backslidden condition." It is the opposite, of course, of walking in the light. Do we not unconsciously think of walking in the light as being perfect, as having everything right? If we are behaving as we ought to as Christians, that is walking in the light. The opposite of that would be walking in darkness, that is, not behaving the way we ought. But to view this phrase that way is to confuse cause with results. The fact is, we sin because we are walking in darkness! Walking in darkness is not an equivalent term to sinning. We are sinning because we walk in darkness. That is the problem.

Well, then, what is darkness? We must answer that first on the physical level. How would you go about getting a room dark that is filled with light? Would you have to somehow scoop out the light and shovel in darkness? Of course not, you need only to turn off the light. Darkness is simply the absence of light. Wherever there is no light there is darkness. That is precisely what John means here. To walk in darkness means to walk as though there were no God, for God is light. It is to be a practical atheist—not an actual one, of course. We believe there is a God, we know he is there, but we live as though he did not exist. We do not expose ourselves to him. That is walking in darkness.

This is what John is describing here. It is possible to be a Christian and yet walk in darkness by turning God off. When you turn off the light the darkness comes flooding in, instantly. As I suggested, this is not a rare condition at all. John starts with this problem because it is one of the most widespread and commonplace of problems. It is evident on every side. You can miss the benefits of God's presence in your heart and life by ignoring the light.

How do you do this? I wish to be very practical about

this. Sometimes these biblical terms are so familiar to us they fall upon our ears without meaning. Therefore, it is sometimes very helpful to put them in other ways. How, then, do people actually turn off the light and walk in darkness?

Lights Off

Some people stop attending church. That is one way. The Word of God, if it is proclaimed from a pulpit, is a channel of God's light. The Word itself is light. It penetrates and searches, it seeks out our inner life and exposes it to our view. If we stop coming to church we escape the light that way. We are no longer made uncomfortable by the Word. We discover that if we stay away we do not experience that pricking of our conscience which the light awakens. The writer of Hebrews warns of a tendency to do this as we draw near the close of the age. He says, "Let us consider how to stir up one another to love and good works, *not neglecting to meet together,* as is the habit of some" (Heb. 10:24,25, emphasis added). The delusions of the age are such that they tend to make us want to stay away from the light. It is much more comfortable to sit around in the old slippers of the flesh and enjoy oneself at home. That is one way to turn off the light.

Another way is to stop reading the Scriptures. There are many who do this. An amazing number of Christians have simply turned off the light by ceasing to read the Scriptures. They seldom open the Bible. They only hear a verse now and then, and are content with what they get in church or Sunday school, but they seldom open it for themselves. Underneath all the excuses that are given for this—no time, lots of pressures, and so on—there is really a desire to escape the light. The Word is light, but we want to walk in darkness. As Mark Twain put it, "It isn't the parts of Scripture that I don't understand that bother me, it's the parts I do."

There are other, more subtle ways to walk in darkness; for example, never take a long look at yourself. Never examine yourself. Nod your head at the right places when the sermon is being expounded, but never apply it or ask questions of yourself about what is being said. This is an almost certain way of walking in darkness, and one of the most common evasions of our day. I would suggest to you that perhaps the greatest cause of weakness among evangelical Christians is that we seldom stop to examine ourselves. We never ask ourselves searching and penetrating questions as to where we are in the Christian life.

The apostle Paul says, "Examine yourselves, whether you be in the faith"! He urges this kind of activity upon us. He says, in effect, do not go on taking it for granted that because you are hearing the truth, you are obeying it. Ask yourself, "Where am I?" John says, "Test the spirits whether they be of God." Examine what you are listening to and how you are thinking, and lay it alongside the Scriptures. Put to yourself life's most basic question: Where am I? Do it periodically and frequently. What kind of Christian am I? Am I better than I was six months ago? Am I easier to live with? Am I a more gracious, compassionate, outgoing kind of person than I was a year ago? That is walking in the light, and to avoid it is to walk in darkness.

There is yet another way. You can walk in darkness by comparing yourself with other Christians. Again, this is a very common way. You can find a favorite person, someone who is obviously lower on the scale than you are, and what a comfort they are! Any time you find yourself getting uneasy about your own spiritual condition, remind yourself of him—or her. "At least I'm better than him." If you keep this up you can go on for years walking in darkness without the light ever once shining on you.

Another variety of the same thing is to blame others. Be sure to find an excuse for your wrong behavior in what others have done to you. Blame the church. Blame the

Sunday school. Blame the teachers. Blame your father or mother. Blame your children. Blame the boss. Blame the Internal Revenue Service. But never blame yourself! This is another sure way to walk in darkness.

A variant way is never admit that anything is wrong in your life. Always appear to be what you want to be when you are out among others. At home, of course, because of the strain of this kind of living, there must be times when you relax and are yourself. Try to be alone when that happens. But otherwise, keep up appearances. This is a way to walk in darkness.

Spiritual Make-up

Put on what I call "moral cosmetics." Did you ever see a woman making up her face? She examines it first, and then she applies a bit of color here and a bit there, a touch of blue here and brown there, patting it and arranging it to look the way she wants it to look. This is a rather harmless matter when it occurs only at the physical level, for the physical is somewhat remote from us—but the closer we get to the real us the more deadly this kind of a practice becomes. We can do it not only on the physical level, but on the soulish and spiritual level as well. We make ourselves up when we go out among others in the kind of image we want them to see.

That practice is absolutely guaranteed to abruptly halt all Christian growth. If you appear to be mature when you are not, then you cannot ever be seen as needing anything. So, when you are out with other Christians it must always appear that you already have everything. You cannot listen, you cannot really seek for anything yourself, you cannot admit any need. If you are already fully grown, of course, you cannot appear to need any food, and so you do not grow. You cannot grow, and you never will grow. This is why the Lord Jesus said, "Blessed are they which do hunger and thirst after righteousness, for *they* shall be filled" (Matt. 5:6, KJV).

Is it not very instructive that the first miracle of judgment in the New Testament occurred shortly after the Day of Pentecost when Ananias and Sapphira were judged for pretending to be what they were not, pretending to have a holiness that they did not actually possess? The Holy Spirit is trying to arrest our attention by this account, to show the deadliness of pretense. It is a most dramatic scene, when these two fall dead. Furthermore, this kind of pretense makes it impossible for you ever to help a younger Christian, even the younger Christians in your own home. They are helped by seeing you overcome the problems of life by the reaction of faith. If you do not admit there are problems, if you never talk about them or never appear to have them, then your image to your children is simply one of achieved perfection, and it is the most discouraging thing they can ever run into.

One day a woman took me aside and for two and a half hours poured a tragic tale into my ear. As a young Christian she admired another Christian woman. This woman appeared to her to be the acme of Christian perfection. She longed to be like her, but she confessed that whenever she was with her she came away totally depressed. She found the standard apparently set before her was impossible to achieve in her immature Christian relationship. But one day she discovered a terribly serious flaw in that other person—who immediately tried to cover it up. All the delusions of years came crashing down around this young woman's head. She realized that the other woman had been pretending all the time. It resulted in a terrible crisis in her experience. She was overwhelmed with feelings of bitterness and resentment, and cried out to me. "Oh, if she had just admitted some need, what a help it would have been to me!"

One of the most serious problems among Christians stems from never admitting that anything is wrong, or that we have problems, or that there are times when our faith is tested. We never tell anyone about these. Therefore, we walk in darkness. Remember, darkness is the absence of light. To walk in the light is to have everything open, exposed to God, or to anyone else who is interested. But to walk in darkness is to talk about love and joy and power, but to live a lie. It is fellowship, the sharing of the life of Christ, from which strength comes. To ignore light is to choose weakness.

Now what is the answer? John says, "Walk in the light" (1:7). That does not mean to behave perfectly, but to examine ourselves; to be willing to look at ourselves, listen seriously to what others say about us and ask ourselves how much truth there is in it, and not immediately to grow defensive. If we take down our fences and facades and open up to others, tell them what we are going through and encourage them to open up to us, admitting faults—this is walking in the light. As James puts it, "Confess your faults one to another, and pray one for another" (James 5:16, KJV). If we share these and ask for prayer about them, John says, "We have fellowship with one another" (1:7), you and Christ. Immediately you have fellowship. That is the important thing, is it not? You immediately discover that when you are willing to look, to listen, and to examine, that the light is shining on you. If you walk in the light it does not matter what your actual condition is; immediately you will have fellowship with the Son of God.

But not only that, our fellowship is also with one another. Fellowship with other humans will surely follow. In other words, you become approachable, sympathetic, and uncritical. You lose your blaming, demanding, critical spirit. You give up your perfectionism, your demand that everyone else measure up. You become human, and oh, so much easier to live with.

Cause of Depression

That is not all, however. There is more, and it goes much deeper. Listen to this. ". . . and the blood of Jesus his Son cleanses us from all sin" (1:7). Why does he put that thought in there? Is it not extraneous? Is that not introducing some other idea? We have been talking about fellowship and now suddenly he talks about cleansing. Well, of course, it is not out of place. Nothing in God's Word is out of place. This belongs right here because the inevitable accompaniment of evading light is guilt. You cannot walk in darkness without being guilty, feeling guilty. Guilt is the underlying cause of Christian depression. It is the thing that creates that somber, wet-blanket approach so many Christians demonstrate. They are suffering from suppressed guilt and trying to make up for it in a rigid, demanding code to punish themselves for not being what they know they ought to be. Walking in darkness also results in actual physical afflictions at times, such as insomnia, obesity, nervous habits, and even asthma and ulcers, aphasia, and other afflictions.

To walk in the light means to hide nothing. You do not defend yourself from the light of God nor in any way try to appear to be something you are not. It means to come instantly, without defensiveness, to the light and deal with it before God. If you see something wrong, say so. You are not going to lose face. You are not going to lose status. The amazing thing is that your friends will still love you. In fact, they love you more when you begin to admit there are things wrong in your life. You will discover that you are far more approachable, far more human. Your family begins to be comfortable around you instead of being uncomfortable. And there comes the sweet relief of the cleansing grace of God that always accompanies walking in the light. It is almost automatic. If we walk in the light, the blood of Jesus Christ is continuously cleansing us from all sin. It is the present tense there; it is done instantly, continuously, all the time.

You could walk through a great, dark cloud of soot, and if it were dark enough and thick enough, you would come out completely covered with black—face, hands, everything—except for two spots that would be clear:

your eyeballs. Why? Because a continuous cleansing action goes on all the time, keeping the eyes clear. And this is the provision God has made in Christ. If we walk in the light, if we do not try to deceive ourselves, pretending we are something we are not, the blood of Jesus Christ is continuously cleansing us so that the problems of the immediate past, as well as the distant past, are taken care of in the cleansing, forgiving grace accomplished in the death of Jesus Christ, the blood of Christ outpoured for us.

Many have told me that they had been Christians for years, but had seldom experienced fellowship because they had been walking in darkness. But I also have a long list of those who have come to me and said what a joy, what a sheer, dramatic relief it has been to get rid of all this posturing, this pretending, and admit that they have problems. When they did this, they were open to have people pray for them even though they had been Christians for years, and to feel the burden of pretense roll away. It is a glorious freedom, the cleansing grace of the Lord Jesus Christ.

4

The Man Who Denies Sin

We have just looked at one way of avoiding light. But there is a second obstacle which can keep us from walking in the light and thus cause us to miss out on fellowship. It is given in verses 8 and 9 of chapter 1.

If we say we have no sin, we deceive ourselves, and the truth is not in us. If we confess our sins, he is faithful and just, and will forgive our sins and cleanse us from all unrighteousness.

It is necessary to note first the difference between the word "sin" and "sins." In verse 8 it is singular: "If we say we have no *sin*"; in verse 9 it is plural: "If we confess our *sins.*" This marks a very important distinction between the root, which is "sin," singular, and the fruit, which is "sins," plural. Sin is that in man which makes him want to play God on every occasion. We know how this is: we want the world to revolve around us, that we may always be the center of things. That self-centeredness is sin. It goes by other names as well: pride, selfishness, or independence. That is the root, the twist in human nature which makes us commit sins.

Sins, therefore, are those specific forms which this inward bent makes us take. There are many kinds of sins, but they all stem from one root, sin. John says if we say we have no sin, that is, no capacity to commit sins, if we deny the very possibility of sins, then we deceive ourselves. Obviously, this case is worse than the previous one. In the first instance, John says, "If we say we have fellowship with him while we walk in darkness, we lie and do not live according to the truth" (1:6). There, we are trying to deceive others and to some degree we often succeed. But if we say we have no ability to sin at all we are only deceiving *ourselves*. Others are quite aware that we are lying to, and deceiving, ourselves. They are not fooled. The man who ignores the light deceives others but seldom himself. He knows that he is not living as he ought; he knows he is ignoring light. But this one deceives himself, and that is always pathetic. He actually believes that he can no longer sin, that there is no longer any possibility of evil in him.

You ask, does this really happen? Are there people so deluded that they have come to the place where they really think they cannot sin? Unfortunately we must reply yes, it often happens. John would not have brought this up if it did not happen. It happened in his day and it happens in our day, and for several reasons. But whenever it happens, the one who makes this claim immediately loses that glorious fellowship which makes Christianity so vital and unforgettable. He loses his power, his influence, his vitality, and his effectiveness as a Christian. His life becomes lusterless, dull, and deadening.

Victim of False Teaching

Now how does this happen? There are primarily three ways in which this occurs. First, a Christian can become the victim of one of the cults which deny the reality of sin, saying that sin is but "an error of mortal mind." Sin, they say, has no real existence; it is a mere figment of the imagination, and all that is necessary to deal with sin is to correct one's thinking. This widespread teaching is represented by groups such as Christian Science, the Unity School of Christianity, and Religious Science. Also, it is prominent in non-Christian religions such as Theosophy, Hinduism, and Buddhism. These all teach that sin does not really exist; it is merely in the mind. Truth exists and good exists, but sin does not have objective reality.

Unfortunately, many who are really Christians have fallen into this trap and believe that to correct the problem of sin merely calls for an adjustment in their thinking. But John says, if you believe that the truth is not in you, there is no light in you, for light is truth and truth is light. The truth as it is revealed in Jesus says something quite different. According to the word of the Lord, both directly from his own lips and through the apostles that followed, the truth is that sin is a very objective reality. It does exist; it is always a present possibility. It finds its original expression in the great hosts of satanically controlled beings who are at work in the world, influencing and controlling the thinking of men. Sin is personified in the person of our adversary, the devil, but it exists as a very powerful and persuasive factor in life. To treat it as though it is not there is to practice self-deception and to become the victim of the saddest of delusions.

There is nothing more pathetic than the person who denies the reality of sin. In this regard, I always remember the story of a young woman who was attending a meeting with older women. They were discussing the effects of prenatal influence upon a child, and some gave rather strange accounts. One said that when she was carrying her baby she saw a red fire engine, and the baby was born with a red blotch on its forehead. This young woman said, "I don't believe all this. My mother told me that before I was born she dropped a whole pile of phonograph records and broke every one, but it didn't affect me, affect me, affect me, affect me." So those who make this claim of being free from the universal taint of sin are constantly saying by their very lives that it did affect them, as it affects all.

The Root Removed

Now that is the first way of denying sin; those who succumb to the false teaching of the cults. Then there are those Christians—and very devout Christians, for the most part—who have come to believe that the root of sin with which they were born has been somehow eradicated. By the activity of the Holy Spirit in the outworking of their salvation it has been completely torn out, lifted out, and they are freed from the root of sin. There are a considerable number of Christians who follow this teaching today. They group themselves in denominations that usually bear the name "holiness." They interpret sanctification as a digging out and eradicating of the root of sin. Often they even base this idea upon a verse in 1 John. Many of them quote 1 John 3:9, "No one born of God commits sin; for God's nature abides in him, and he cannot sin because he is born of God." At first glance this verse does look like a confirmation of that view. But it is clear from the Greek that John is referring to *habitual* sin in that verse. A Christian cannot persist, on a continuous basis, in sin, because he is born of God. He cannot sin without a sense of grief so powerful that ultimately, despite his struggles, he will be brought to repentance.

Quite a number of years ago, in Pasadena, I went into a certain barber shop for a haircut. I went because I had heard that the barber was a Christian. After I sat down in the barber chair, he began his work. It was not long before I discovered that he was indeed Christian, but he was a member of a holiness group. He personally believed that he had come to the place where he did not any longer have the possibility of sin. Unfortunately for him, I was that most knowledgeable of creatures, a seminary student in his second year, and we got into an argument that waxed hotter and hotter as it went along. Finally he became so perturbed over our discussion that he began yelling and shouting at me and waving his fist in front of me, until another customer who was waiting got up in disgust and walked out. I felt that was quite an adequate commentary on the theology of the barber, for he was himself demonstrating the folly of his position.

Here again, those who do this are self-deceived. They walk in darkness and therefore they are without fellowship, for the key to fellowship with Christ is to walk in the light. If you have reached the place where you say there is nothing for the light to reveal any more, all sin is taken away, there is nothing to look at any more, then, of course, you are deceiving yourself and you walk in darkness—and it always results in loss of fellowship.

But there is still a third way of denying sin, even more subtle, but perhaps more widespread, that occurs among the best instructed Christians: those who have learned that there is a possibility of being free from sin by walking in the Spirit. They have fully grasped the implications of the great verse in Galatians that says, "Walk in the Spirit, and ye shall not fulfil the lust of the flesh" (Gal. 5:16, KJV). They are aware of the mighty possibilities for freedom from the control and power of sin, and they enter into this with all their hearts. They give themselves diligently to understanding how to walk in the Spirit in every circumstance until they believe that they have so mastered the process of being free from sin that they invariably fulfill it: therefore, they do not, and even cannot, sin.

Theoretically Possible

It seems a perfectly logical position to take, does it not? Theoretically it is possible, for any given period of time, to so walk in the Spirit that we are free from sin, we do not sin. This is the whole purpose of salvation in its present tense. When we manifest the life of the Spirit, we do not sin. This is true. But the remarkable thing is that as you read the pages of the New Testament you discover that no New Testament Christian ever makes a claim to sinless perfection. The only one who could say, and did say, that he was without sin was the Lord Jesus himself. All others remind us that though we must face constantly the challenge of walking without sin, nevertheless, the subtlety of the flesh, the cleverness of the wiles of the devil, the ease by which we can deceive ourselves and be deceived, is so prevalent and powerful that there will be times when we succumb, times when we fail.

As Paul warns his readers, "Let any one who thinks that he stands take heed lest he fall" (1 Cor. 10:12). This is why the Christian is always exhorted to walk in fear and trembling. When we think we have come to the place where we have mastered the processes of walking in the Spirit, then we need to think again. We have not yet learned it all. Even the apostle Paul can say of himself at the close of his ministry that he regards himself as the chief of sinners—not because he sees sin abounding in his life, but because, as his conscience is sensitized, his awareness of transgression multiplies. He is fully aware of the ease with which he can fall into an attitude that is contrary to the things of the Lord. He is aware of the fact that not until he stands in resurrection life with a redeemed body will he be totally free from the taint of sin. This is why our Lord himself taught in the great Lord's Prayer that we are daily to pray, "Lead us not into temptation" (Matt. 6:13). The pressures are so great, the opposing forces so subtle, that it is easy to succumb.

Let us not take this stand. If any man deny sin, if any man says he cannot sin, he deceives himself, and the truth is not in him. Then what is the remedy? It is always the same thing; it is to walk in the light—to face reality. Specifically, as the apostle puts it, it is to confess our sins. Regardless of whether we have deluded ourselves into thinking there is no root of sin in us any more, it will still be there and it will keep right on producing sins, and all the more if we think there is no need to guard against it. Well then, face the sins, John says. Take a good look at them and agree with God about them. The light reveals them to be there.

Remember the word of the Lord himself? Out of the heart of man, he says, proceed murders, adulteries, fornications, evil thoughts, and so on. All these things come from within. The root is still planted deep within our physical natures, and we shall not escape it until the body is redeemed. Of course, we do not need to yield to it—that is the point of redemption. As we learn to walk in the Spirit there can be protracted periods of time when we walk free from the taint of sin. Ah, but when we do sin, do not try to hide it, do not cover it over, do not, out of some mistaken notion that you will lower yourself in the estimation of someone else, refuse to acknowledge sin. Confess it, say what it is—anger or malice, envy or lust, jealousy or selfishness or ambition—any of these things. Do not deny them and do not deny the root. Face the reality, the apostle says, confess these fruits when they do appear.

Agreeing with God

Now the word *confess,* as you may know, does not mean to ask for forgiveness, and we will see why in a moment. Christ's work for us upon the cross has already done all that is necessary to forgive us. What God wants us to do is to look at the sin before us and call it what he calls it. That means to agree with God about it. The word *confess* comes from a Greek word which means "to say the same thing." To say with God what he says about this thing is to confess sin. There is a popular song which you sometimes hear in Christian circles:

If I have wounded any soul today,
If I have caused one foot to go astray,
If I have lived in my own selfish way,
Dear Lord, forgive.

That is not confession at all. The "if's" take it out of the realm of confession. Do not say "if," say, "Lord, I have caused some foot to go astray, I have lived in my own selfish way." That is confession, that is agreeing with God.

When you agree with God about these things, what happens? We are told, "If we confess our sins, he is faithful and just, and will forgive our sins and cleanse us from all unrighteousness" (1 John 1:9). Sometimes, I might add, there is need for confession not only to God, but to others who are injured by what we do. There is need, often, for restitution. If we are honestly saying what God says about it, then we need to do something about it. We need to remedy the harm we have done as much as possible, and God will sometimes demand this of us. Often, no sense of forgiveness is granted to us until we have moved in restitution. Ah, but when we look at it as he does, then he says we are cleansed. The cleansing is not based upon God's mercy or his kindness or his love; it is based upon the work of Jesus Christ. On that basis God is "faithful and just" to forgive us, and he would be utterly unjust if he refused to forgive a penitent sinner. God himself would be wicked if he refused, on the basis of the work of Christ, to forgive one who confesses his sins. That is how certain we can be of the cleansing that comes when we agree with God about these things.

Do you remember how our Lord himself dramatized this for us in the solemnity of the Last Supper, before he went to the cross? Gathered with his disciples in the upper room, he took a basin and a towel and girded himself and set about to wash the feet of his disciples. You recall, as he came to Peter, Peter shook his head and said, "You shall never wash my feet" (John 13:8). Jesus then said these significant words, "If I do not wash you, you have no part with me" (John 13:8). Peter did not understand all that meant until years later. But we can see that what our Lord meant was, "Peter, here is the key to fellowship. You can be related to me by sharing my life, but you do not have any fellowship with me unless you let me wash your feet." Peter, in his impetuosity, always plunging himself to the full into everything, replied, "Lord, if that's the case, then wash me all over." Again the Lord had to correct him. "No, Peter, he that is bathed does not need to wash again." That first cleansing of redemption, that coming to Christ which washes away the guilt of the past, the Adamic guilt, that is "bathing all over." Jesus said he who is so bathed does not need to wash all over again, but he does need to wash his feet. This is what John is talking about here, this repeated washing of the feet. Whenever we are aware of having fallen into a fleshly reaction, into sins, then let us stop right there and in our hearts before God agree with God about it and experience anew this wonderful cleansing, this faithful and righteous cleansing of our lives, "cleansing from all unrighteousness." That is keeping the feet clean.

Do you know what happens when you do not keep your feet clean? You become very unpleasant to live with. As a schoolboy in Montana I endured many bitter winters when the temperature would sometimes go down to 60° below zero for a week at a time. In those homes where we had no running water, no indoor plumbing, and no electricity, taking a bath was akin to major surgery. We had to go out and get the c-o-l-d galvanized iron washtub off the wall, bring it in and put it on the kitchen floor, then pour heated water into it from the stove. Where the water touched the tub, it was hot, but where it did not, it was cold. In that painful setting we performed our ablutions. It was difficult enough and distressing enough that some people did not think it necessary to bathe at all during the winter months. If you went into the heat of a one-room schoolhouse on a cold winter's day, with about 50 or 60 sweating bodies there, you became very much aware of this fact.

Now I do not mind living with someone who knows his feet get dirty and who therefore frequently washes them, but it is terribly distressing to live with someone who thinks his feet never get dirty. That is what John is saying. If we say we cannot get dirty feet, we deceive ourselves, and the truth is not in us. But if we face up to it and confess it and agree with God about it (and that is sometimes hard to do because we want so desperately to get him to agree with us), well then, the cleansing that the Lord Jesus has fully and abundantly provided for on the cross is immediately ours, and we are as though we had never sinned.

5

The Man Who Rationalizes Sin

Now we come to the third of these ways of avoiding light, the case of the man who rationalizes the sin which the light reveals. It is described for us in chapter one, verse 10, and, ignoring the chapter break, the first two verses of chapter two.

If we say we have not sinned, we make him a liar, and his word is not in us. My little children, I am writing this to you so that you may not sin; but if any one does sin, we have an advocate with the Father, Jesus Christ the righteous; and he is the expiation for our sins, and not for ours only but also for the sins of the whole world.

Here is the person who rationalizes sin. I do not hesitate to say that this is the most common obstacle of all, the most common failure in Christian experience. In the first case we referred to, the man does not like what the light reveals so he keeps himself too busy ever to see it. In the second case, the person says there is no need for light because, he says, I cannot sin, therefore I shall just go on living the Christian life as I see it, since there is an automatic something in me that keeps me from falling into sin. But in this third case, the person is saying, of course I can sin as a Christian; I know this. I do need

51

light. But when I stop to look at my life and examine myself what I see is not sin. Weakness and failure perhaps, but not sin. I may have to admit that I have been weak, but I have not sinned. Now that is what John means. "If we say we have not sinned, we make him a liar, and his word is not in us."

Essentially this is an evasion of fact, an avoidance of reality. It is the exercise of that terrible power of the human mind which we call rationalization, the ability to clothe wrong so that it looks right, and evil so that it looks good. Who of us has not experienced this? We are all experts at it. We know well how to invent reasons to do what we want to do, and how to invent equally valid-sounding reasons to avoid what we want to avoid. There are always perfectly understandable circumstances that keep us from doing these things. That is rationalization. In other words, it is the tendency to tone down an unpleasant, or unacceptable reality. We do that with the word "sin." Many people really do not know what the word means, but all of us have an uncomfortable feeling about it. We know that it suggests something bad and we do not like to use it about ourselves. So we have invented some very fancy names for it.

By Any Other Name

What the Scripture calls sin, we call human frailty, or bad tendencies, or simply weakness, or a hereditary fault, or an environmental kick-back. The fancier the name the more we like it, because it sounds so much better than that simple, ugly, three-letter word, sin. It is just as if you went through your medicine cabinet, took out all the bottles of poison, and relabeled them "perfume," "hand lotion," and so on. It does not change the character of the poison, but it does make it sound a lot better. The evil twist of our fallen natures is revealed in the fact that what others do we call sin, but when we do the same thing, we have a different name for it. Others have prejudices; we have convictions. Others are conceited; but we have self-respect. When another man is lazy, we say so; but when we do not want to do something, we say we are too busy. When someone else goes ahead and acts on his own, we say he is presumptuous; when we do the same thing, we have initiative. When someone else gets angry and blows up, we say he has lost his temper; but when we do that, we are merely showing righteous indignation. As long as we can find a nicer label we will never treat the thing like the poison it is.

Now we may laugh at these things, but these are the reasons why we are weak as Christians. As long as we laugh at them, we will never do anything about them. We say, "Oh well, everyone does it. It is so common, even the Christians at church all do it." As long as we take that attitude we shall always be in the grip of evil. We will never treat these things as the poison they are as long as we permit ourselves to paste perfume labels on them. Also, we will never understand why we still go around crippled and ailing ·and acting as though some poison were sapping the spiritual strength from our lives.

Another way we rationalize our sins is to excuse them because of the pressure of our current circumstances. We say it is nerves that causes us to speak impatiently to one another. Or it is tiredness, fatigue, that makes us utter sharp words at home. We blame the pressure of work for losing our peace and making us worried, troubled, and harassed. We say it is our difficult neighbors who make us resentful and bitter. If it were not for them we could be sweet, lovely, and kind. We do not need the cleansing of the blood of Christ. Obviously, if we sinned we would need that, but what we are saying is, we do not sin. Rather, we need to have our tensions unraveled by our psychiatrist. We are saying, "I know I shouldn't have said that, or done this thing, but it's not really my fault. I can't help it. It's because of the circumstances and therefore it's not really sin. Sin is deliberate, sin is willful, but I can't help myself and so *I have not sinned.*"

Put the Blame on God

Now put that alongside what John has said. "If we say we have not sinned, we make him a liar, and his word is not in us" (1:10). He says this is not only an evasion of reality, but it is also a direct accusation against God. We make him a liar, he says, and his word is not in us. In other words, we are not shifting the blame to some unknown, unstated individual, we are putting it squarely on God. The Christian always lives in direct relationship to God. There are only two people in life, as far as your basic relationship is concerned—you and God. So if we say it is not our fault, we are saying it is his fault. "It's your fault, God, not mine. These circumstances that you've allowed me to get involved with make it impossible for me to obey you. Therefore, you're to blame. I want to do it. You know my heart; you know that I really want to be what I ought to be, but because of these circumstances I can't, so it's really your fault."

That is the oldest excuse in the world; it goes back to the Garden of Eden. When God came looking for man, he said to him, "Why did you do this thing?" And man said, "It's the woman you gave me. It's your fault." And when God said to the woman, "Why did you do it?" she said, "It is the serpent. It's your fault because you let him talk to me." So, the blame comes right back to God. We are, in effect, calling God a rascal and a double-crosser. But John uses even a worse name. He says, "we make him a liar." The Word of God makes clear that the Christian has a source of strength in Christ that is imparted to him from within. We are inwardly strengthened by him. As Paul puts it, "the inward man is [being] renewed day by day" (2 Cor. 4:16, KJV). The outer man can perish but the inner man is being renewed daily. Therefore, nothing *outward* should hinder us.

In Romans, Paul cries, "Who shall separate us from the love of Christ?" (Rom. 8:35). Then he goes through the list of possibilities. Can life, or death, or things present (your circumstances), or things to come (the pressure of the future), or height, or depth, or time, or eternity, or anything else in all creation, separate us from the love of Christ? His answer is, no, none of these things can cut us off from the strength of Christ, the love of Christ. But that is not what we say. We say to God, yes, there are many things that cut me off from you and make it impossible for me to do what you ask me to do. Difficulties cut me off, and fatigue, and sickness, and pressure. Therefore, God, you're a liar. You say that none of these things will do it; I say they do. Now one of us is not telling the truth; one of us is lying, and I know who it is, it's you!

Now think of the enormity of that charge! Here is what we are constantly saying to God! Lord, it is your fault; you are not true. Here we are, mere human pigmies, standing before the faithful and unchanging God, the God who has revealed himself as without a shadow of turning, absolutely faithful; and we are charging him with faithlessness. We glory in the unchangeableness of God when it adds to our comfort. We love to speak of the unchanging God, the Refuge from every kind of pressure. Yet, how strange it is that we can stand before him the next moment and defiantly assert that the reason for our weakness is not our failure, but his. We declare he is not faithful to his word, he does not keep his promises, he denies himself, he is a liar.

I have often quoted 1 Corinthians 10:13 to Christians in difficult circumstances, "No temptation has overtaken you that is not common to man. God is faithful, and he will not let you be tempted beyond your strength, but with the temptation will also provide the way of escape, that you may be able to endure it." I have had people look me right in the eye and say without batting an eyelid, "That's not true. I have been tempted already above what I've been able to bear. I can't stand this thing." How many times do we say that, in one way or another? But what is that but calling God a liar? Do we realize it is impossible for God to be wrong and us to be right? If that were true, we would be God, not he. It is simply an impossibility. We need to read again the Book of Job and see how Job learned this great lesson. Because he was going through terrible pain and hardship, his heart protested and cried out against God. There came a time when God said to Job,

> "Shall a faultfinder contend with the Almighty?
> He who argues with God, let him answer it."

> Then the Lord answered Job out of the whirlwind:
> "Gird up your loins like a man;
> I will question you, and you declare to me.
> Will you even put me in the wrong?
> Will you condemn me that you may be justified?
> Have you an arm like God,
>   and can you thunder with a voice like his?" (Job 40:2,6–9).

In that amazing fortieth chapter God puts to Job a series of test questions, asking Job if he can perform even the simplest functions which God performs every day. And Job's answer is,

> "Behold, I am of small account;
>   what shall I answer thee?
>   I lay my hand on my mouth.
> I have spoken once, and I will not answer;
>   twice, but I will proceed no further.

> therefore I despise myself,
>   and repent in dust and ashes" (Job 40:4,5;42:6).

The blunt truth is, we do not like where God puts us. We do not like the people or the pressures we have to live under, we do not like the circumstances that surround us, and we refuse to accept them. That is the real problem. Therefore we are not interested in Christ's power to live *in* them. We do not want it. We have set our will against God's will.

Now let us be honest and admit that we fall because we

do not choose to meet the circumstances with his strength. Rather, we run away from them and blame it all on God. No wonder we lose fellowship. No wonder God seems to be our enemy, and things all go wrong. We find that peace has fled our hearts, we are troubled, harassed, worried, and upset. We find ourselves flying off the handle even more easily, and losing our patience, and we are baffled by it all, not knowing what is causing all this. Does this sound familiar?

Me for the Defense!

John explains what the trouble is. In verse 1, chapter 2, he says,

> My little children, I am writing this to you so that you may not sin; but if any one does sin, we have an advocate with the Father, Jesus Christ the righteous; and he is the expiation for our sins.

What does he mean? Just this. There is never any need to sin, but if we find ourselves doing so we have a perfect defense available to us; a defense which the Father will gladly receive, one that he already assures us will be welcomed. We have an Advocate with the Father, who will rush to our defense immediately. But his defense is of no avail to us as long as we are still defending ourselves. There cannot be two advocates in this case. You either rely on his defense of you—the manifestation of his work on your behalf which has wiped away every stain, every sin which you ever will commit or ever have committed— or you must rely upon your own defense. Here you are, standing before God, defiantly telling him that you are not to blame, that you have a defense. You are not guilty. You can explain all this by the pressure of circumstances.

Now, you see, as long as you remain defiant or evasive, you are still justifying and excusing yourself and therefore the Judge can only condemn you, and permit the inevitable, built-in judgment that follows, to upset you, overthrow you, harass you, baffle you, and leave you in weakness and folly. But if you will stop justifying yourself, he will justify you. The blood of Jesus Christ cannot cleanse excuses. It only cleanses sins. If we will say, "Yes, it wasn't the pressure, it wasn't the circumstances, it wasn't that these things are not as bad as you call them; it's that I chose to be impatient, I chose to be resentful. I decided to be worried and to let anxiety grip me." If we come to that place, then we discover that there is One who stands before the Father and reveals to him the righteousness of his own life, and God sees us in him, and we are cleansed and accepted. Strength again flows into the inner man, peace comes back to our hearts, we are cleansed of our sin, washed and restored to the grace of God. Then we can go back into the very same circumstance, under the very same pressure, in the very same disagreeable relationship, and find our hearts kept by the grace and strength of God.

Paul puts it so beautifully, "Have no anxiety about anything, but in everything by prayer and supplication with thanksgiving let your requests be made known to God. And the peace of God, which passes all understanding [you cannot explain it; someone says to you, how can you be so calm in the midst of these circumstances? And you say, I don't know, but it must be because I'm trusting Christ, resting on him], that peace will keep your hearts and your minds in Christ Jesus" (Phil. 4:6,7 personal paraphrase). Is that not practical? That is not designed for church, that is designed for life, for home, for work, for your relationships with your neighbors and your boss and your mother-in-law, your children, everyone.

For Every Man

Now why does John say, "He is the expiation for our sins, and not for ours only but also for the sins of the whole world" (2:2)? Why does he put that in? Obviously he is drawing a contrast between Christians and non-

Christians. He is reminding us that when the Lord Jesus
died upon the cross 1900 years ago he not only paid the
debt of our sins, he not only took our guilt, as Christians,
but he took the guilt of the whole world. He paid the
price for every man. There is no man who will be kept
away from God because of his sins, if he accepts the work
of Christ on his behalf. Sin can never separate an
individual from God, because of the cross of Christ. No
matter how bad the sin is, no matter how extreme it may
be or how long continued, sin can never separate
anybody, anywhere, in any time or any age, from the
heart of God, if the work of the cross be received. That is
the extent of the expiation mentioned here.

But why does he remind us of that in this context? It is
to help us see ourselves. Why is it that all the world is not
reconciled to God? Why is it that these others, whose sins
have already been paid for on the cross, are living in
estrangement and hostility to the God who loves them
and who seeks after them? Why is it that men are still
defying and blaspheming God and turning and running
from him, experiencing the death, darkness, and degra-
dation that comes from not knowing God? You know the
answer. Because they will not believe him. They will not
accept his forgiveness. He has forgiven them, but they
have never forgiven him. As Paul puts it to the Corinthians, "In Christ God was reconciling the world to
himself, not counting their trespasses against them. . . .
We beseech you [therefore] on behalf of Christ, be
reconciled to God" (2 Cor. 5:19,20). We do not have to
say to God, be reconciled to men; we are saying to men,
be reconciled to God.

Now that is the very reason why we Christians are not
enjoying the full flow of the Spirit of power, life, love,
and wisdom in our experience. It is all available to us, but
we will not receive it. That is what John means. Like the
world, we are turning our back on it. We are saying to
God, "I'm not interested in cleansing because, you see, I
really don't need it. After all, this is not a sin, it's simply a
weakness, just an inherited tendency, something I got

from my family. I can't help it." That kind of rationalization is cutting the ground out from under the whole redemptive work of Jesus Christ done on our behalf.

Now let us bow before him. In a moment of quietness before God, let us confess this terrible tendency that each of us has unquestionably experienced: to rationalize sin, to excuse it, justify it, call it something else, doll it up, sprinkle perfume on it and make it look better, instead of calling it exactly what it is. Christ has found a way below, around, and above our circumstances. He can reach us despite the pressures; it is just that we do not want him to do so.

Our Father, search our hearts. We do not want merely to play at being Christians, we want to really be Christians. We need this probing, searching, finger of the Spirit to touch us and to unveil to us the closeted areas, these closed doors that we have shut away from you. Make us open, make us honest, make us stop this eternal excusing of ourselves and face up to the wonderful reality of your challenge and promise, that nothing and no one can keep us from being what we ought to be. May we begin to live in that way, Lord, that the world might see your light breaking out, your sweetness, your love, your fragrance in Jesus Christ. We pray in his name, Amen.

6

Counterfeits and Reflectors

We are considering, in his first letter, John's great analysis of the way to maintain unbroken fellowship with the Son of God. Such fellowship is described to us by Jesus himself as the flowing of rivers of living water out of the center of life. It is something that cannot be hindered by anything outward because it comes from within. Jesus said, "If any one thirst, let him come to me and drink. . . . 'Out of his heart shall flow rivers of living water.'" John adds, "This he said about the Spirit, which those who believed in him were to receive . . ." (John 7:37–39).

We have seen that there are two ties we may have with Christ. There is the tie of relationship which is established by the response of our faith to the invitation of his Word. But there is also fellowship, as John is making clear here, the actual experience of his power and wisdom, his love, and his life at work in you. Fellowship is to come into a day-by-day experience of Christ working, living, and manifesting himself through you. There is nothing more exciting than that! And this experience of fellowship is continually yours if you live honestly before God and call the reactions of your life what God calls them, shunning all pretense and deceit. In other words, walking in the light is the secret of fellowship. Fellowship is the secret of power, and walking in the light is the secret of fellowship.

We have examined the three conditions which, John indicates, block the light that shines to us from the person of God. First, we can evade the light, refuse to examine ourselves. Then, we can close our eyes to the light by denying the possibility of sin. And finally, we can obscure the light by rationalizing the sin which is revealed in our life, by excusing it because of circumstances, or calling it another name that does not sound so bad.

Now in verse 3 of chapter 2, John pauses in the flow of his discourse to deal with an inevitable human reaction to this kind of searching examination of our spiritual life. When I was a boy we had on the shelf of our library at home a big, thick, book called *The Journal of Home Medicine.* It had many fascinating pictures in it—fascinating to me, because I was hoping at that time to become a surgeon. And it gave a brief description of all the sicknesses that afflict the human race—their symptoms and certain suggestions as to the cures. I remember reading in that book many, many times, and feeling a kind of macabre fascination at descriptions of such horrendous things as cancer, diabetes, heart failure, perforated ulcers, and other equally horrible diseases. Inevitably, after each reading of that book, I became aware of the very symptoms I had just read about, and I spent some hours of intense anxiety over the suspicion that I was developing one of these terrible diseases.

Spiritual Hypochondria

Is that not what often happens when we start reading about sickness? We all have a bit of hypochondria in us, and perhaps it is true on the spiritual level as well. Since John is examining our spiritual lives as a doctor would examine our physical lives, pointing out the sicknesses of the soul, it is only natural that he would expect a reaction of spiritual hypochondria, in which some of us might feel we had some of these diseases, or even worse. He evidently feels there may be many who are saying to themselves, "Am I really a Christian at all? Can I even claim a saving relationship with Christ?" If the Spirit has convicted us and we sense a lack, the question at the back of our mind may be, "Perhaps my trouble is not merely a break in fellowship; perhaps I am experiencing a total lack of relationship." Of course, the Tempter is quick to suggest this very thing. He is alert to push us into such feelings, to arouse such fears within us whenever we examine ourselves. So John stops to handle that very question.

> And by this we may be sure that we know him, if we keep his commandments. He who says "I know him" but disobeys his commandments is a liar, and the truth is not in him; but whoever keeps his word, in him truly love for God is perfected. By this we may be sure that we are in him: he who says he abides in him ought to walk in the same way in which he walked (1 John 2:3–6).

Here he is making a careful distinction between relationship and fellowship. He wants us to be quite clear that there is a distinction between *union* with Christ and *communion* with Christ. The division is marked by the phrase, twice repeated, "by this we may be sure." The first part is in verses 3 and 4:

> And by this we may be sure that we know him, if we keep his commandments. He who says "I know him" but disobeys his commandments is a liar, and the truth is not in him. . . .

John is talking here about an experience in the past for any believer in Christ. The original Greek makes that even clearer; what is said here is, "by this we may know that *we have known him* (perfect tense—something done in the past), because *we are now keeping* his commandments (present tense)." The present willingness to keep his commandments, John is saying, is a sign of a valid *relationship*. It is proof that an act of union with Christ has already occurred; we have been born again. Our actions have changed, and because they have changed and we do not behave as we once did but now have a desire to obey him—we can be sure we have indeed been born again.

Now please do not reverse this! Do not change it around. We cannot know God by attempting to keep his commandments. That is impossible. Let us be clear on that. We never come to know God by trying to keep his commandments, for the knowledge of God comes by faith in Jesus Christ. That must be first. Martin Luther made the mistake of trying, as an Augustinian monk, to find God by keeping his commandments. He made a desperate and sincere effort to do anything that he felt God required of him, that he might discover and know God. This is always the hunger of the human heart, to know God. Luther would beat himself, spend days in protracted fasting, lie for long, weary, agonizing hours on the cold floor of his cell in the monastery, and try in every way he could to discover God by keeping his commandments. But it only drove him to despair. As you know, it was only when those words from Paul's letter to the Romans, "the just shall live by faith," came alive to him, that he found God and then spent the rest of his life actually keeping God's commandments.

Desire to Obey

Now it must always come in that order. We receive Christ by faith, by believing his invitation, and accepting him. When we do, he comes quietly and invisibly into our lives and begins his delivering work. The sign of that delivering work is a change in our attitude about obeying him. John suggests there is a *desire* to obey God. Notice that Jesus himself declared this to us in the great message called "the Upper Room Discourse" when he said to his disciples (John 14:15), "If you love me, you will keep my commandments." And (in verse 21), "He who has my commandments and keeps them, he it is who loves me. . . ."

Years ago I recall hearing a friend say that in a short while after he had become a Christian he had listened several times to others giving their testimonies. He was struck by the number of times he had heard Christians express a love for Christ—how much they had fallen in love with the person of Christ. He said, "You know, I don't think I can say that. I've been a Christian about a year but I don't think I've ever had any deep sense of love for Christ. This bothered me for a while. I didn't seem to have what others had. But then I ran across a verse that has comforted me a great deal." And he quoted the verse I have just referred to, the words of our Lord in John 14:21, "He who has my commandments and keeps them, he it is who loves me." My friend said, "I don't know that I have the feeling, but I do have a great desire to obey the Lord, and therefore I must love him." Now that is exactly what John is saying here. Are you willing to obey him? Whenever he makes clear his will, are you already pre-committed in your own heart to do it? You may have many problems as a Christian, you may have a sense of weakness or lack in your life, but one thing is clear; if you are keeping his commandments, if you desire to obey him, then you know him. You can be sure that you know him; that is what John declares.

He puts this also in the negative in order that we may make doubly sure.

> He who says "I know him" but disobeys his command-
> ments is a liar, and the truth is not in him . . . (v.4).

Have you ever seen a counterfeit bill? I do not know that one has ever been handed to me. If so, I passed it along without knowing. But I know one thing about counterfeit bills: they never come in $3.00 or $7.00 denominations. You hear the phrase, "as phony as a $3.00 bill," but I have never seen a $3.00 bill and I never hope to see one.

Counterfeiters are smarter than that. At a superficial glance, a counterfeit bill appears to be perfectly normal and in a common denomination. But there is always something bogus about it; there is always something phony. There is a lack of exact correspondence. There is a blur somewhere, or something is omitted from it which marks it as a counterfeit bill.

It is the same with a phony Christian—and there are phony Christians, many of them. As John indicates, they *say* the right things. If you were to judge them by what they say you would never know they were phonies. They go to the right places, they mingle with the right crowds, and they *say,* "I know him," but, as John indicates, there is something wrong with their lives. They disobey his commandments. They have no apparent desire to do what he says, to keep his word. Their lives are unchanged. Their actions are no different than they were before. As a dairyman once said to me, "They preach cream, but live skimmed milk."

Paul also warns of this in his letter to Titus. He speaks of some who, he says, "profess to know God, but they deny him by their deeds; they are detestable, disobedient, unfit for any good deed" (Titus 1:16). It was Charles Spurgeon, the prince of English preachers, who once said, "An unchanged life is the sign of an uncleansed heart." The Scripture is extremely clear on this. If the thief has not stopped his stealing, if the liar has not quit lying, if the alcoholic has not stopped drinking, it is useless for him to claim that he is a Christian. If there has been no basic change in his life, there is nothing that indicates, to him or to anyone else, that he has been delivered from the bondage of Satan and the power of evil into the kingdom of God.

Now let me make something clear. There are many reasons why men may quit something evil, if for no other cause than that it is bad for their health. You can stop these things without being born again, but you cannot be born again without stopping them. That is the claim John makes.

He goes still further in verse 5.

. . . but whoever keeps his word, in him truly love of God [this translation is preferable to "love *for* God"] is perfected.

He declares that if we keep his word, if there is a willingness to do what he says regardless of whether we see the reasons for it, then something else is also happening to us: The love of God is gradually taking over our lives and changing us, it is being perfected within us. In Romans 5:5 the Apostle says, "the love of God is shed abroad in our hearts by the Holy Ghost which is given unto us" (KJV). If we have been born again, if we have received Christ and we are willing to obey him, then the love of God is doing something to us. It is being shed abroad in our hearts by the Holy Spirit and it is leading us on, step by step, toward the goal the Lord desires in our lives—the experience of continuous, unbroken fellowship with him.

Do you see now how relationship leads on into fellowship? The act by which we began the Christian life is intended to precipitate a process that leads us into the experience of the fullness of Christ. It will, and it is, for God is at work in your life to do this very thing, for this is the goal of love. The love of God is being perfected, it is being completed, but it may take awhile. For some of us who are particularly resistant, it takes long years, and on this I speak from full experience.

The Sign of Fellowship

Now if an obedient will is the sign of relationship, what is the sign that we are beginning to move into the experience of fellowship? The answer is in the latter part of verse 5 and in verse 6.

By this we may be sure that we are in him: he who says he

abides in him ought to walk in the same way in which he walked.

This phrase, "abides in him," means exactly the same thing as "fellowship with him." They are one and the same experience. The Lord Jesus made that clear when he said, "As the branch cannot bear fruit by itself, unless it abides in the vine, neither can you, unless you abide in me" (John 15:4). You can be in Christ, as a member of the vine, and only bear leaves. That is mere relationship. But if you want fruit in your life, there must be that further attitude of abiding in him, resting in him. That, he says, is what produces significant results in life. Without that, "you can do nothing." The sign of abiding, as John says here, is to walk in the same way in which Christ walked. ". . . he who says he abides in him ought to walk in the same way in which he walked." That does not mean to do the same things that Jesus did; that means to act from the same principle upon which he acted, to reflect the same kind of relationship to the Father that he had. That is the sign of fellowship.

How did our Lord walk? How did he do the things that he did? How did he manage to speak such matchless words, convey such challenging ideas, do such remarkable things among men, and change lives so consistently? What was the secret of his power? You can be sure that while he was ministering, this was the question everyone was asking. "Wherein lies this man's power?" That is what brought Nicodemus to him by night, to try to ferret out the secret, if he could. Many others came wondering what the secret of his power was. The amazing thing is that he kept telling people what it was, as he keeps telling us. But we skip over it with easy disregard. He said, "the Son of Man does not do these things of himself." That is, "I'm not doing this; it is the Father who dwells in me; he is doing it. I do not speak these words of myself, but I speak only that which I hear the Father say. It is the Father who speaks the words; it is the Father who does

the work. I am a man, available to him, but he is in me
and his working in me is the secret of the things that I do.
I am simply counting on him every minute to be at work
and to do these things, and he does them."

That is the great secret, and that is one of the hardest
things for Christians to learn. How did he walk? He
walked in total, unrelenting, unbroken fellowship and
dependence upon the activity of the Father who indwelt
him. But that seems so hard for us to learn. With us, it is
the Son of God who lives within us and he has come to
reproduce in us the effect of his death and the power of
his resurrection—to live again his life in us. But we have
such difficulty with this.

Our attitude is, "Please, Father, I'd rather do it
myself!" We are brought up with this idea that we have in
ourselves an ability to act significantly, that God is
looking to us to act on his behalf and if we fail him the
whole program will fall apart, but if we do it God should
be eternally grateful to us for our faithfulness. Does this
not represent our attitude? But this is not Christianity.
This is not what a Christian is called to do. If we ever
learn the great secret that John is trying desperately to
impart to us it will revolutionize our lives. We will never
again be the same persons. When we begin to see it and
act on it our lives are immediately changed. A quiet,
unrelenting dependence upon an indwelling God to be
always at work in us, reproducing the value of his death
and the power of his resurrection—that is what Christianity is, that is what fellowship is, that is what abiding in
him means. We are continually to expect him to do this,
and *we are to consent to its being done.*

But there is where the rub comes! We want him to do it
despite us. We do not always want to consent to it; his
death means that we must absolutely renounce *all* the
self-life, *all* the self-centeredness around which our lives
have for so long been built. His death cuts off the old
man, with its egocentric ways. We do not like that. If we
were arranging the Christian plan for living, we would

devise a different process. In fact, we try to do just that most of the time. We want to make it some of us, and some of him. A little bit of glory, fame, power, and favoritism for us, and quite a bit for him. We are glad to let him have the lion's share, but we hang on so desperately to something for us.

All of It Has to Go

That is the problem, do you see? But his death absolutely eliminated the natural man. When he became man and died in our place he cut off, he ended, not merely *part* of the old life, but *all* of it. Therefore his death, reproduced in us, means that all of it has to go. That is tough, hard for us to take, but what draws us on is the rest of the transaction. His *life* in us means the reproducing in us of the power of his resurrection, the kind of power that works in the midst of death.

When everything else has ceased to work, when nothing man can do can be performed any longer, when all hope is gone, when all possible avenues of human endeavor have been blocked off, resurrection power begins to work. That is wonderful. That is a different kind of power than the world has ever seen, a kind that works when everyone else is discouraged. It keeps on blossoming, growing green and bright, full and productive. When everyone else's life seems dead and dull, and for them life is monotonous and boring, this power keeps one alert and alive and interesting and fascinating. Resurrection life! How we long for it. But, you see, the two go together. It is a package deal. As Paul puts it, "that I may know him and the power of his resurrection, and may share his sufferings, becoming like him in his death" (Phil. 3:10). That is fellowship. That is what the love of God will lead us into, step by step, little by little, as we grow along with him.

And the sign of it? We learn to be dependent upon the Father. We learn to walk as Jesus walked, in a complete and unbroken dependence upon another to work within us. That is the sign of fellowship. Where does this leave us? Let us not be counterfeits, denying the faith by an unchanged life. Let us rather be reflectors, reflecting the character, the quality, and the principle by which the Lord himself lived his life. Read this description of that reflecting process from Paul's second letter to the Corinthians:

> And we all, with unveiled face, beholding the glory of the Lord [seeing the secret of Jesus and his life], are being changed into his likeness from one degree of glory to another; for this comes from the Lord who is the Spirit (2 Cor. 3:18).

7

Visible Christianity

People often say today that when Christianity has been rejected by the world it is on the basis of a caricature which has been mistaken for the real thing. We twentieth-century Christians tend to say that as though it were something new, as though it had never happened before. But this is something that has been true ever since the first century. We have seen it in a new form, perhaps, in our own generation, but the phenomenon is a common one and has been true in every century. The work of the devil is always to distort and to twist truth.

The ministry of the apostle John is to call us back to original things, to foundations, to fundamental issues, to repair that which is broken. In this first letter John is correcting the twisted caricature of Christianity which existed in his day, and exists equally in our day. If you know the reality, you will be able to detect the false and twisted form, the counterfeit.

The caricature, for instance, says that Christianity is primarily a religion concerned about the behavior of men. But we see in the Scriptures that the primary concern of real Christianity is not with behavior at all, but with being, with character, from which all behavior must ultimately come. The caricature tells us that Christianity's attitude toward life is essentially negative—don't do this, don't do that, stop doing this, stop doing that. That is the view of the Christian faith held by the average man on the street. But the genuine article says that in Christ we are discovering the secret of the fullest, freest, most satisfying life that could possibly be experienced by anyone. As Jesus himself said, "I came that they may have life, and have it abundantly" (John 10:10).

The caricature says that the facts upon which Christian faith rests, the death and the resurrection of our Lord, are mere stories, legends that centered upon the figure of Christ in the early church, which Christians must accept by blind faith without any confirmation or support. But the real article says these are actions of God in history that can be tested by the normal means of testing evidence and that they form, therefore, a solid ground of faith based in history. The caricature says that the goal of the Christian faith is to produce a heaven filled with stodgy, hymn-singing saints. But the real thing says the goal of Christian faith is to produce love-filled homes right now, filled with strong, manly men, and gracious, sweet-tempered women, and orderly, alert, admirable children, who live together facing the normal, useful problems of life with thoughtfulness and mutual dependence upon the activity of a living God in their midst. That is real Christianity.

As God Loves

In this introductory section of the apostle John's first letter we have been noting what he has to say about maintaining fellowship with the Son of God. That is the secret of this abundant life. In chapter two he comes to the practical goal toward which all this is moving. You will find this in verses 7–11. But let me first point out that all of this section is a commentary on one phrase in verse 5 of chapter two. John says there, "But whoever keeps his word, in him truly love of God is perfected." God's love is finding its completeness, it is being fulfilled in him who keeps God's word. Now in verses 7–11 he takes that phrase, "the love of God is being perfected," and explains it, indicating that it is the supreme goal of the Christian life. I hope you catch the importance and urgency of his word. What the apostle is saying is that the goal of the Christian life is for us to love *as God loves.*

The single, most desperate need of humanity is for love. Yet, the twisted paradox of our lives is that we increasingly find it impossible to give what another one desperately needs. Therefore, because others have the same trouble, we find ourselves unable to have what we cannot live without—love. There you have the whole pathetic tragedy of human life today. A hunger for love, on the one part, and an inability to satisfy it on the other. That is the dilemma of human life.

Recently I received a packet in my mail, a large manila envelope. I opened it, and found it was a letter. The reason it came in such a large envelope was that it was 25 single-spaced typewritten pages. It was a letter from a lonely man who, writing in the loneliness of his hotel room in the loneliness of a big city, was simply putting down his thoughts, reactions, and attitudes. I could not help but feel that was typical of our day. The hunger expressed in loneliness is simply a cry out of the human heart for love.

Both Old and New

Now the glorious news of Christianity is that, in this strange, impossible dilemma in which we live, a tremendous breakthrough has been achieved. A way has been found, through the death and the resurrection of Jesus and through the process of union and fellowship with him, by which we may fulfill these demands made upon us, and in doing so, satisfy the needs of our own hearts. See how John describes this in verses 7 and 8 of chapter 2.

Beloved, I am writing you no new commandment, but an old commandment which you had from the beginning; the old commandment is the word which you have heard. Yet I am writing you a new commandment, which is true in him and in you, because the darkness is passing away and the true light is already shining.

Do those seem strange words—"an old commandment," "a new commandment"? What does he mean? What is old and yet new? There is a clue here in his words, "an old commandment *which you had from the beginning,*" that is, the beginning of our Christian life, as this phrase most frequently means in John's letter. This is something that you learned when you first came into the Christian experience. It accompanied or was part of "the word which you heard," God's word to man. What is the first note of God's word to man? Well, it is written all through the Scriptures. You find it at the beginning of the Bible, and it runs like a river all the way through the inspired text, from beginning to end. Jesus called it the first and great commandment, "Thou shalt love the Lord thy God with all thy heart, and with all thy soul, and with all thy strength, and with all thy mind; and thy neighbor as thyself" (Luke 10:27, KJV).

That was the first commandment to be broken. Adam violated it in the Garden of Eden when he chose to love his wife more than he loved his God and, following her into temptation and sin, the race fell in him. The second part of it was violated by his son Cain, whose contemptuous response to God's inquiry about his brother has become the classic expression of loveless unconcern, "Am I my brother's keeper?" (Gen. 4:9). It is the violation of love toward God and toward men. Now John is indicating that this old commandment is, in some sense, new. What does he mean, "yet I am writing you a *new* commandment, which is true in him and in you . . ."? If you are familiar with his Gospel you know this is an echo of our Lord's own words recorded in the thirteenth chapter of John, in the Upper Room, "A new commandment I give to you, that you love one another; even as I have loved you" (13:34). That last phrase, "as I have loved you" is the key. To love one another is an old commandment, as old as the human race. But "as I have loved you" is new. The manner by which we love, the process by which this can occur is new.

Did you ever think how difficult it was for our Lord to love the disciples? As you read the New Testament, how do you think of these men? We are so apt to see them through the aura of twenty centuries of admiration that I'm afraid we often overglamorize these disciples and see them only as saints, almost plaster saints. But these were no plaster saints—these were ordinary men. There was Peter, with his tendency toward boasting, always a bit overbearing, very difficult to get along with at times, and so utterly unreliable, given to boastful commitments that he could never fulfill and then falling flat on his face when the hour of testing came. And there were James and John, those two young men whom our Lord called "the sons of thunder." That is a revealing description. I do not know exactly why he called them that, but it evidently reflects something of their disposition, their temperament. We do know that they were somewhat spoiled and a bit selfish. It was they who came with their mother and asked Jesus for a place, one at his right hand and one at his left, when he came into his kingdom.

Then there was stubborn, unmoveable, doubting Thomas, and mousy, retiring, introspective Philip, and the practical, hardheaded Andrew, and all the others. They were sometimes most disappointing and frequently quite disagreeable. There are even occasions when the Lord, almost in exasperation, says, "How much longer must I put up with you?" So if you think these men were easy to love, you are mistaken. There is that occasion in Luke 17:3 when the Lord said to them, "If your brother sin against you, rebuke him; and if he repent, forgive him. And if he sins against you seven times in one day, and repents, then seven times you are to forgive him." If your imagination fills in the details of that, you can see the apostles looking at one another and thinking of the difficulty they have in forgiving one another even once. As one man they turn to the Lord and say, "Lord, increase our faith!" There was Judas, too, who betrayed him. The Lord knew Judas was working against him from the very beginning. Yet the wonderful truth is he loved every one of them. He was sometimes displeased with them, he was irritated by them, he was exasperated with them, but he loved them. And he said to them, "a new commandment I give to you, that you love one another; even *as I have loved you*" (John 13:34).

Out of a Shared Life

There, hidden in that last phrase, is the wonderful process that John is now explaining to us. He says this is the new commandment. "I am writing you a new commandment, which is true in him and in you, because the darkness is passing away and the true light is already shining" (2:8). How did our Lord love these men the way he did? As Paul says in Romans, "the love of God is shed abroad in our hearts by the Holy Ghost which is given unto us" (5:5, KJV). That is also the way the Lord loved his disciples. The love of God was shed abroad in his heart by the Holy Spirit who was given unto him without measure. That is the only way anyone ever loves another the way God loves. Only God can love that way.

It is the same way for us. That is why John says, "which is true *in him and in you*." It comes out of a shared life. The fact that you and he share together the same life makes it possible for you to love another who may be difficult, disagreeable, or hard to live with. It is because the love of God is shed abroad in your heart by the Holy Spirit who is given unto you. That is the only way it can be done. This, therefore, is the new thing. The old commandment was there from the beginning. We *are* our brother's keeper. *No man is an island.* We have a responsibility to love each other. But we have never found the way until we find it in the sharing of the life of Jesus, the fellowship with the Son of God. In the light of that new power it is now possible to perform the old commandment. Therefore, John says, the darkness is passing away.

Do you find that true in your life? He does not say the darkness is past, because obviously there are still times of weakness. There are times when we become angry, and even hateful toward one another, as Christians. But the darkness of hatred and indifference is rapidly passing away as the light of the nature of our Lord, the light of the character of God, is possessing us, gripping us, as we grow in grace and fellowship with him. This is the secret of love and there is no other.

Now comes the question, how do you measure your progress in this? How do you know how far along you have come, or whether you have even begun? John answers that in verses 9 and 10. You can test yourself by asking, "What is my attitude toward my fellow Christian, my brother in Christ, the man who, like me, professes faith in Jesus Christ?"

> He who says he is in the light and hates his brother is in the darkness still. He who loves his brother abides in the light, and in it there is no cause for stumbling (1 John 2:9,10).

What does he mean here by hate, "He who hates his brother"? The dictionary tells us that hate is a feeling of extreme hostility or extreme dislike of another. That suffices as far as the definition is concerned. Ah, yes, but it can be expressed in two different ways. It can be active, in that we indulge in malicious talk or injurious actions toward another. We can strike them or beat them or throw our garbage over their fence or mistreat them in some way. All these are active expressions of hate, and perhaps most of us think of hate only in that sense.

But hate can also be expressed passively and still be hate. It can be expressed by indifference, by coldness, by isolation, by exclusion, or by unconcern for another. Someone has well said that indifference is the most cruel form of hate. You only need to read the gospel records to see how true that is. What hurt our Lord most was not the active enmity of those who were trying to accomplish his death, but the coldness and indifference of those who once followed him, as they stood idly by while he was put to death.

A Basic Denial

Now John says that he who hates his brother is not a Christian. He is "in the darkness until now," i.e., he has never come out of it. He is in the state of darkness in which the whole race is plunged and into which we all are born. He has never been removed from that. To say you are in the light and yet hate your brother is a basic denial of faith. We have seen this all along. Notice also verse 11.

> But he who hates his brother is in the darkness and walks in the darkness, and does not know where he is going, because the darkness has blinded his eyes.

Such an attitude of hostility, indifference, or unconcern toward another is a mark of an unregenerate life. But notice that the apostle is careful to make a distinction between walking in the darkness and being in the darkness. To be "in the darkness" is to be unregenerated, as you see also from chapter 3, verse 14:

> We know that we have passed out of death into life, because we love the brethren. He who does not love abides in death.

Darkness and death are the same thing. He who hates

has never been born again, has never passed into life. To return to verse 11, chapter 2, he says "He who hates his brother is *in the darkness*"—unregenerated—"and *walks in the darkness*"—he experiences the effect of this in his daily life as he goes along.

Walking in the darkness is not to know where you are going, not to be aware of where hate is leading. Our papers today are filled with crimes of violence, unusual incidents of appalling, senseless brutality. People are asking where this is all coming from. Why is it that this kind of activity is breaking out all over the country? Remember the word of our Lord in Matthew 24? "Because wickedness is multiplied, most men's love will grow cold" (Matt. 24:12). There is an inevitable sequence here. When the moral life of a nation degenerates to the place where immorality and wickedness abound, then there is a hardening, a stultifying of the life of that nation. The love that is intended to be like a fire in the heart of man grows cold and unresponsive and, as a result, there come outbreaks of senseless violence.

The apostle John is tracing the same thing here. He says that he who hates his brother is in the darkness. Such a person does not know where he is going. He has no understanding that this can easily lead to murder or to mayhem, to heartache and heartbreak. Stumbling blindly on, he proceeds in his hateful attempt to do evil to his friend or brother or companion, whoever it may be. But the result is that he is only damaging himself and all he loves. He has no idea where he is going. He is blinded, John says; "the darkness has blinded his eyes." The word used here is a word which means "to make insensitive," and it implies that if we live in this way, we ultimately come to the place where we no longer can respond. Hatred grips us and hardens our heart and it is no longer able to be softened by any force that comes upon us. This is the warning that runs all through the Scriptures about the nature of human life. When we give way to feelings of hatred we inevitably harden our own hearts.

Only the Worldling

Now John says only the worldling can do this. A
Christian may temporarily succumb to this kind of thing
(and we see this; otherwise there would not be these
pleas in the New Testament for the Christian to put away
malice, anger, hatred, and all the other things). Yes, he
can *walk* in darkness, temporarily, but he is no longer *in*
the darkness. He is no longer a child of darkness. The
light of God's love has come into his heart. If he is not
aware of a struggle between the expression of hate and a
sense of concern, and conscious of guilt over his attitude
of hate, then he ought to wonder whether he has really
passed from death into life. It is possible for a Christian
to walk in darkness, as we find in chapter 1, verse 6: "If
we say we have fellowship with him while we walk in
darkness. . . ." But he is not in the darkness. This is
something that the Spirit of God will inevitably deal with
in the Christian and break, and it may sometimes be by
difficult measures. I know some Christians who have had
to come almost to the end of their lives before they would
face up to the power of hatred within them.

I remember counseling a woman about a physical
problem which really had a spiritual basis in her experience. I discovered that she hated another person and had
hated her for years. She told me the circumstance, and
she had without doubt been treated unjustly, but the
thing had eaten like a canker in her heart for years and
years. Hate had turned her bitter and rancid and had
poisoned all her thoughts. I said to her, "You must find it
in your heart to forgive this person, as God has forgiven
you." She looked at me and said, "I can't forgive her, I'll
never forgive her!" I said, "But God says you must." She
said, "But I can't." I said, "If you can't, then you need to
face the fact that you are not a Christian. Because if you
can't forgive, then you've never been born again." She
looked at me and said, "I guess you're right. I know I am
a Christian, and I see I have just been deceiving myself. I

need to forgive." And she did! There came a change in that woman's life which was like a turning from night into day.

Now a Christian can forgive. He can, of course, delude himself into going along with the world's attitude that he cannot forgive, for it is true that the worldling often cannot forgive. When the worldling hates, he finds himself locked in an unbreakable grip. Hatred, bitterness, and resentment will follow him down through the years. But when the Son of God comes into his life, the power of the evil one is broken and he is delivered from this and can forgive.

But we still must agree to it. God is not going to make us forgive apart from our own will, though the ability to do so is there. Notice the contrast the apostle draws here in verse 10: "He who loves his brother abides in the light." That is, the fact that he loves is proof that he is abiding in the light, he is in fellowship with the Son of God. He is walking in openness and honesty before God, and the proof of it is that he loves all the disagreeable brethren around him. Though he may be irritated by them, or upset by them, he does not cut them off, he does not exclude himself from them, he does not go away and say, "Let them go their way and I'll go mine." Or, "I'll forgive, but I'll never forget." No, he still shows that heart of concern which is born of the Holy Spirit, the love of God which is shed abroad in our hearts by the Holy Spirit who is given unto us. In the Sermon on the Mount our Lord said we are to love our enemies and do good to those who hate us and despitefully use us, and thus, he said, "you will be the children of your Father in heaven." You will demonstrate, you will manifest the fact that you are the children of the Father, "who is kind to the ungracious and the selfish."

That is God's kind of love, not the love of the lovely but the love of the unlovely, a concern and manifest willingness to mix with, talk with, deal with, and help those to whom naturally you find it difficult to respond.

That is the love of God. "He who loves his brother abides in the light, and in it—the light—there is no cause for stumbling." If we walk in love toward one another there is no problem that cannot be worked out, there is no reason for division or schism among us, there is nothing that can separate us if we walk in the light as he is in the light.

Oh, the hunger of men for the manifestation of love. And oh, the hunger of God that those yearnings of the world might be satisfied by Christian hearts that reflect the heart of God.

8

Growing and Maturing in Grace

Now that we have seen how we may keep God's ancient, but yet new, commandment to love our brother, John introduces us to a third factor which follows relationship and fellowship: maturity, full growth—or, as in the King James Version, perfection. The curse of the church has always been immature Christians, Christians who never grow up, Christians who cease their progress soon after beginning the Christian life. It reminds one of that familiar story of the little boy who fell out of bed. When his mother asked what happened, he said, "I don't know, I guess I went to sleep too close to the place I got in."

The Christian life is much more than a beginning in conversion; it is what happens after that which is of supreme importance. Christians who have never grown up are always a problem and cause many difficulties. If you are a brand-new Christian, still rejoicing in the thrill of a new-found relationship with Jesus Christ, I am not speaking of you. You are not a problem, particularly, for there is always room and provision for babies in a family circle. But Christians who are still babies after ten, twenty, thirty, even forty years of Christian life, these are the problem. They are immature, they refuse to grow up.

John now comes face to face with this problem and in

the text before us he describes three stages of spiritual development, three levels of growth in the Christian life:

> I am writing to you, little children, because your sins are forgiven for his sake. I am writing to you, fathers, because you know him who is from the beginning. I am writing to you, young men, because you have overcome the evil one (1 John 2:12,13).

There are the three groups: children, fathers, young men. These have no relationship to physical age whatsoever, or to sex. It is possible for a man sixty years old in the flesh to be six months old in the Lord. It is possible for a woman to be a father in the sense used here, a mature, developed, full-grown Christian. A young man of thirty can be either a babe in Christ, a father, or a young man according to the terms John uses here. These have no relationship to the time that you have been a Christian, the years since your conversion, or even to the position you may hold as a Christian.

Born Ones

Now let us look at these more closely. These successive stages of the Christian life (and if you are a Christian you belong in here somewhere) are introduced by the title, "little children." John uses a word in Greek which means "to be born." It is almost the exact equivalent of the Scottish word *bairns,* born ones. He is referring to the fact that though they are young and immature, they are in the family. They have become part of the family of God. You cannot get into a family without birth. That is true on the physical level, and it is true on the spiritual level. Jesus said to Nicodemus, "You *must* be born again." As John Wesley went about England, everywhere he would preach on that text, "You must be born again." Someone said to him once, "Mr. Wesley, why do you so continually repeat that text, 'you must be born again'?" Mr. Wesley said, "Because you must be born again."

Now John immediately describes the experience of all Christians subsequent to this new birth. "Little children, I am writing to you *because your sins are forgiven for his sake.*" That is the basic Christian position. It is forever true of all Christians that their sins are forgiven, and it is always the first thing of which they become aware. There is the lifting of the load of guilt, the solving of the problem of destiny, the forgiveness of sins. In *Pilgrim's Progress,* John Bunyan describes this experience as Christian is struggling through the Slough of Despond. He is terribly discouraged, with a great and heavy burden on his back. Then he sees a cross a long way off, and, when he finally comes up to it, he feels the burden roll off his back. He has a great sense of release and freedom. That is the experience of the forgiveness of sin.

It is often a time of tremendous emotional release. Some of us look back to it and remember well how our emotions were stirred by a wonderful sense of relief. God had laid upon Christ the burden of our sins, and we were set free from the awful load of guilt that harassed and hounded us. I remember a lady, years ago in Denver, who became a Christian after a very worldly life. When she sensed the glory of the truth that her sins were forgiven, she wanted to say something that would express it but she did not know what to say. She had yet to learn words like "Hallelujah," so she cried "Whoopee!" There are many who feel that way. Others have a more quiet experience. To them forgiveness is a deep, sweet sense of peace. No wonder they sing "O happy day, that fixed my choice, on Thee my Savior and my God." It has been many years since I first experienced the joy of the forgiveness of sins, but I will never forget the wonderful sense of the lifting of the load of guilt.

Only a Beginning

John does not mention here some of the negative aspects of spiritual infancy. He merely marks this one consistent, positive condition that is true of all who come to Christ—their sins are forgiven. He does not mention that, like physical babies, new Christians can often be rude and egotistical, emotionally unstable and overly dependent on other people. That is the way babies are. They display many negative qualities but the one thing that is universally true of them is that they are in the family, they have life.

I conducted an amateurish and unauthorized study of my youngest daughter when she was a baby and noted several things about baby personalities. I found, first, that she was very lazy. She did nothing but lie around the house all day, and contributed absolutely nothing to the household except to make a lot of trouble for everyone. And she was rude. She would burp right in your face and never apologize. She was utterly unconcerned about another's reaction or welfare. She was also highly uncooperative, often waking us up in the middle of night for demands that could well have waited for morning. But there was one thing about her that kept me intensely interested in her—she knew her daddy! So John says here, in the latter part of verse 13, of these spiritual babes, "I write to you, children, because you know the Father."

But you know, there was one thing I did not say about that little lassie. I did not say, "Look at her. Rude, uncooperative, lazy. If that's what a human being is, I don't want to be one." No, I realized that all she needed was growth. She needed to have her human life developed, properly trained. I knew that as she grew she would move into maturity. And that is what John is after here. There must be a beginning in the Christian life, but it is only a beginning, it is not an ending. We are intended to move, to go on, to "grow in grace and the knowledge of our Lord Jesus Christ," as Peter said. This is what all the apostles aim for. Paul said, "Him [Christ] we proclaim, warning every man and teaching every man in all wisdom, that we may present every man mature in Christ" (Col. 1:28).

Now John moves on to look at the other end of the

growth process, the fully matured Christians, the fathers:

> I am writing to you, fathers, because you know him who is
> from the beginning (2:13).

That is the chief characteristic of one who could be called
a father, "You know him who is from the beginning."
Who is that? Well, that refers to the word with which this
epistle opens.

> That which was from the beginning, which we have heard,
> which we have seen with our eyes, which we have looked
> upon and touched with our hands, concerning the word of
> life—the life was made manifest, and we saw it. . . .

In other words, this "one who is from the beginning" is
Jesus Christ; the mark of a father is one who has come to
know Jesus Christ. The word "know" is a word which
carries the implication of coming to know by experience.
A father is one who has come to know, by long
experience, the Lord Jesus Christ.

There are two inescapable factors about that kind of
knowledge. There is, first, personal acquaintanceship; it
must be intimate, close, and personal. And it must
extend over a long period of time. No one can become a
father, in this sense, overnight; there must be years spent
in fellowship together. The inevitable result of that kind
of activity is resemblance, a mutual identity that grows
out of such close personal acquaintance.

You often see this on the physical level, do you not? If
two people live together a long time, know each other
well, and are communicating—talking back and forth—
they grow to be like one another. Thus fathers are
Christlike. That is their chief characteristic. They possess
in great measure the disposition of Jesus Christ. They
have left behind the signs of immaturity. Remember Paul
says, in that great love chapter of 1 Corinthians 13,
"When I was a child, I spoke like a child, I thought like a

child, I reasoned like a child; when I became a man, I gave up childish ways" (1 Cor. 13:11). That is maturity, to put away childish things. Fathers are no longer juvenile in their attitudes, no longer unstable, petty, flippant. They are steady, thoughtful, competent, easy to live with. We will see more of this as we come back to John's second survey of these classifications.

The third stage he indicates is that of young men:

I am writing to you, young men, because you have overcome the evil one (2:13).

The distinctive mark here is that a young man has overcome the devil. This is the mark of those who are growing, who are strong, who are moving into maturity. They have overcome the evil one. What does that reveal? First it reveals that their eyes have been opened to the true nature of the struggle of life. As Paul put it in Ephesians 6, "We wrestle not against flesh and blood." Our problem is not people. It is the immature Christian who says, "If so-and-so would just leave me alone—my boss, my mother-in-law, my daughter, my son, my husband, my wife, the Internal Revenue Service—if they would just leave me alone I would be fine. It's people who are my problem." But anyone who has learned to overcome the evil one knows differently. He knows "we wrestle not against flesh and blood but against principalities and powers, against wicked spirits in high places, against world rulers of this present darkness." The battle is in the mind, with ideas, with attitudes, with subtle and alluring temptations that come in hidden ways. Here is the true battle, and these young men have had their eyes opened to the struggle and have come to grips with these powerful invisible forces that wreak such havoc today.

Furthermore, they have learned to live deliberately and consistently in fellowship with the Son of God, for that is the only way to overcome the evil one. You cannot do it by your own might, you cannot do it by your own intellectual power, you will be beaten every time you try. How do you overcome? Well, as Paul puts it again in Ephesians, *"Be strong in the Lord* and in the strength of his might"* (6:10). These young men have learned how to walk in the Spirit.

Spirituality is the Process

Yet they are not fully mature. They *are* spiritual, but they are not mature. They still lack the full range of Christian experience. There is great confusion in Christian circles at this point. There is a difference between spirituality and maturity. Maturity is the final goal, and spirituality is the process by which you get there. Maturity is produced by time spent in fellowship, in spiritual relationship with the Son of God. That is why you can live for years as a Christian and never mature if the years are not spent in fellowship with the son of God.

See how this works on the physical level. You fathers, suppose your little boy came to you and said, "Daddy, I want to grow up to be big like you are. I want to be a man. How do I do it?" Would you say to your son, "Well, go and try hard to grow. Think about growth. Strain at it all the time. Chin yourself every morning when you get up; constantly be stretching and thinking about growth. That's the way to grow." No, you would say, "Son, if you eat well, exercise, sleep, and keep healthy, you can't help but grow. Growth is automatic when health is present. Don't worry about growing but give yourself to the conditions that make for growth and you'll get there."

That is equally true when you apply it to the Christian life. The key to growth is fellowship with the Son of God. Do you want to be a mature Christian, able to take whatever comes, able to keep your head when all about you are losing theirs and blaming it on you? Then give yourself to the conditions that make for health. Eat

Christ, absorb his Word, grow in the knowledge of him; think, talk, communicate with him. And sleep; rest in Christ. Learn how to rely on his strength, not yours, and live in constant expectation that he is working in you to do his good pleasure. And exercise! Serve him, obey him, move out, take on things to do, open your eyes and step out to meet the needs that call out all around you, the cries of suffering and anguished hearts, the lonely and discouraged. When you do, you will discover that you have overcome the evil one; he cannot get at you. And bit by bit you become like Christ, the most attractive, the most fascinating, the most compelling personality who ever lived.

To me, the true glory of the Christian message is not the fact that it is a way to get to heaven (though there was a time in my early Christian life when that was all important to me; and it certainly *is* the way to get to heaven), but the richness of the Christian proclamation to me is that in Christ I discover a way to become a man. God is not interested in making saints, period. He is interested in making saints, but only as one step in the process of producing men. After all, that is what God is after—men and women. The goal is not sainthood, but manhood and womanhood, as God intended them to be.

Now in this passage John has told us there are three stages in the process of becoming what God intends us to be: little children, fathers, and young men. Other scriptures confirm this threefold process in fulfilling manhood. In our Lord's parable of the sower he reminds us that when the good seed (which is a picture of the Word of God, the gospel itself) falls onto good ground, it brings forth in three degrees: some thirtyfold, some sixtyfold, and some a hundredfold. There are these three stages of spiritual growth: little children, young men, and fathers. These are evident also in the three types of food the Scriptures mention as available to Christians. Both Peter and Paul speak of the "milk" of the word for babes in Christ, because milk is the proper food for infants. John describes our Lord as the "bread" of life, that which makes for strength in the Christian experience. Again, Paul speaks of the "strong meat" of the word, which only the mature can handle. In those three you have a reference to these three stages of life.

They are evident also in Romans 12, where Paul speaks of the Christian's experience of understanding, and knowing, the will of God. He says we are to present our bodies as a living sacrifice unto God, holy and acceptable to God, which is our spiritual worship, for by this we come to know, he says, "what is the *good* and *acceptable* and *perfect* will of God." To an infant, spiritually, the will of God is good, but he does not see much beyond that. It is not always pleasant, but as he grows he learns that it is acceptable, that it is the right way to work it out, though he still has not learned to enjoy it. Then at last he comes to the place where he understands that what God chooses for him is perfect. It is exactly what he should have. Although he is still, perhaps, not enjoying it in the flesh, yet in the Lord he rejoices in what God is doing.

You can see these stages again in the three degrees of rewards promised to believers in Christ. In 1 Peter he says that at the appearing of Christ we shall receive "praise and honor and glory." The apostle Paul says that every Christian receives praise from God. And the Lord Jesus says, "If any man serve me, him will my Father honor," while both Peter and Paul speak of the glory that awaits those who have learned to walk in the Spirit. Peter describes the Chief Shepherd who gives us "a crown of glory, which fadeth not away."

Again these three are strongly suggested in those three abiding things that Paul mentions in 1 Corinthians 13— faith, hope, and love. Is it not true that to the new Christian, faith is the preeminent thing with which he is concerned? It is the elementary factor in Christian living, believing God and doing what he says. But as the Christian goes on hope lays hold of his heart. He sees the possibility of fulfilling all that he dreamed of being and doing. He realizes that, in Christ and by means of the life of faith, there is a way of entering into all the promises of God, and that hope makes him strong, as a young man should be. But as he goes on he discovers that the one thing above all that marks him as Christ's and fills his own heart with satisfaction, making him easy to live with, is the pouring forth of love. "So abide faith, hope, and love, these three; but the greatest of these is love." Thus all the Scriptures testify to these three stages of growth.

Explaining Why

Now, coming back to John, we find him addressing each of these classes again. Going back over them he adds another word, this time not to describe what they are like, but to explain what made them this way.

> I write to you, children, because you know the Father. I write to you, fathers, because you know him who is from the beginning. I write to you, young men, because you are strong, and the word of God abides in you, and you have overcome the evil one.

There are the same three classifications; again he first addresses the little children, "whose sins are forgiven." Why forgiven? Now he makes it clear: "Because you know the Father." That is why sins are forgiven. They have joined the family of God and come to know the Father. They have come to God through the only way anyone can come to God, through Jesus Christ. Remember that the Lord Jesus himself said so, in that oft-quoted passage in John 14, "I am the way, and the truth, and the life; no one comes to the Father, but by me."

John does use a different word here for children than he used in the previous verse. Here he uses a word which means children under instruction, students. "Now little children (who are under instruction), I write to you because you know the Father." The first lesson the Holy

Spirit teaches a new Christian is that he has come to a Father. He has not come to a stern and austere Judge, as many think of God before we know him in Christ. And certainly he has not come to a senile, sentimental Grandpa who gives him anything he wants. But he learns that he has come under the care and affection of a strong, tender, true Father, with a father's heart. Is it not beautiful the way Paul puts that in the letter to the Galatians? "Because you are sons, God has sent the Spirit of his Son into our hearts, crying, 'Abba! Father'"! That is a baby's word for his father—"Abba." Even baby lips can say that. What a glorious thing it is to see the birth of a new life in Jesus Christ, and to watch the joy of a babe with his Father, and the Father with the babe.

Arrested Development

But even that joy soon turns to sorrow if the babe remains forever an infant. A major problem in Christian circles is that we are constantly trying to cling to the joys of spiritual infancy. We remember the glory of that moment when we came to know the Father, the warmth of it, and the joy of entering the family circle, and we are constantly trying to get back to that. That is why many of our hymns seem to look backward into the past with evident nostalgia and an obvious desire to return. But you cannot go backward, and it is wrong to try. To do so is to become a case of arrested development, to remain an infant in many, many ways.

But permanent infancy is hard to live with. Any of you who have a baby in your house know that you are looking forward to the day when he begins to sleep the whole night through, and gets off this awful cycle of the bottle, in which he seems to demand attention every twenty minutes! Some of the problems concerning spiritual infancy are listed in Hebrews 5. The author says the mark of an immature Christian, a babe in Christ, is threefold. First, he cannot tell the difference between good and evil.

Therefore, he is always getting into trouble. He goes charging ahead, thinking he has the answers to everything, and he ends up in trouble because he has not yet learned the difference between good and evil—good, when it looks bad, and evil, when it looks good. Second, he does not know how to apply the word to his behavior. He is "unskilled in the word of righteousness," that word which results in right conduct. And third, he cannot teach or help others, but needs to be taught again himself. These Hebrew Christians have been Christians long enough to be able to help others, but, instead, they are in desperate need of being taught themselves. These are the marks of infancy.

Now John goes on to the fathers. He says, "I write to you, fathers, because you know him who is from the beginning." That is exactly what he said before, is it not? It is word for word the same; he adds nothing here. He described them as those "who know him who is from the beginning." That is the mark of a father. Now he explains how they became fathers. They know him who is from the beginning! In other words, both the way to maturity and the mark of maturity are the same thing. After all, when someone, by years of walking in the Spirit and testing the faithfulness of God, has come to know the eternal God, the One who is from the beginning, to really know him, what else can you say of such a man?

In grade school I learned the hard way that you cannot compare the word "perfect." I was sent to the board one day by the teacher, who gave us certain words to write on the blackboard. Then we were to write the comparative and superlative forms of that word, such as "good, better, best." She gave me the word "perfect." She did it deliberately, trying to trap me, and I fell into the trap. I wrote "Perfect, more perfect, most perfect." She said, "You're wrong." I said, "Well, it can't be 'Perfect, perfecter, perfectest.'" She said, "No, it is just 'perfect.' If a thing is perfect, it can never be more perfect, or most perfect; it is just perfect." That is the word used here about these fathers. It is also translated "mature," or "full-grown."

Of course, no Christian ever comes to perfection in the sense of being without fault in this life; the Word of God makes that clear. But one can become perfect in the sense of having mastered the fundamental principles of spiritual life. Having understood the growing process, these come to full growth, and the rest of their lives are devoted to the joy of experiencing God in a thousand ways, seeing God at work. We use the word this way in physical life. When a child reaches the age of 21 we say he is full-grown, mature. But do we mean he is ready to stop living? No, he is just ready to start. This is not the end of progress in other ways, at all. More than anything else, it is the beginning of the enriching of his life. He now has all the physical equipment he needs. Ah, but he needs to learn a great deal in the way of using this equipment, and this is what John means here. The fathers are those who are mature because they have learned how God operates, they have mastered the techniques of faith.

Instrument of Growth

Now we come to the last class, the young men. "I write to you, young men, because you are strong, and the word of God abides in you, and you have overcome the evil one." I believe John placed this last for a very important reason. He has already described these young men as those who have overcome the evil one. He repeats that again, but he adds this explanation, "you are strong, and the word of God abides in you." He put that last because here is revealed the secret of growth. What makes a spiritual child become a young man, spiritually? Why, the Word of God abiding in him! That is the secret of growth. That is what will move him from one stage to another until at last he becomes a father, able to reproduce himself in others.

Here, then, is the divinely designed instrument of

growth, the Word of God. It is absolutely impossible to grow up as a Christian or as a real man or woman, unless the Word of God abides in you. This is why the devil fights the whole matter of Bible study, the building of your life around the centrality and the authority of the Scriptures. Though the devil cannot stop us from being Christians, he can certainly keep us from becoming strong Christians. The way he does it is to introduce false methods, trying to divert our attention and get us off onto spiritual sidetracks. He brings in certain apparent shortcuts which offer to bring us to maturity in an instant. Instant spirituality, instant maturity! That is up-to-date, is it not? He suggests that if you can just get the experience of speaking in tongues, or if you can have visions of Christ, then you will be mature. If you give yourself to exploring the realms of human knowledge, this will bring you to maturity. But all these things are cleverly designed ways to arrest Christian growth. Across the years I have watched these things prevent maturity by diverting attention from the divinely designed instrument which will bring it about, the knowledge of the Word of God.

Now do not misunderstand that. I am not talking merely about Bible study. There is a very mechanical, wooden approach to Bible study which gets you acquainted with the teachings of the Bible, but that is not enough. This passage, remember, says the Word of God "abides." That means a knowledge of the Bible plus obedience to the Spirit. When the Scriptures speak of knowing the Word of God, it is never merely talking about the instrument of the Bible, it is always the Bible plus the Spirit. It is the Word understood in the light of the illuminating, searching power of the Holy Spirit. It takes these two, together, to produce maturity. We first lay hold of the Word, and then it lays hold of us. Thus the Word abides. It penetrates to the conscience, it lays hold of the will, it exposes the thoughts and the intents of the heart. That is what produces maturity.

Diligence Required

Now this means, of course, that our studying must be deliberate. The knowledge of the Word must be more than a hobby with us, or a diversion, an option in life, a kind of low-calorie dessert which we can take or leave as we please. No, this demands time and strength. The exhortations of Scripture are to "grow in grace *and in the knowledge of the Lord.*" Be diligent about searching the Scriptures and studying the Word. Notice how the apostles labored to make these things clear. When the apostle Paul met with his dear friends from Ephesus on his last visit with that church, going up to Jerusalem, he was facing the possibility of bondage and imprisonment there for Christ's sake. His closing words to them were, "Now I commend you to God and to the word of his grace, which is able to build you up" (That is what we need, is it not? What is the instrument? Why, the word of God.) "and to give you the inheritance among all those who are sanctified" (Acts 20:32). That is, to open the door of experience into the realm of walking in fellowship with Jesus Christ. What does it? The Word of God! As Paul wrote to Timothy, his son in the faith, "All scripture is inspired by God and profitable for teaching, for reproof, for correction, and for training in righteousness, that the man of God may be complete, equipped for every good work" (2 Tim. 3:16).

Surely this means we must deliberately give ourselves to the study and knowledge of the Word of God. You cannot treat this as something nice to have if you like it, or something you can adequately get from the pulpit on Sundays. This requires opening the Book, digging into it, and understanding these vital things. You must be able to explain to another what is meant by justification, and sanctification, and all these other great words of Scripture. What if someone were to come to you and say, "I don't believe in the resurrection of the body." What are you going to say? Have you worked through Paul's great argument in 1 Corinthians 15, so you can answer that statement as he does? That is what makes us strong, that is the maturing process which ultimately makes us fathers.

Further, our knowledge of the Word must be permitted to govern our conduct and attitudes in the normal encounters of life. Here we touch upon the whole problem of social unrest and the moral decline of our day. These things have come about because Christians react to the unpleasant situations they get into exactly the same way as the world does, with grumbling, quarrelsomeness, resentments, with vengeance and attempts to get even, and even with open revolt and rebellion. The result is this: the salt in society has lost it savor and, as the Lord said, it is good for nothing but to be cast out and trodden under the feet of men. By and large, that is what is happening in the world today. The message of the church is regarded as useless, worthless, not good for anything, irrelevant, meaningless, trodden under the feet of men. Why? Because the Word is not abiding in our hearts and there is no salt in society.

Sometimes I see Christians pointing the finger at the moral decline around them saying, "Oh, what terrible things are happening, how fast we are going down the hill to apostasy." I know I am listening to someone who is not allowing the Word to judge his own heart. A denunciatory attack is a revelation of a lack of sympathy, and therefore a lack of love, since sympathy is a form of love. There is no understanding of the pressures that grip men and hold them in bondage today, the awful power of these demonic forces that are let loose in our world and society. The only thing that can break through is the love of God in Jesus Christ, and the revelation of the Word of God. When someone spends his time denouncing these things, I know he has not yet let the Word get down into his own heart to judge him.

Do you want to be an immature Christian all your life, a problem to others, constantly needing to be helped along with this or that crutch? Or are you earnestly desirous (and I know God has placed that desire in your heart), to be a strong, mature, fully God-dependent man or woman, able to walk through life and face its problems without being overthrown or tossed about with every wind of doctrine that blows, fulfilling your manhood and your womanhood in Jesus Christ? That is what he calls us to. That is what fellowship in Christ means. The instrument that is given to us by God is the Word of God in the hands of the Spirit of God. Without that we have no hope of fulfilling the divine program. God has called us to diligence in this. Let us begin.

9

The Enemy Around Us

Now, in a final word on the subject of maintaining fellowship, the apostle deals with the supreme peril to fellowship and therefore, the greatest peril to Christian maturity. It is the world and its allurements. Here is a great enemy of the Christian, the siren voice that seeks to lure us aside, trap us, delude us, and ultimately defeat us in our Christian experience.

> Do not love the world or the things in the world. If any one loves the world, love for the Father is not in him. For all that is in the world, the lust of the flesh and the lust of the eyes and the pride of life, is not of the Father but is of the world. And the world passes away, and the lust of it; but he who does the will of God abides for ever (1 John 2:15–17).

Surely this is a much-abused passage. Each of us has heard it used to denounce everything from buttons to beer, from opera to operations, from the waltz to the watusi. Anything that is currently the subject of Christian disfavor has been crammed into this passage, labelled "worldliness," and denounced. I am not interested in adding to that list. I am not interested in denouncing, but understanding. Surely the apostle desires to warn us; there is clearly something very dangerous about the

101

world, otherwise he would not speak as strongly and as sharply as this. "Do not love the world or the things that are in the world."

Now what is it that is dangerous about the world? That is what we must discover. The first step is to note that the apostle divides this enemy into two major divisions. "Love not the world," he says, "nor the things that are in the world." Two things: the world itself, and the things that are in the world. Now why does he make this distinction, and what difference does it make? Does it need to be said that the world which the apostle is talking about is not the physical world, the world of nature? There is nothing wrong with loving the physical world. God has given us the world of trees and mountains, of skies and seas. We sometimes sing,

> This is my Father's world,
> I rest me in the thought
> Of rocks and trees, of skies and seas—
> His hand the wonders wrought.

There is nothing wrong with that world. Nor is the dangerous world the world of humanity, of people with their many different practices, customs, and interests. We know it is not wrong to love that world because God himself loves it. That most famous of all scripture texts says so: "God so loved the world that he gave his only Son, that whoever believes in him should not perish but have eternal life" (John 3:16). That is the world of humanity, the world of people.

Enemies of Jesus

Nevertheless there is a world that we must not love and John expects his readers to know what that world is. It is something he has evidently talked over with them often and described to them. He does not need to define it for he knows that they know what he means. This would suggest that the world which John has in view here is clearly defined for us in other parts of Scripture. We shall find it most clearly in John's previous writing, the Gospel of John. In the Upper Room Discourse John records our Lord's words, as he speaks in warning about the world.

> If the world hates you, know that it has hated me before it hated you. If you were of the world, the world would love its own; but because you are not of the world, but I chose you out of the world, therefore the world hates you (John 15:18,19).

Here is a world that hated Jesus Christ. What world is that? Obviously, the representatives of that world were the enemies of Jesus. Who were they? It is most striking to recall that the enemies of Jesus were basically religious men. This world which the Christian is not to love is therefore primarily a religious world, although there was a secular world which hated Jesus as well—not with outright enmity but with callous indifference, which is worse. In either case, our Lord said that the world would hate us because it hated him, and John says this is the world we must not love. We must not love that which hates Christ.

The world hated him because he constantly challenged its basic philosophy. He was in continual protest against that to which the world was irrevocably committed. Our Lord put the whole matter plainly one day when he said, "You are those who seek, not the honor which comes from God, but that which comes from man." There is the philosophy of the world, the world that John says we must not love. It does not look beyond this life; it is concerned only with the honor which comes from men and unconcerned about the honor which comes from God. It is a philosophy which is bounded at one end by a cradle and at the other by a casket. It is centered only in this life and this world. Jesus challenged that concept wherever he went and whenever he spoke. Because he thrust so decisively against this, he was hated, and men banded together to put him to death. It was this philosophy which was ultimately responsible for nailing the Son of God to a bloody cross.

Think about that for a moment—this philosophy that says the only important thing is *this* life—think how widespread it is today. Are we not constantly exposed to this idea? Does it not subtly penetrate everything we touch today? We see it underlying all of life. It makes its appeal in every magazine. It is blazoned on every billboard. It is shouted abroad by radio and television, every time we turn a dial. It can be summed up in this precise way! "There is nothing better, there is nothing higher, there is nothing more precious than what this earth can give you: its money, its pleasures, its fame. You had best eat, drink, and be merry, for there is no nobler life than that."

Now John says, do not love that idea, do not love that philosophy, do not think it important. Be careful that you do not give yourself to that way of thinking. If you do, you will lose out on the fullness of Christian experience. You will be deceived by the devil. You will be trapped, deluded. You will become the victim of the Big Lie, and your very humanity will be wizened and withered by that philosophy. Well, you ask, how do you battle this? What can you do about this? If it pervades everything around us, where does the battle begin?

Reduced to Specifics

The battle begins with "the things that are in the world." It is not enough to say, love not the world. To reject a philosophy we must take certain specific actions, related to that with which we actually come in contact. So John adds, "the things that are in the world," and he defines these. He gives a list of them and says, "these are not of the Father but are of the world." They are what is wrong.

First, he says, there is the lust of the flesh. In the Scriptures this word "flesh" is usually something other than the body. It refers to the sinful nature, the sinful tendencies of humanity, the fallen condition of man which is present *in* the body. What is this lust of the flesh? Certain things which our body desires are perfectly proper, God-given. God has made us to have certain urges and hungers, and to satisfy these is not wrong. But the "flesh" always seeks to add something, to go beyond the satisfying of God-given desires.

For instance, God has so made our bodies that they hunger for food, in order to maintain life. This is as it should be. But the flesh goes beyond and craves special foods, delicacies. It urges us to gluttony. It demands the best, the softest, the most flavorsome. This is what John is speaking of. God has made us to have need of shelter, as human beings. But the flesh demands that it be luxurious shelter. There is a constant craving for ease and luxury. This is the lust of the flesh. God gives us the wonderful function of sex, which produces the most enjoyable sensation the body can experience. But the flesh wants to indulge this in any direction at any given time. It urges us to license. This is the lust of the flesh.

The second division John sets before us is the lust of the eyes. What is this? The eye symbolizes that which pleases the mind or inner life. The lust of the eyes, like that of the flesh, goes beyond simple needs. Our minds, for instance, were made by God to search and inquire, to take the great facts which revelation or nature sets before us and to explore them, analyze them, and systematize them. But there are certain limits within nature, and there are certain limits within revelation. There are certain areas of knowledge into which God has said we, as fallen men, are not to enter because they are exceedingly dangerous. But the flesh takes this basic permission of God and pushes it beyond God's will to extremes we are forbidden to follow. We demand to know everything. We will not accept facts unless we can understand everything about them. We seek to probe into the world of the occult, and the world of the future. We even give ourselves to superstition and the dark powers in order to explore these areas. This is the flesh, the lust of the eyes.

God has given us the gift of acquisitiveness, that is, the desire to own things, to possess things as our own. But the lust of the eyes pushes that into greed that is never satisfied. We want more! more! more! This results in the common phenomenon of "keeping up with the Joneses," the desire to have things we do not need, bought with money we do not have, in order to impress people we do not like! God has given us a love of beauty, but the lust of the eyes perverts this into vulgarisms, the love of the erotic, pornography, and that covetousness of another's body which the Scripture labels outright as idolatry.

To Awaken Envy

There is still a third division, which is the pride of life. Basically, this is the desire to awaken envy or adulation in other people. The first two divisions had to do with satisfying ourselves beyond God's intention for us. But they were directed toward us and only incidentally involved others. The pride of life, however, cannot exist except as it relates to others. It seeks to create a sense of envy, rivalry, and burning jealousy in the hearts of others. It is the desire to outshine or to outrank someone else. Perhaps the chief symbol of it today is the automobile, with its shiny exterior, its luxurious cushions, its beautifully designed interior, and its tremendously powerful engine, those instant horses that can be released with a touch of the toe to send us flying down a highway. What a thrill it gives us. You only have to study the habits of a human with an automobile to see how it is far more than simply a means of transportation. It is a symbol; a symbol of pride.

Why do we trade our cars in every two years? Well, of course, we have very carefully designed rationalizations that can show, beyond the shadow of a doubt, that it is much cheaper to do so. But actually, do we not do it because we want to be admired? We do not want to fall behind in the race. We want to have that which is new and excites admiration in others, even envy and jealousy. That is what John calls the pride of life. The automobile is not the only expression of this, but it is certainly a graphic one.

Now notice again the warning. What does John say about this? Notice that he does not say: touch not, taste not, handle not. Writing to the Colossians, the apostle Paul says such an attitude is legalism. John does not say, "Do not have anything to do with any of this," for we live in a world that is devoted to this outlook and we must use the things of the world. But what he does say, what he wants to bear home to our hearts, is *do not love* these things, do not set your hearts on them, do not think of them as important. Do not give yourselves to amassing things, do not love luxury and ease, and do not strive to outshine others. God help you, keep from that at all costs! Oh, the subtlety with which this whole philosophy makes its appeal to us! When the love of these things, the importance of them, occupies our major interest; when we find them using up most of our money; when we find them looming large in our thoughts so that we are constantly dreaming of that new "something" we hope to get, then we are in danger, terrible danger. This is what the apostle wants to make clear.

This condition is often revealed in the way we make our choices. I read recently of a pastor who said that a man from his congregation actually came to him and said, "Pastor, I know you've been wondering why I haven't been at the Sunday evening meetings lately. My favorite television program has been changed. It now appears at the same time as the Sunday evening meeting, and I had to choose between the two." He said this openly, evidently feeling that the pastor would fully approve of his action. It was a tremendous revelation of how subtly the love of the world had taken over his life.

You can see this in your emotional reaction when you

have lost something, or been disappointed in a business venture. Are you depressed, discouraged, defeated? What a contrast with that passage in Hebrews where the writer reminds those Christians, "You joyfully accepted the plundering of your property" (Heb. 10:34). That does not sound like many Christians today, does it?

Mutually Exclusive Loves

What is wrong with all this? Why must we not love the world and its things? John gives two very searching and important reasons. First, because love for the world and love for God are mutually exclusive. You cannot do both—it is one or the other. Man is designed to love (and therefore serve), but one master. Remember how Jesus put it? "No one can serve two masters" (Matt. 6:24). He is not stating a moral choice there. He is not saying, no man *should* serve two masters. It is an impossibility. It cannot be done. We only delude ourselves if we think we are doing it. No, we are made to be mastered by a greater power than ourselves. This is the underlying, elementary function of humanity. But that master is either the world, as the channel and activity of the evil one, or it is God. It is God or mammon. Therefore, John says, "if any one loves the world, love for the Father is not in him" (2:15). You cannot do both.

If we give ourselves to loving the world we are utilizing all the potential of our humanity to a false and grievous end. There are two powerful forces constantly making their appeal to us. Both of them offer to fulfill us, to satisfy us, to make life rich for us, but one is a lie and one is the truth. You must decide which is the lie and which is the truth, for you cannot do both. This is where we fail so often. Many of us say there must be a way of having the best of both worlds. But the entire testimony of Scripture and experience is that this is impossible. That is why the apostle Paul writes that the mark of the last days is that men would be lovers of pleasure rather than lovers of God. These are two absolutely antagonistic ideas.

This love of the world can get into the heart even of a dedicated Christian, and let us not forget it. Godly companionship is not enough to defend against it. Even the companionship of the apostle Paul was not enough, for the Scriptures record that he had to write in sorrow these revealing words, "Demas, *in love with this present world,* has deserted me" (2 Tim. 4:10). That is how subtle, how deceitful this thing can be.

Change and Decay

Now there is another reason we must not love the world. Not only does it exclude the love of God completely, but it is an utterly foolish choice, because the world, John says, is passing away. It is only a temporary thing; "but he who does the will of God abides forever." Martin Luther wrote, "I have held many things in my hands and I have lost them all. But the things I have placed in God's hands I still possess." How true that is. We all know the glory of this world is rapidly turning to dust. The power of it soon passes from our nerveless fingers into the hands of another. Nothing lasts very long; everything is changing. "Change and decay, in all around I see." That is the characteristic of the world.

Shall we give ourselves to that temporary, fleeting, ephemeral thing? Must the best issues of our life be built on that kind of a shaky foundation? No, John says, it is he who does the will of God who abides forever. One of these days the world and all that we see in it and all that history records of it, will have passed into the silent dust of the centuries. But according to the Scripture, one day the Lord shall stand with his own and view a universe where all things have been brought together and reconciled in Christ, made one in Jesus Christ. What a thrilling thing it will be to stand there and see that come to pass and say, "Thank God, I had a part in that, in the reconciling of all things in Christ."

Our Lord divided the issues of life into two words. He says there are two things, and only two things, you can do with your life. "He who does not gather with me scatters" (Luke 11:23). Which are you doing? Are you gathering or scattering? Are you uniting and reconciling, or are you dividing and breaking up and severing? All the issues of life funnel down into those two things. This is also where John puts it. If you are living for the world, loving its glory, seeking its fame, counting important the things it can give, clinging to these desperately, letting your emotions get wrapped up in them, you are scattering, you are breaking up, you are dividing.

But if you are walking with Christ, if the things that he loves are most important to you, if a cup of cold water given in his name is of far more value than another dollar in the bank, if time spent in comforting or encouraging some lonely person is to you a far greater treasure than a killing on the stock market, then you are gathering. You are building that which will endure, which will last forever. You are laying up treasures in heaven. Remember the word of that superb young missionary, Jim Elliot, who died at the hands of the Auca Indians? "He is no fool who gives what he cannot keep [i.e., his life], to gain that which he cannot lose." That is where John rests his case.

Book Two

Maintaining Truth

10

The Nature of Heresy

The first note sounded in this letter of the Apostle John is one of power, the power of a Christian (which is Jesus Christ himself), living within a human being today. Power is Christ living in you, being God again in you, expressing his life in terms of your personality. The key to this is fellowship, the sharing of the life of Jesus Christ. This is the note on which this letter begins (1 John 1:1–2:17).

The second note of the letter is one of purpose. What is the purpose of every Christian in the world? The answer is to tell the truth! Every Christian exists to be an instrument and channel by which the truth is to be made known—the wonderful, delivering truth which is in the gospel of Jesus Christ. It may sometimes be unwelcome, but it is the one thing for which men search, and the one thing they desperately need. The task of the Christian is to declare and demonstrate the truth as it is in Jesus.

There is no question but that a charge of heresy is justified against ecclesiastical leaders who renounce this truth, though heresy is an exceedingly serious charge. We tend to discount its seriousness because in our age we have made an idol of tolerance. We are told it does not really matter what anyone believes; it is what they do that counts. But it does matter what people believe, if only because action invariably follows belief. It is belief which produces action; therefore belief is supremely important. This is why the practical sections of the Epistles of the New Testament always follow the doctrinal sections. Each practical section begins with the word "therefore," for action must follow belief. Belief is a supremely important matter.

The apostle John was called to be a mender. Toward the close of the first century, when John wrote this letter, Christian truth had already come under severe attack and heresies had come into the church. John's function as an apostle was to call these early Christians back to fundamental issues, back to the essentials. That is why he centers upon this theme of maintaining truth. It is introduced to us in verses 18 and 19 of chapter 2:

> Children, it is the last hour; and as you have heard that antichrist is coming, so now many antichrists have come; therefore we know that it is the last hour. They went out from us, but they were not of us; for if they had been of us, they would have continued with us; but they went out, that it might be plain that they all are not of us.

This whole passage, which continues on to the end of the chapter, is a tremendous study on how to recognize a heresy when you hear one. I suggest that there is nothing more needed today in this age of abounding confusion in this area. The whole passage is a foundational study on the difference between truth and error.

Far Off But Near

John begins by setting forth certain characteristics of heresy. First, he indicates that heresy makes its appearance in certain repetitive cycles in the Christian era, cycles which mark the possibility of the coming again of Jesus Christ. This is what he means by his phrase, "the last hour." We will look at that more closely in a moment, but the very phrase has in view what James Russell Lowell has called "that one, far-off, Divine event toward which the whole creation moves," the second coming of Jesus Christ. The poet calls it "far-off" because some 1900 years had gone by in the Christian era before he wrote those words. But, in a sense, this event has never been far-off—even in the first century.

John, of course, was present when our Lord himself said to his own disciples, speaking of his coming again, ". . . of that day and hour no one knows, not even the angels of heaven, nor the Son [i.e., himself, as a man], but the Father only" (Matt. 24:36). John was present also when, after the resurrection, our Lord gathered with his disciples and said to them, "it is not for you to know times or seasons which the Father has fixed by his own authority" (Acts 1:7). These passages indicate that there were to be certain portents of the coming of Christ, but the exact hour and day no one would know. Our text says here, "Children, it is the last hour." But that is exactly the thing John did *not* say. He did not call it *"the* last hour." Here the translators have inserted an article which does not appear in the original language. What John said was, "Children, it is *a* last hour," and it is very important to note that distinction.

Read through the prophetic writings of the New Testament and you will note that the whole time between the comings of Christ, his first coming in the flesh and his second coming in glory, is called "the last days." Contrary to the popular view, this term does not refer to the end immediately preceding his coming. See, for instance, Hebrews 1:1,2. The whole period, running now well over 1900 years, is called "the last days." Even in this letter the apostle has said the age to come has already dawned. Twice he has reminded us that the world is passing away, the darkness of it is disappearing; the last days have already come and we are moving toward the end of them.

Descending Spiral

Also, as you read these prophetic passages, it is apparent that the movement of the last days is in a constantly contracting spiral of repetitive events. There will be cycles of events repeating themselves through these last days, moving at last to the coming again of the Son of God to earth. Paul describes these cycles very clearly and accurately in 2 Timothy which, by the way, was the last writing from his hand. He says, in chapter 3, "But understand this, that in the last days there will come times of stress." Now he does not mean these "times of stress" will occur only at the end, just before the coming of the Lord, but these will be characteristic of the whole period of the last days. There will come times when "men will be lovers of self, lovers of money, proud, arrogant, abusive, disobedient to their parents, ungrateful, unholy, inhuman, implacable, slanderers, profligates, fierce, haters of good, treacherous, reckless, swollen with conceit, lovers of pleasure rather than lovers of God. . . ." Then he notes this in particular: ". . . holding the form of religion but denying the power of it" (2 Tim. 3:1–5). Again, that is not something which characterizes only the end; that occurs repeatedly through this whole time, as history confirms.

There was just such an outbreak of heresies, as we see here, in the first century itself. John says, "You have heard that antichrist [the man of sin—the man who will be in control of the world before the return of Christ] is coming, so now many antichrists have come; therefore we know that it is a last hour" (2:18). Another special attempt to twist and distort Christian doctrine came during the fourth century at the time of the momentous doctrinal struggles over the nature of God. These were settled by the great councils of the church, such as the Council of Nicaea, from which we get the Nicene Creed. Another outbreak of heresies, another cycle of heretical ideas, broke out in the seventh century with the rise of

Mohammedanism and the pretentious claims of the Bishop of Rome to supremacy over all of Christendom. Again in the ninth century, there was the rise of strange and deceiving doctrines within Christian circles. During this century there was a widespread false expectation of the return of Christ which for almost a hundred years nearly paralyzed the economy of Europe. Contrary to the very thing that Jesus had said—that no one could know the day or the hour of his return—men were expecting him at the year 1000.

In the eleventh century history records that the Crusades began with an heretical fomenting of zeal for a false religious objective which captured the attention of men and turned them from the things God wanted them to know. For several centuries these Crusades dominated the thought of Europe. In the thirteenth century an outbreak of heretical concepts came in again, as the papacy consolidated its power over the ecclesiastical world. Then began the terrible days of the Inquisition with its persecution of the Waldenses and the Albigeneses, those people hidden away in the valleys of Italy and in the Alps. In the fifteenth century we can trace another outbreak, a heretical cycle, when "the papal antichrist," as Martin Luther termed him, reigned unchallenged in his power. This was answered by the Reformation and the stirring days of Martin Luther, whose great hymn, "A Mighty Fortress Is Our God," is so well known. Then again, in the eighteenth century, came the rise of German rationalism which undermined the supernatural characteristics of the gospel, and reduced the whole Christian message to nothing but an appeal to the intellect, leaving it dull, drab, and lifeless. In the nineteenth century there was another outbreak. Think of the cults which exist today. How many are "Made in America"—Jehovah's Witnesses, Mormons, Christian Science, Unity, and so on. These all began in the nineteenth century. Thus these cycles are narrowing, coming faster and faster.

Now, in the twentieth century we have seen such an outbreak in the "Death of God" theology, the de-mythologizing of the Scriptures, the rise of new cults, and the goals of the ecumenical movement to establish one world-wide church, wielding vast political power. These are the issues of the hour. All these, John says, are "last hours" when it looked, from the standpoint of the individual who lived through those days, as it looks to us now, that it was an hour when Christ could come. He himself had predicted that the days before his return would be marked by false christs, false prophets, and false teachers who would teach heresies in the name of Jesus Christ. We must remember, as Dr. Blaiklock has put it, that "nothing is so damaging in the study of New Testament prophecy as to imagine that the eternal God, who stands above and outside of time, is bound by the clocks and the calendars of men." This is why our Lord warned that the factor of time in predictive matters would be impossible to establish.

But we can note certain things. We can see that as the centuries roll by, the pace of events is picking up. Things move with frightening rapidity today. The pace has been accelerating and the spiral has been widening geograph-ically so that now it involves the entire earth. We are linked together as one people in these present times of crisis, this "last hour" which now appears in human history. All this suggests that we are rapidly moving closer to that final "last hour" which will occur before Christ's return.

Within the Family

Now note the second thing John has to say about heresy. In verse 19 he continues a rather general descrip-tion of heresies, which is true in any age. The second thing he indicates is that they all begin with the Christian family.

They went out from us, but they were not of us; for if they had been of us, they would have continued with us; but they went out, that it might be plain that they all are not of us.

The implication is clear that the beginning of heresy was within the circle of Christian truth and doctrine. That is where heresies have their root. That is what the word "antichrist" suggests. We often take the term to mean someone who is against Christ, much like the attitude we see in communism, where there is a blatant denial of God and Christ. But that is not the thought here. It is true that the eventual outcome of any antichrist is that he is against Christ, but *anti* can also mean "instead of." It is someone who comes in Christ's name, someone who claims that he is Christian and is declaring the truth of Christianity. Yet, as you analyze his teachings, it is contrary to what God, in Christ, has said. This is antichrist.

Our Lord himself predicted the activity of antichrists in the parable of the wheat and the tares. He said (speaking of himself) that a sower went forth to sow, sowing the good seed of the word of God, in human history. But, he said, an enemy came at night and sowed evil seeds as well "among the wheat," that is, in the midst of the wheat, and the two grew up together—the wheat *and* the tares. They looked so alike at first that it was very difficult to distinguish between them. Our Lord said that as they grew men would ultimately recognize them as evil and say to the Lord of the harvest, "What shall we do about them? Shall we go in and root them out?" And his word is, "No, let them grow together until the harvest." To try to root them out, he said, would also root up the wheat along with the tares (Matt. 13:24–30). How often this has been fulfilled in human history by zealous attempts to purify the church in false ways.

The apostle Paul also recognizes the fact that heresies will arise within the church. In Acts 20, in his farewell to the Ephesian elders he says,

> I know that after my departure fierce wolves will come in among you, not sparing the flock; and from among your own selves [i.e., from among the elders of the church, the bishops, if you like] will arise men speaking perverse things, to draw away the disciples after them (Acts 20:29,30).

All this is foretold. It is well known. Therefore let us not be surprised by those heretics who arise within the Christian circle in our day and say false things. It has always been so.

Same Words, Different Meaning

Notice the third thing the apostle indicates as a mark of heresy. He suggests that heretics adopt Christian terminology for their errors. That is, they begin within Christian circles and at first they sound truly Christian. You cannot tell what they are until they begin to break away. "They went out, that it might be plain that they all are not of us." Their terminology is correct, but they substitute another meaning for the words. How widespread this is in our own day. Perhaps the classic illustration of this is the book by the founder of Christian Science, Mary Baker Eddy. Though she uses perfectly normal Christian words she invests them with an entirely different meaning, and in order to explain that meaning she must publish a glossary of terms at the end of her book. Words which in the dictionary are universally taken to mean one thing are, in her book, given a specialized meaning which is a departure from essential Christian doctrine. This is common practice in many cults today.

Take, for instance, the way the word *resurrection* is being widely used among so-called Christian leaders. They say, "We believe in the resurrection of Jesus Christ; we believe in the resurrection of the believer." But what do they mean by that? They mean that the soul survives death in some way, that the spirit of Jesus somehow survived the experience of death and his spirit is abroad today, though his body lies mouldering and rotting in the grave. They do not believe what the New Testament states as the meaning of *resurrection*—the raising of the body of Jesus. It was his body which came from the grave. Paul hinges the whole of the Christian faith upon this doctrine and says that if it did not happen, our faith is in vain and we are yet in our sins.

Take, also, the use of the term *evangelism*. We hear much about evangelism, and many talk about the need for evangelizing to the uttermost parts of the earth. But in many circles that has a different meaning than we ordinarily understand. To many it means engaging in social work, doing beneficial things in foreign countries. Such ministry is called "evangelizing," preaching the gospel. But it is a far cry from what the New Testament means by evangelism, helpful and necessary as these things may be. Take, too, the use of the word *prayer*. People use the term so glibly today. You can hear programs on the radio about prayer and many articles about it are being published in Christian magazines. But analyze their meaning and prayer is often only the thinking of helpful thoughts. People talk about gathering together in a room and praying for someone, and all they mean by that is to think beneficial things about that individual. What a far cry all this is from the Christian use of these terms. One of the marks of heresy, then, is that it evacuates the meanings of biblical words and substitutes other meanings in their place.

Or perhaps such heretics may simply give a different emphasis to certain aspects of the Christian message from that given in the New Testament. Take for instance the purpose of the church and the reason for the preaching of the gospel. What is it? Why, it is to change men from death unto life. The purpose of the gospel is to give men the gift of life. That is its supreme thrust. Without that it is not the gospel. Now along with that there come many other wonderful benefits—peace of heart, even health of body, a sense of guidance through life, and so on. But heresy seizes upon these secondary benefits and makes them primary, and offers the gospel only as a means of producing peace of mind. But this is the error of heresy; the truth is, none of these things are permanently possible unless there is first an imparting of life by Jesus Christ.

Break-off from Truth

Notice that the fourth mark of an antichrist is that he will finally break away from New Testament Christianity. All such invariably do. And when they do they will insist that *they* are the true mainstream of Christian truth and that *we* are living in the backwaters of Christian doctrine. John puts this very plainly, does he not? "They went out from us, but they were not of us; for if they had been of us, they would have continued with us." The mark of genuineness is continuity in the truth, continuance in true faith. What does he mean by "us"? Surely not Christendom in general. He means, of course, as he makes clear in the context of this whole letter, those who love the Word of God and who possess the Spirit of God, those who seek to obey the Word in the power of the Spirit. This is the emphasis he has been making all along. Heretics will invariably cut themselves off from those who share the life of Christ, by the Word of God, in the power of the Spirit of God.

If you suggest studying the Scriptures together with people who are involved in heresy, you will immediately feel their scorn of the Scriptures, their dislike of the Word of God. If they read it at all they cull out certain portions, carefully edit them, omitting the parts they do not like. If you read what they are studying, you find it to be emasculated of essential truth. We need not fear heresy if we find someone who wishes to study the Scriptures as they are. There are many people today who are utterly ignorant of the Scriptures, who do not know anything about them and perhaps have quite peculiar viewpoints about them, but they are quite willing to learn. They want to study; they want to know what the Bible says. Then do not worry about the fact that they are way off about a lot of things now. Get them into the Scriptures. The Word of God has a marvelous ability, in the hands of the Spirit of God, to correct error and to channel interests into vital matters. They will soon be brought into line with the great, marvelous, glorious, all-pervasive truth of God, these tremendous themes which grip the hearts of men wherever they are set forth in power.

What a defense this has been against error through the centuries. Through the centuries there have been these cyclic outbreaks of heresy arising within Christian circles to twist, distort, and pervert the truth. What a wonder this Word is, which has been given to us that we might understand what is happening in our world. We can thus realize that history is utterly in the control of God and is moving exactly the way he planned. Our own individual lives can be brought into line with this to produce not that which is transient and ephemeral, but to be engaged in that which abides, that which will end up at last fulfilling the purpose of God in history.

11

The Hard Core of Truth

John began his theme of how to maintain truth on a rather negative note. He talked about perversions of truth that will exist from time to time, in repeating cycles, throughout history. He went on to give us certain general characteristics of these heretical ideas. These anti-Christian doctrines come disguised as Christianity, but are often caricatures of Christianity which most people, upon hearing, reject and therefore think they have rejected the real thing. Later, John will give us certain specific details which characterize counterfeit Christianity, but in between he gives us a positive word of reassurance and hope.

> But you have been anointed by the Holy One, and you all know. I write to you, not because you do not know the truth, but because you know it, and know that no lie is of the truth (1 John 2:20,21).

The King James Version, in verse 20, says, "But ye have an unction from the Holy One, and ye know all things." Now that is certainly not what John wrote. He did not say of Christians, "You know all things." That would make Christians "know-it-alls" and there is nothing more universally obnoxious than a "know-it-all."

Christians obviously do not know all things. The correct rendering, adopted by the Revised Standard Version, is "you all know." Because of the anointing which you have received from Jesus Christ, the Holy One, you all know. There is no doubt that this anointing is the Holy Spirit whom the Lord Jesus gives to those who believe in him. In the seventh chapter of John's gospel we read,

> On the last day of the feast, the great day, Jesus stood up and proclaimed, "If any one thirst, let him come to me and drink. He who believes in me, as the scripture has said 'Out of his heart shall flow rivers of living water'" (John 7:37,38).

Rivers of power, rivers of energy, refreshing, changing and affecting the lives of others—out of his innermost being shall flow these rivers. John adds, "Now this he said about the Spirit, which those who believe in him were to receive" (7:39). When you received Jesus Christ, you received the indwelling of the Holy Spirit. Perhaps you did not know it for you did not feel anything. This is what often leads people astray. They are often expecting some strange sensation when the Holy Spirit comes in. But the Holy Spirit is life—moral life, spiritual life, God's life—and just as there was no sensation when physical life began, so there is no sensation when spiritual life begins. Yet it is there.

To Know the Truth

If you have believed in Jesus Christ you have received this anointing from the Holy One, the gift of the Holy Spirit. Now, having received him, John says "you all know," i.e., you have now been rendered capable of knowing as God intended man to know from the very beginning. Now that which was taken away in the Fall, that which has been missing in your heart and life until you came to know Jesus Christ, has been restored to you.

No longer must you walk on in confusion, darkness, and uncertainty, unable to find your way through the maze of contradictory opinions and forces. Now you have something by which you can know. For the first time in your life, you have received the necessary equipment to know. To know what? To know the truth! As he says, "I write to you, not because you do not know the truth, but because you know it." You have the equipment to know truth at the very center and, ultimately, using the mind and emotions and will which God has given you, and under the tutelage of the Holy Spirit, to know truth out to the farthest reaches of its limitless shores, not only in time, but in eternity. That is a tremendous program, is it not? Yet that is the amazing program of God, which he has begun in those who have come to know Jesus Christ.

Look back at the Upper Room Discourse in John 16, where the Lord is unfolding to his amazed disciples this fascinating, almost unbelievable, program of God for the future. They do not understand what he means and are puzzled by what he says. It is not until the Holy Spirit comes on the Day of Pentecost that the pieces of this strange puzzle begin to fall into place. But in verse 12 he says to them, "I have yet many things to say to you, but you cannot bear them now." Why not? Well, because they did not have the equipment. That is the trouble with fallen men. God has many mysteries hidden in the universe, mysteries about ourselves, mysteries about the world around us, but we do not understand them yet because we do not have the equipment. Unregenerate men lacks what it takes to explore himself adequately, not to mention to explore the universe in which he lives. Thus these men, not yet having the Holy Spirit, did not have what it takes to understand what Jesus was saying.

But "when the Spirit of truth comes [the Spirit of reality, the Spirit who gets right down to the basics, the fundamentals, the essential issues of life], he will guide you into all the truth; . . ." How will he do it? What is the curriculum, what is the course of study for this?

". . . for he will not speak on his own authority, but whatever he hears he will speak, and he will declare to you the things that are to come [to you]. He will glorify me, for he will take what is mine and declare it to you." This is the only way we can know Jesus Christ. By means of the Holy Spirit, the anointing which we have received from him, we can know him who says, "I am the Truth." "All that the Father has is mine." What a fantastic course of study! All that the Father has he will take and reveal unto you. ". . . therefore I said that he will take what is mine and declare it to you" (John 16:13–15).

God's Hidden Wisdom

Paul enlarges on this same remarkable curriculum of truth in 1 Corinthians 2. He is explaining to these Corinthians why he did not come to them discussing philosophy and the teachings of the Greek thinkers. He says, I deliberately set these things aside. I did not come to engage in debate with you in these areas. I came to preach Jesus Christ and him crucified. Then in verse 6, he says, "Yet among the mature we do impart wisdom, although it is not a wisdom of this age or of the rulers of this age, who are doomed to pass away. But we impart a secret and hidden wisdom of God, which God decreed before the ages for our glorification" (1 Cor. 2:6,7). Read that now in Phillip's translation.

> We do, of course, speak "wisdom" among those who are spiritually mature, but it is not what is called wisdom by this world, nor by the powers-that-be, who soon will be only the powers that have been. The wisdom we speak of is that mysterious secret wisdom of God which he planned before the Creation for our glory today. None of the powers of this world have known this wisdom—if they had they would never have crucified the Lord of glory!

What is missing from man's knowledge today? Why do we have a world so filled with such obvious confusion and uncertainty? No one seems to know the answers to the overwhelming problems that face us. Why is it that we cannot solve world problems, even on the material and physical level? Take, for instance, the matter of smog. What causes it? They tell us it is primarily the automobile, these sleek chariots we enjoy so much and spend so much time and money on. The obvious answer is to get rid of the automobile, or change it. But the problem is that our whole economy is geared to the internal combustion engine and the petroleum industry. To change these would wreck the American economy. How do you solve that problem?

Obviously, there is something missing in man. He does not know enough, he does not understand himself. The New English Bible rendering of this verse in 1 Corinthians 2 reveals that what is missing is "God's hidden wisdom, his secret purpose framed from the very beginning to bring us to our full glory." That is what is missing. Man does not know how to bring himself to the glory God intended for him. He has lost the key, he has lost the program because he has lost the understanding of himself, and, lacking this, he gets involved in what seem to be perfectly right things but which end up as very serious problems. That is why he can build an automobile, complete in its technological perfection, but if he puts a driver in the seat who cannot handle it, within moments that beautiful automobile is a mass of wreckage. With the automobile we are killing thousands of people a year, but instead of solving the problem with the driver we are trying to solve it by improving the car.

Right here is where philosophies and pseudo-Christian heresies come in. Every philosophy, every cult, and every heresy is an attempt to reveal how man can achieve greatness, how he can fulfill himself. Each is offering to unfold the secret of the nature of man, how he can operate correctly, how he can achieve what he longs to do. Each of these takes for granted that fallen man already has in himself all that it takes to understand himself and to explore the secrets of life: that is, his reason and his observation. Therefore, each of them launches upon what they call "a search for truth." They are looking for the key to all things. They are examining the mystery of existence, both living and inanimate, to discover the secrets of the universe, looking for that which can give purpose and meaning to life. Lacking the necessary equipment and refusing to acknowledge the need for another teacher beyond man, superior to man, they became those whom Paul describes as "ever learning, and never able to come to the knowledge of the truth" (2 Tim. 3:7, KJV).

Why not? Because truth is a Person. Truth is Jesus Christ. The fundamental characteristic of truth is consistency. It must fit every fact, every known and unknown situation. If you have what you think is the truth but you must force things to make it fit, or squeeze pieces in, then you do not have the truth. The glorious thing about knowing Christ is that the longer you live and the more you observe life with him at the center, you find that everything fits. Without struggle, without pressure, without twisting or turning, all of life fits, *for he is the truth.* You know that truth, John says, "that is why I write to you."

That is why man without this knowledge hasn't a clue as to the secret of his own existence. The only principle he knows is that of demonstrating his inherent ability. Is that not what you see around you? Did you ever hear someone say, "Just let me show you what I can do"? If he only has the opportunity to show what he can do, he can demonstrate his greatness. Now that works just well enough to give the appearance of actually being the secret, and most men are thus deluded. But man cannot understand why he cannot ultimately solve his problems. He is baffled and bewildered when he sees this principle work in certain areas but not in others.

The apostle says it is because he is forever ignorant, apart from Jesus Christ, that the secret of man's greatness is not that of trying to demonstrate our inherent ability but that of declaring our utter dependence upon Another. The one who learns that God is living in him, and of his utter dependence upon that God to make life full and rich, is the one who discovers what he is here for. The apostle Paul says that because men did not know this they crucified the Lord of glory. If they had known it, as the Lord Jesus kept constantly setting it before them, they would never have crucified him. But because they rejected the principle he presented, because they would not believe what he said, they became the murderers of the Son of God, and their hands were stained with the blood of the Lord of glory.

Now John says, this is why I am writing to you Christians. You are now equipped to understand and know. I can point out to you the nature of error. You are worth writing to, for two reasons. He lists these for us in verse 21. First, "I write to you, not because you do not know the truth, but because you know it." That is, you now have the ability to grasp and understand truth. There is no longer any reason for weakness in your life. If you will pay attention, if you will give heed to the anointing, the Secret Teacher within who will take what I write and explain it, you can fully lay hold of life, life in all its fullness. That is why I am writing to you.

There is no use writing to someone who does not have this anointing. You cannot explain life to those who have never met Jesus Christ; they cannot understand it. To them what you say is threatening, and they reject it. It looks to them as if you are cutting the ground out from everything they have built their lives on. They must start with receiving Christ before you can explain life to them.

No Possible Harmony

John adds a second reason: You "know that no lie is of the truth." Have you learned yet, as a Christian, that there is no possible harmony between a lie and the truth?

In other words, there are no gray areas in life. A thing is either black (a lie) or it is white (the truth), and there are no gray areas, though there may be a mingling of black with white. By virtue of the anointing, every Christian has an ability to exercise moral judgment, to distinguish right from wrong. It is amazing how many Christian have not learned this yet, and still go on echoing the lie of the world that there can be a shading of truth and error. John utterly negates that; he says it is not true. I write to you, he says, because you have found this out, if you know Jesus Christ. You may not have thought through the implications but you must know that there is no possibility of blending a lie with the truth. "God is light and in him is no darkness at all" (1 John 1:5).

One of the glorious things about God's secret purpose, that is, the restoring of the life of God to the spirit of man, is that it also reestablishes standards of absolute values and makes possible moral judgments. It shifts us from control by a conscience of convenience to control by a conscience of conviction, from fear of consequences to faith in a Conqueror. That is the great difference. These days we are hearing much about what are called "situational ethics," relativism in the realm of moral judgments. If the boss sees you take fifty cents from the petty cash drawer, then obviously you have disgraced yourself and the company's name, having been caught red-handed, and that is wrong. But if you do it without getting caught, it is all right. That is situational ethics.

If you cheat on an examination because you do not like the teacher, then that is wrong, that is not reason enough. But if you do it because you are desperate to get a good grade—you have been letting the whole thing slide until exam time and there is no other way but to cheat, and obviously, the important thing is to get a good grade—that is right.

It is this relativism that results in a double standard in life. You borrow a book from your buddy and when you have finished reading it you put it in your own library.

Later on, as you are running around together with the gang, he suggests to you that you steal a sports car out of the parking lot. You look at him in horror. "What kind of a guy do you think I am? I only steal books!"

It is what makes it possible to stand in church and sing with full-throated soprano, "Be like Jesus, This my song, In the home and in the throng, Be like Jesus all day long, I would be like Jesus." But when you finish the song, you put the hymn book down and turn to the one beside you and say, "Get a load of Susy Jones—boy, how fat can you get!" That is situational ethics, lumping together right and wrong, smoothing over the difference between truth and error.

John suggests that once you could do that without any concern at all, once all you needed was a desire to do something, and you would soon find a way to justify doing it, even making it look necessary. That is the terrible power of the human mind called rationalization. But, John says, no more. Now you know One who is the truth and you cannot get by so easily any more. Sooner or later you must explain your actions to him, and all those wonderful excuses that went over so smoothly with your wife or husband or friends or neighbors sound very lame when repeated to him. He is totally unimpressed by them. He does not say anything; he simply folds his arms and looks at you, and when you feel his eyes upon you all your excuses sound watery and weak. You start stammering and pretty soon you stop. Because, as John says, "no lie is of the truth," and you know that now. Therefore, he says, I am writing to you because you can be helped. You are not like these people who are caught up in human falsehood, swept along by a lie, carried about with every wind of doctrine that blows. I am writing to you because you can learn, you can grow, you can be helped, you are worth writing to.

Now give heed to these things. Begin to examine the voices you hear, the philosophies around you, the suggestions and explanations of life that are presented to you.

Measure them according to the truth. Bring them to the One you have learned is the Truth. That makes you worth writing to. Have you come to know the truth as it is in Jesus? Are you ready to listen to the Word of God, unfolded by the Spirit of God, in order that you might understand the world in which you live and the person who lives in it—you? Are you willing to understand how God made you, how he intends you to function, how he wants you to react to situations? Will you let him teach you no longer to depend upon the false sense of ability that you have lived on all your life, but to renounce that, and rely instead upon his life within? That is why John is writing. He writes these things, he says, because he knows the necessary equipment is there. All that remains for us is to use it.

12

No Son, No Father

Resuming his analysis of heresy, John now unveils to us the nature of error, in two verses. He exposes here the fundamental issue of error, that is, the goal toward which all lies trend, and also the reason why error is diabolically terrible and destructive in its character.

> Who is the liar but he who denies that Jesus is the Christ? This is the antichrist, he who denies the Father and the Son. No one who denies the Son has the Father. He who confesses the Son has the Father also (1 John 2:22,23).

Did you ever ask yourself, Why is it wrong to lie? Many of us have a secret admiration for, if not agreement with, the little boy who defined a lie as "an abomination unto the Lord, but a very present help in time of trouble." We do take a serious view of lying, at least when it is done by other people. Why is it that parents often say to their children, "I'm not punishing you because what you did was wrong, though it was. What I'm concerned about and what I'm punishing you for, is that you lied about it"? Why do they look so seriously upon lying? Do they not unconsciously sense that all lies are a pathway which can lead to the ultimate lie? That ultimate lie is the supreme expression of lying, of falsehood, of error. John says, this is *the* liar, the one who has fallen victim to the supreme delusion, he who denies that Jesus is the Christ. That is the supreme lie of all ages.

It is evident that the name "Jesus" and the name "Christ" have somehow become fused together in our thinking. I have met people who think Christ is Jesus' last name. The word "Christ," however, is a Greek word which translates the Hebrew word "Messiah"; Christ means exactly the same as Messiah, "the Anointed One." It is this same root which forms the word John has spoken about a few verses earlier, the "anointing" which has been given to each Christian. The Holy Spirit is that anointing. The disciples were first called "Christians" in Antioch, because it was obvious they were anointed with the Christ, that Christ shone through their lives. They were called "Christ's ones"—Christians—because the anointing was so evident upon them.

Anointed for Work

This word, therefore, refers not to Jesus' last name but to his work. It is a reference to the office he fulfilled. Jesus is the Anointed One. In Isaiah's great prophecy there is a passage which speaks specifically about this. In chapter 61, the servant of Jehovah, whom Isaiah has been describing, says

The Spirit of the Lord God is upon me,
   because the Lord has anointed me [Here is One anointed to do a certain work. What is that work?]
to bring good tidings to the afflicted;
   he has sent me to bind up the brokenhearted,
to proclaim liberty to the captives,
   and the opening of the prison to those who are bound;
to proclaim the year of the Lord's favor . . . (Isa. 61:1,2a).

Luke tells us that our Lord himself, in the synagogue in his home town of Nazareth, quoted this passage and stopped at a comma. The verse goes on to speak of "the day of vengeance of our God," but our Lord stopped before that because his first coming did not include the day of vengeance. Closing the book at this point he said to these people in the synagogue, "Today this scripture has been fulfilled in your hearing" (Luke 4:21). He had reminded them that the Lord had anointed him to proclaim the gospel, to give release to the captives, to bind up the brokenhearted. This is his appointed work.

This passage makes clear that the baby named Jesus, who was born to Mary in the stable in Bethlehem—that human baby—*is* the predicted Anointed One whom Isaiah saw 725 years before the angels sang over Bethlehem. He is the same one. Jesus *is* the Christ. He was named Jesus because, as the angel announced to Joseph, "He will save his people from their sins." That is the work of the Messiah, of the Anointed One, of the Christ. He is anointed to save. The great heart of the Christian proclamation is that Jesus, the human being who was born in Bethlehem, who grew up and lived in Nazareth, who walked and ministered on the hillsides and byways of Judea and Galilee, that human Jesus is the Christ. He is the Messiah.

In the Old Testament, three kinds of men were anointed. Prophets were anointed when they entered upon their office of proclaiming the Word of God. Priests were anointed when they began their ministry of cleansing, healing, and forgiving. And kings were anointed when they ascended to the throne. If you read through the Old Testament and gather up the predictions concerning the coming of Jesus Christ, you can see clearly that Jesus was to be God's prophet, God's priest, and God's king. Moses said, "The Lord your God will raise up for you a prophet like me from among you . . . him you shall heed" (Deut. 18:15). It was announced to Eli, the father of two wicked sons, that the Lord would raise up for himself a faithful priest who would fulfill all his word (1 Sam. 2:35). And scattered through the Old Testament are many predictions that speak of the coming of Christ as God's king. There is that one so familiarly connected with Christmas:

> For to us a child is born,
>   to us a son is given;
> and the government will be upon his shoulder,
>   and his name will be called
> "Wonderful Counselor, Mighty God,
>   Everlasting Father, Prince of Peace."
> Of the increase of his government
>   and of peace there will be no end (Isa. 9:6,7).

Jesus is that Mighty One; he is the Messiah. He is God's prophet, he is God's priest, and he is God's king. When he is born again in your heart as God intends should happen to any man or woman who is ready to believe, that is what he will be: God's prophet, priest, and king. Through the Holy Spirit he will speak to you the word of God as a prophet. He will cleanse you, as God's priest, and he will rule your life, as God's king. This is because what he is, is what he was. Everything that he was, he still is. Remember that word in Hebrews, "Jesus Christ is the same yesterday and today and forever" (13:8). Everything he was he still is and everything he will be he is now and all that he is he will be, in you. When he comes into your life, he will be exactly what he was. Jesus is the Messiah, Jesus is the Christ, the Christ is Jesus.

Desperate Distortions

The devil hates this truth above everything else. He is constantly exerting every wile, stratagem, and clever ruse he can devise to distort this basic truth of the Christian message. The history of the Christian centuries is an account of how the devil, in one way or another, succeeds in taking this fundamental truth of Christian faith and twists it to make it appear to be something else.

One of the early forms of heresy, and one that is

reflected here in John's letter, is that Jesus was nothing but a man upon whom the spirit of Christ came. The Christ is the Eternal Spirit from God, but Jesus was nothing but a man. As he grew up and came to the days of his ministry, he was baptized, and then, according to this theory, the Christ Spirit came upon him and dwelt within him. He still remained Jesus the man, but the divine Spirit came to him and rested in him, dwelt in him, and this was the explanation of his amazing ministry. That same divine Spirit who came to Jesus when he was baptized, left him on the cross. Thus when he was buried, he was buried as Jesus the man, no longer the Christ. It is the Christ Spirit which is available to men today. We have nothing to do with a historical Jesus but with a Christ spirit.

That early heresy is unfortunately still with us. It can be found today in the doctrines of Christian Science, which teaches that Jesus was a man upon whom the Christ spirit came. But this is what John calls "the lie." According to such teaching, Jesus is not the Christ, he is only possessed by the Christ. This denies the incarnation, the fact announced in John's gospel that "the Word became flesh" (1:14). The truth is that Jesus *is* the Christ, he is that predicted One. The man Jesus is identical in every respect with that One whom the prophets saw.

A modern form of this heresy says that the virgin birth of our Lord Jesus, the shining of the star, and the song of the angels are legendary accretions that have been added to the essential story of the humanity of Jesus. These are all myths, beautiful but incredible ornaments, that have been added to make the story more attractive, and that Jesus was but a natural man. John labels that "the lie," and says that the one who denies that Jesus is the Christ is "the liar." A final form of this lie is found in the predicted one referred to here as the antichrist, and whom Paul calls "the Man of Sin." In Paul's second letter to the Thessalonians he says:

Let no one deceive you in any way [Note that word; we are constantly warned that the enemy is exceedingly clever in his ability to deceive]; for that day will not come, unless the rebellion comes first, and the man of lawlessness [the man of sin] is revealed, the son of perdition, who opposes and exalts himself against every so-called god or object of worship, so that he takes his seat in the temple of God, proclaiming himself to be God. Do you not remember that when I was still with you I told you this? [This is nothing new, says Paul, I am simply reminding you of what I taught you when I was with you.] And you know what is restraining him now so that he may be revealed in his time. For the mystery of lawlessness is already at work [John says the same thing: "Even now many antichrists have gone out among us." This is characteristic of all the Christian centuries: the mystery of darkness, the mystery of evil, the mystery of iniquity, the lie, is already at work.]; only he who now restrains it will do so until he is out of the way. And then the lawless one will be revealed, and the Lord Jesus will slay him with the breath of his mouth and destroy him by his appearing and his coming. The coming of the lawless one by the activity of Satan will be with all power and with pretended signs and wonders, and with all wicked deception for those who are to perish, because they refused to love the truth and so be saved. [Then he adds this very significant phrase] Therefore God sends upon them a strong delusion, to make them believe what is false [literally, *the lie*], so that all may be condemned who did not believe the truth but had pleasure in unrighteousness (2 Thess. 2:3–12).

The Underlying Lie

There again is *the lie*. Why is it so terrible? Why such strong language? John explains that behind the denial of Jesus as the Christ is hidden a deeper, more significant lie. "This is the antichrist, he who denies the Father and the Son." That is the problem. To deny that Jesus is the Christ is to deny the Father and the Son.

Here we are encountering something of the mystery of the nature of God, this tremendous, eternal wonder to the human heart. I grant immediately that there is much that we cannot understand about God, about the Trinity. We know there are three persons who eternally exist as one God. Our minds boggle when we try to understand fully what that means and to grasp its implications. It is nevertheless the truth, and John says the one who denies that Jesus is the Christ always, inevitably, goes on to deny the Trinity, the Father and the Son. He does not mention the Spirit here because in this particular reference John is dealing with an apostate (a religious person who is without the Spirit). He is without the Spirit because he denies the testimony of the Spirit that Jesus is the Christ.

In that profoundly significant passage which we call the Upper Room Discourse, when our Lord is gathered with his own (and it is John who records it for us), our Lord himself reveals to us something of the wondrous relationship that has eternally existed between the Father and the Son. We know that in the beginning was God—God in three persons—Father, Son, and Spirit. It is a supreme characteristic of God that he loves; God *is* love. Therefore the Father loved the Son, and it was always the Father's delight, through the eternal Spirit, to give of his fullness, of all that he is, to the Son. Love always gives, and God is forever giving. All that is in the Father is, through the Spirit, given to the Son. This is why Jesus said, "All that the Father has is mine." Paul adds in Colossians, "In him [the Son] all the fulness of God was pleased to dwell" (Col. 1:19). Therefore, as man, he became "the image of the invisible God." All that the Father was, given to him, became visible in the Son, as man.

But the Son also must love and give, for he too is God, as the Spirit is God. This is where creation comes in, for John has told us, "All things were made through him [the Son]" (1:3). Why? In order that all the fullness which is in him, which the Father has given to him, might be given to the whole creation, headed by man. Paul says, "all things were created through him and for him" (Col. 1:16). He is the full expression of the Father, and the creation is to be the full expression of the Son. Everything that we see about us, the universe in all its wonders of complicated structure, is but an expression of the life of the Son.

A Limited Expression

But now limitation is very evident. The Son can receive all the fullness of the Father, but the lower creation cannot receive all the fullness of the Son. We know that inanimate matter does not express anything of the love of God. You cannot find any expression of God's love in nature. Nature will treat you exactly the same when your heart is grieved and crushed and broken as it will when you are filled with buoyancy and joy and blessing. There is no expression of God's love in nature. Of his wisdom and power, yes, there is very much. Analyze the structure of natural things; both animate and inanimate, and you can see the amazing wisdom of God, how marvelously he puts all things together. He creates animals with an instinctive drive that causes them to travel thousands of miles to a place they have never seen before. This migratory pattern repeats itself generation after generation. This is the wisdom of God.

Also the power of God is evident in nature. We have released some of it now with our vast array of nuclear weapons. God never made a hydrogen bomb, but he made the atoms from which it comes, and the power of it is there. Even among the animals you can see the wisdom and power of God. They are governed by an instinctive interlock that makes them do what God wants them to do. In them you can see the goodness of God and the kindness of God, but you see nothing of the self-giving love of God. Only in man, in all the visible creation, is there a being who can receive the fullness of the Son and return it again. This is because man has the power of will. He can make a voluntary choice, and love, of course, is always voluntary. You cannot compel love.

Thus the whole program of creation was intended to be the Father, taking of the fullness that was in him and, through the eternal Spirit, imparting it to the Son. He in turn takes of the fullness he has received and through the eternal Spirit imparts it to man and the whole creation, to the end that this fullness may be reflected back visibly to the Father. So the whole created world would glorify God. There will come a day when, as Paul tells us in 1 Corinthians 15, all things have been put in subjection to the Son. Then he to whom all things have been subjected will, in turn, subject himself to him who puts all things under him (the Father), "that God [the threefold God: Father, Son, and Holy Spirit] may be everything to every one" (1 Cor. 15:28). That is God's design for the universe.

As you know, this program was interrupted by man's deliberate choice to repudiate his dependence upon the Son, through the Spirit, and to be his own god, to turn creation to his own purposes. Then the Spirit of God was removed from the spirit of man, and man lost his ability to love God, and lost his capacity to know God as Father, for the heart of fatherhood is love. Thus man had lost his awareness of the love of God. When he chose, by a voluntary exercise of will, to shut himself away from the love of God, he lost the experience of the fatherhood of God. Without a capacity to love God, he fell to the level of the animals, retaining only his mental cleverness and his superior emotional sensitivity. He thus became nothing but a very clever animal, made by God, intended for God, but living without God except as the animals receive, without worship, the goodness and the kindness of God. That is the way man is living today.

Thus, when a man denies the testimony of the Spirit that Jesus is the Christ (i.e., the eternal Son become flesh to die and to rise again in order that God may live once again in man), he also shuts himself off from the possibility of knowing God as Father and he cannot experience the love of God. This is why the devil attacks so vehemently the truth that Jesus is the Christ. Through a denial of this he can get at that relationship which God desires for his people, the glory of knowing the Father. At a pastors' conference once I heard Dr. Joe Blinco say that he has long since learned that the devil is no "pimple squeezer." He always strikes for the jugular vein. That is why these devilish, diabolical heresies that appear from time to time are forever striking at the heart of the Christian message. These are not insignificant things; these are not trivialities. They are aimed at the very heart of the thing God wants. They are an attempt to keep man from understanding and entering into the realization of the desire of God for man, that he may discover the true fatherhood of God and the true brotherhood of man.

Restored to the Family

When a man receives Jesus the Christ as his Redeemer, as the Lord who came to save him, and the Holy Spirit is by that process of receiving Christ restored to a man's spirit and heart, then the first word that he teaches that man to utter is "Abba!" Father! He is restored to the love of God and to the family of God. So John can say, "He who confesses the Son has the Father." The fullness of the Father is forever being given to the Son; therefore, all that is in the Father belongs only to the Son, and to him to whom the Son will reveal himself. Jesus said this himself.

In the Upper Room he was amazed by Philip's request: "Lord, show us the Father." Jesus said, "Philip, have I been with you all this time and still you do not know me? He that has seen me has seen the Father. If you have me, you also have the Father. As you come to know me you discover that in knowing me you know also the Father, for all that the Father has is mine." John says of him, "Of his fullness have we all received." The amazing, revolutionary aspect of the Christian message is this: the fullness that is in God is given to us who receive the Son.

Paul confirms this again in Colossians, where he says, "In him the whole fulness of deity dwells bodily, and you have come to fulness of life in him" (Col. 2:9,10). As he puts it in his prayer in Ephesians, you are intended to be "a body wholly filled and flooded with God himself." That is the secret of Christian living. The Lord Jesus described that, in terms of our experience, as a well of living water within us from which we could drink at any moment of pressure, trial, heartache, or sorrow. It is not something we go to church to get; it is something God has already put within us. Jesus said this to a woman at the well in Samaria, a poor troubled woman, a seeker after romance who had already had five husbands, was living with a sixth man, and still was not satisfied. Obviously her heart was tremendously athirst. Jesus said, "If you know who it is who asks of you, you would have asked of him and he would have given you living water . . . welling up to eternal life" (John 4:10,14).

Not only would it be a well, but in another place he said it would become a river, flowing out in blessing to others. The heart in which the Son dwells has all the fullness of the Father, and that fullness will be evidenced by a manifestation of the attributes of the character of God; a heart filled with love, with peace, with blessing. That means to become easy to live with, a delight to be around, someone whom people love to see and to talk to—as they loved to see and talk to and share the presence of the Son of God. That is true Christianity.

Do you see why the lie is the most hateful thing that could come into the world? It cuts man off from the blessing God has for him. All there is of God is available in Christ. There is no other channel; there is no other way. There are those who point to certain people who do not believe in Christ and say, "Look at them, look at the blessing they have, look at the goodness of their life, look at their moral character." But they never seem to see the flaw in that argument. As we have seen again and again, part of the power of the devil is that he can so cleverly imitate for a while the goodness that is in Jesus Christ. It will fool anyone—for a while. But we only need to stop and think through the implications of saying that some people can come to God other than through Christ to see how wrong such a statement is. Anyone who says that is essentially denying the Christian faith. He is saying there was no need for the cross; there was no need for the Son of God to come, or for the death on Calvary and the resurrection from the grave. These things are of no value, of no significance. If a man can come to God in any other way than through Jesus Christ, then this whole story is a foolish fable and ought to be discarded. It is simply a wild, imaginative tale that deserves no intelligent consideration whatsoever.

But then how do you explain Jesus Christ? And how do you explain the fact that through twenty centuries men and women, living in darkness, confusion, bewilderment, and despair, have found in Jesus Christ the satisfaction of their hearts, the fullness of God, the riches of God imparted to them? It is only through Christ that these come. "This is antichrist, who denies the Father and the Son."

13

The Living Word

The great announcement of the Christian faith is that God can only be discovered as Father, and known as Father, through contact and fellowship with the Son of God. As Jesus put it, "I am the way, the truth, and the life; no man comes to the Father but by me." I realize that this claim to uniqueness on the part of Christian faith has given rise to a great deal of criticism. There are many who regard Christians as essentially bigots, narrow-minded religious fanatics, in their refusal to admit that any other line of approach to God is valid. But this uniqueness is essentially true because of the nature of man himself.

Man consists of body, soul, and spirit. God is the Creator of the body and the soul, but, according to Hebrews 12:9, the God with whom we have to do is the "Father of spirits." Although he made us body and soul, he breathed into us a spirit, which was part of himself, since he is the Father of spirits. The problem is that in fallen man, as he now exists, as he is born into this world in his so-called "natural" state, the spirit is unresponsive. Man is dead spiritually. He is unresponsive spiritually, dead in trespasses and sin.

What a Dead Spirit Needs

Therefore, he cannot know God as Father because it is in the spirit that man understands fatherhood, and can know and appreciate the fatherhood of God. Just because man is dead in spirit it is also true that no teaching can help him. After all, teaching only instructs the mind. No philosophy can touch that dead and unresponsive spirit because philosophy is nothing more than an intellectual pursuit of truth. No ritual, no sacramental hocus-pocus, is able to change man spiritually, for these are things done to the body or the soul, and do not touch this realm of the spirit. That is the reason why all teaching, all philosophy, all religious performances of any kind are absolutely useless and bankrupt to help man in his spiritual need. They do not touch the heart of the problem; they do nothing to solve the basic difficulty.

The one thing a dead spirit needs is life, and the unique claim of Jesus Christ is that he alone has life. "In him was life," John says, "and the life was the light of men" (1:4). Later on in this very letter he says, "And this is the testimony, that God gave us eternal life, and this life is in his Son" (1 John 5:11). Therefore it is only by the touch of the Son of God that life is imparted to the unresponsive spirit of man. Paul writes to the Ephesians, "You he made alive (in spirit)"; as they believed in Jesus Christ they were born again, made alive in spirit. And when the spirit is made alive by receiving the Son, then God is known as the Father, and we begin to experience the father-heart of God. That is what John is saying in verse 23: "He who confesses the Son has the Father also."

Having led us to that place of understanding, John goes on to show us how to experience this. It is one thing to *have* the Father (and everyone who has come to know Jesus Christ has the Father indwelling him, as well as the Son, as Jesus promised would happen), but it is another thing to *know* the Father, to experience the fullness of God. John now unfolds in two short verses the process by which all of God's intention may be realized in your experience, right where you are—in your home, in your family, on your job—right now.

> Let what you heard from the beginning abide in you. If what you heard from the beginning abides in you, then you will abide in the Son and in the Father. And this is what he has promised us, eternal life (1 John 2:24,25).

Here is the process. These are the three logical steps that lead to the enjoyment of all God's intention for you. The first step is an admonition to you. "Let what you heard from the beginning abide in you." What is this that you heard from the beginning? That takes us right back to the very first verse of the letter. John begins, "That which was from the beginning, which we have heard, which we have seen with our eyes, which we have looked upon and touched with our hands, concerning the word of life—" That is the message of Christ, all that concerns him. It includes, primarily, what he said, what he came to unfold and manifest about God and about man—all the words and deeds of Jesus Christ.

The Whole Thing

That message, of course, is to be taken as a whole. There is a tendency on the part of many today to take certain of the words of Jesus and to ignore others. I must confess I fail completely to understand an asserted loyalty to Christ that is accompanied by an indifference to his words. For instance, there are some who say that they believe Jesus when he says he is the light of the world, and he is the door, and he is the one who came to bring truth to men. But they feel he is mistaken about the time of his return. Furthermore, he did not understand nature; he was only a creature of his times with regard to scientific knowledge; he did not understand many of the things that we understand today. They say surely we cannot expect him to know the psychology which has been developed by today's eminent thinkers, and that men today know more about man than he knew.

I do not understand that, for if we take the words of Jesus about himself we are confronted with the claim that all power is given him and he is the ultimate answer to the quests of men in any direction. All human knowledge converges at last in Jesus Christ. If we are going to believe him, then let us believe everything he says, on whatever subject. Whenever we set ourselves up as a judge of what he says, we are really saying we know more about it than Jesus Christ. John is simply reminding us here that if we are going to accept the words of Jesus Christ, we must accept everything he said.

A friend showed me a book the other day, *Jesus As Teacher,* in which there was a purported attempt to set forth the teachings of Jesus. But when I examined the book at length I discovered that the author had taken out parts of sentences which Jesus had spoken and linked them with things he had said in another place. He had sometimes dropped out the whole point our Lord was making in a passage only to insert another point from somewhere else until all he had was a hodgepodge of fragmented sayings of Christ, labeled *Jesus As Teacher.* But such is not a study of the teachings of Jesus; that is merely a study of the ideas of some human author as to what Jesus taught.

Sometimes you hear people say, we don't want to follow the Bible, we want to follow Christ. Christ is our authority, not the Bible. But as you read the Bible you find that you cannot distinguish between Christ and the Bible in the area of authority. The words of Jesus form the Bible, and if we are going to receive the words of Jesus we must receive them as they are recorded in the New Testament. Our Lord himself reminds us of this in the twelfth chapter of John:

"He who rejects me and does not receive my sayings has a judge; the word that I have spoken will be his judge on the last day. For I have not spoken on my own authority ["I

did not originate what I came to say." Well, who did?];
the Father who sent me has himself given me commandment what to say and what to speak. And I know that his
commandment is eternal life. [The very thing man is
seeking is all wrapped up in these words which God has
spoken. "And I know that his commandment is eternal
life."] What I say, therefore, I say as the Father has
bidden me" (John 12:48–50).

That is why, when John wants to help us understand
and grasp all that God provides for us, he says we will
find it in the Word, the Word of life. We will find it in the
message which was given us from the beginning.

That not only includes the words of the Lord himself,
but it also includes the apostolic expansion of those words
which we call the Epistles of the New Testament. As you
read these letters through, you will see they are simply a
fuller exposition, given under the direction of the Spirit
of God, of all that Jesus said in capsule form in the
Gospels. There are no departures from Jesus' words, no
contradictions, no divergences. There is no place where
an apostle goes off on his own and says something that
differs from what Jesus said. They are simply taking all
that he said and, under the leadership and inspiration of
the Holy Spirit, are expounding it in fuller detail that we
might understand completely what Jesus Christ came to
say and to be to men. So the apostle Paul writes to the
Ephesians, "Let the word of Christ dwell in you richly,
teach and admonish one another in all wisdom" (Col.
3:16).

Be Possessed

Now look a little more closely at the word which John
employs here. He says, "Let what you heard from the
beginning abide in you." To abide means more than
simply reading your Bible once in a while. That means
more than reading it in a cursory, mechanical way, and

then marking off on your list that you've done your Bible reading for today. This word "abide" literally means "to remain." Or perhaps the closer word would be "to possess." It is exactly what we mean when we say to a guest who comes into our home, "make yourself at home." Of course they know we do not really mean that. It is a polite expression and does not mean, "Take over the house and do what you would like," but rather, "in the rooms that you have already been given access to, feel free to move around a bit, if you like, but don't go into the bedrooms, and stay out of the closets." But if we really meant that statement we would be saying, "Possess this house as though it were yours. Go anywhere you like, do anything you like, make yourself at home as though you were really home."

That is what this word means; John is saying, "Let this message which was from the beginning make itself at home in your heart and in your life. Let it possess you, spirit, soul, and body. Let it grip you, mind, emotion, and will." This is the first and necessary step to the goal he has in mind, the fullness of God manifest in you. See how he links this inescapably with the Word of God. Let the *word* abide in you.

Here is our trouble. When we read the Bible we really do not want it to move into the whole house; we only want it to move into one room or two. We want it to occupy the room of our mental acumen—the library, if you like, the study. Many people read the Bible that way. They study it intellectually for the knowledge of the times in which we live—the prophetic passages, perhaps, because they are simply interested in discovering what the program of God is for the future. Or they study the moral standards and ethical teachings of the Bible, like the Sermon on the Mount, since they are only interested in extracting from it certain intellectual, academic, or moral teachings.

There are others (I am afraid, perhaps, a majority) who read the Bible only for its ability to stir the emotions. That is why we love to read certain favorite passages—the twenty-third Psalm, John 14, or Romans 8. Why? Because these truths, as we read, stir us. These are beautiful passages and beautiful thoughts and they stir the emotions. We love the good feeling we get from reading these passages which have spoken to us in the past, and reading them again awakens memories and we are stirred anew. But that is all. After we have read them and our emotions have been stirred, we close the Bible and go out to live just as we have always lived. Reading the Word has made no difference. We may be religious; certainly we are being churchly, and no one can deny we are reading the Bible, but yet the Word of God is not abiding in us and that is the necessary thing. John is urging us to let the Word grip us.

Let it confront you intellectually first; that is always the gateway through which God makes his appeal to man. Understand what God is saying. Meditate on these passages until you see the truth, and know what God is saying. Read them again and again, and let them burn into you; muse and meditate upon them until they grip you. Then, as you find you understand the truth, you will discover it has done something to your emotions. It has taken hold of you—you are captivated and compelled by it. When that happens, then respond to it; submit yourself, obey it. This is what the Scripture calls acting or living by faith; obeying the truth made known to the mind, gripping the emotions, and thus moving the will. That is the Word of God abiding in you, possessing you. *Let* that happen, the apostle says; make provision for it, set a time for this, make room in your life for this.

That will inevitably lead you to the next step which is an explanation for you.

> If what you heard from the beginning abides in you, then you will abide in the Son and in the Father (2:24).

It is inescapable. If the Word, if the truth of God has possessed you, then you will be possessed by the Son and

by the Father, that is, by the fullness of God which is in
the Son and the Father. Notice that he ends with the
same word: "then you will *abide* in (be possessed by,
gripped by) the Son and the Father." This is nothing
more than what Jesus himself had said to his disciples in
the Upper Room, as recorded in John 14: "If a man loves
me, he will keep my word, and my Father will love him,
and we will come to him and make our home with him"
(v. 23). We will be with him at his work, we will be with
him at his home, we will be with him in his relationships
with others, in his problems, in his joys. We will be with
him when he is confronted with temptations to anger and
temper. We will be with him all the time. We will make
our home with him. This is what John is saying. "If what
you have heard from the beginning abides in you, then
you will abide in the Son and in the Father."

There is a difference between being "in" something,
and "abiding in" something. Our Lord made that clear in
John 15 in the parable of the vine and the branches. He
said, "I am the vine, and you are the branches." The
branch was in the vine by virtue of union, and the life of
the vine (or some of it, at least) was being imparted to the
branch so that it could bear leaves. But it could not bear
fruit under that relationship. He pointed out that if a
branch is to bear fruit, it must *abide* in the vine. The
fullness of the vine must be in the branch. Not just
enough life to sustain it, but all that the vine is, is to be
imparted to the branch, and the result would be fruit, and
more fruit, and much fruit, to the complete satisfaction of
the owner of the vineyard.

To the Same Degree

This, you will notice, is a reciprocal relationship. To
the degree that you act in faith, obeying the Word, to
that same degree the Father and the Son will be in you,
performing the Word. This explains why there is sometimes so much difference between Christians. One Christian, even one relatively young in the faith, can seem to

be so abundantly full of the character of Jesus Christ, manifesting the fruit of the Spirit in much abundance, while another Christian, who has perhaps been a Christian for years, is still crabbed and ugly in temper and disposition, and there is little of the fruit of the Spirit. What is the difference? One has the fullness of the Father and the Son. If you obey little, you will experience little. If you obey much, you will experience much. To the degree that you give yourself to God in understanding and obeying his Word, to that same degree he gives himself to you.

Now if this reciprocal relationship is true, certain conclusions must inevitably follow. Since God gives himself to us in the same degree as we give ourselves to him, then I see three things that result from this. First, you can have all that Christ is, if you are ready to take him. There is no limit to the degree to which he will give himself to you, if there is no limit to the degree to which you are ready to believe and obey him. You can have all he is, in any situation, at any given moment, if you are ready to take it by an act of obedient faith.

Second, if this is true, then it is also true that you will have only as much as you are satisfied with. God will never give you more than you really want. God never forces blessings upon anyone. Christians can live—sometimes for decades—in weakness and folly, in barrenness, fruitlessness, and despair, because they do not really want any more from God. Nothing has awakened them to hunger and thirst after righteousness. They are content to live at that low level, and God will never force more upon them. Oh, he will try to wake them up, by one means or another, but he will never bless them, cannot bless them, beyond what they are willing to take.

The third conclusion is, therefore, that you now have (if you understand this) all that you really want from God. Your present level of life is an indication of what you want. So do not blame God if your life is not filled with the blessing and fullness the Scriptures seem to promise. It is not his fault. You now have all you really want, because you can have from him all that you are ready to take. If your life is not satisfying to you as a Christian, it is not God's fault; it is that you are not yet willing, for one reason or another, to take from him all he is ready to give, out of the fullness of his being.

Now just what is it that he is ready to give us? John describes what this is in one phrase: "And this is what he has promised us, eternal life" (2:25). That phrase is greatly obscured by the traditional view that has been poured into it through centuries of Christian teaching and preaching. Most of us understand these words to mean heaven some day, everlasting life, life that never ends. Now that is not inaccurate. Eternal life is indeed life that never ends, but the essential factor about eternal life is not quantity, but quality. John is speaking here not merely of something we are going to get in heaven some day, but something we can experience and enjoy now. It is fullness of life, the full quality of divine life lived out in your situation, right now, forever increasing in enjoyment. In other words, eternal life, as John is using it here, is the daily adventure of experiencing God's solution to every problem, instead of yours. It is the discovery of God's program for every opportunity, instead of yours.

To Flub or to Fly

Every time we are confronted with a problem, there are only two things we can do. One, we can try to solve the problem in the weakness of our own intellect, relying upon our human resources (much as any worldling does who does not know God at all). When we take that approach, the result is inevitably the same. Sooner or later life dissipates into a drab routine that leaves us utterly uninterested in being involved in anything. That is the result of our program.

Or, we can have God's program, God's solution to any

problem or opportunity. If we are ready to follow this simple formula that John provides for us here, to be obedient and understanding, obeying the Word as God unfolds it to us, then in any situation we can say, "Lord, you are in me and you have come to live through me. This situation has been brought about by your planning and your programming. I wouldn't be in it, if it were not for you. Now Lord, do through me what you want to do." Then we become instantly available to him to move in whatever direction the situation demands. As we do, we discover that his program begins to unfold in that situation. Every obstacle becomes a glorious opportunity. There is no more reason for despair and gloom because every situation, no matter how frightening it might be for the moment, is but an opportunity to display the fullness of glory, wisdom, and power of God.

What a life this is, what quiet excitement it involves! It is described in that well-known passage in Isaiah 40, where the prophet says, "But they who wait for the Lord [those who are expecting God to be at work] shall renew [actually, *exchange*] their strength [for what?—for *his* strength, for *his* power, for *his* wisdom, for *his* under-standing—and then what?], they shall mount up with wings like eagles, they shall run and not be weary, they shall walk and not faint" (Isa. 40:31).

That is a description of the mind, the emotions, and the will of man. "They shall mount up with wings as eagles": They shall be intellectually stimulated, capti-vated by the great range of truth that God is working out through the humdrum, commonplace circumstances of life. Their minds shall be challenged, their mental vision opened so that, like the eagle mounting up, they can see afar and understand what life is all about.

"They shall run and not be weary": We speak of "running" the gamut of emotions. We are never intended to be placid, unmoved people journeying through life, never reacting to anything, dull, stolid, indifferent. We are intended to react: to show joy, to express sorrow, to experience gladness and relief, to run the gamut of emotions. That is perfectly proper, perfectly human. You see the Lord Jesus doing this through the three and one-half years of his ministry. But the trouble is that if we are not doing this in God's strength, it breaks us down. We become anxious, fearful, and trembling. We have a mental breakdown, an emotional breakdown, or a nervous breakdown. Why? Because we are trying to run out of inadequacy, without strength to lean upon. "But they that wait upon the Lord [who are exchanging their strength for his], shall run and not be weary." There is never a breakdown, never any failure in this wonderful experiencing of life—life that is always vibrant and vital, changing constantly, but always joyful.

"And they shall walk and not faint": Walking consists of the steps that we take by the choices of our will, moment by moment. All of life is filled with decision. Sometimes you say, "Decisions! Decisions! Decisions! Nothing but decisions!" Yes, but that is the way life is intended to be, a constant program of decisions which you take step after step after step, walking through life. "But they that learn to wait upon the Lord shall exchange their strength," exchange your deadness for his life, exchange your weakness for his strength, exchange your emptiness for his fullness. You shall walk and not faint. Life will be a constant series of experiencing the undergirding power and strength of God, so that every decision is a strengthening experience.

As a young Christian, I remember reading that great promise in Ephesians, "Now unto him that is able to do exceeding abundantly above all that we ask or think, according to the power that worketh in us . . ." (Eph. 3:20, KJV). I remember looking at that verse and saying to myself, "Is that really true? Does God really offer to do for me beyond that which I can even ask or think at this moment? Why, that's fantastic! I can ask a lot of life. I can dream and imagine a great many wonderful experiences that I would love to have, to bring satisfaction to my life and heart." I even had the program outlined in my mind, just how God could do it. But as I look back across the years I can see that God did not take my program and do it my way, but he has abundantly fulfilled the promise. My life is richer than I ever dreamed it would be when I was a young Christian. My life is fuller, more satisfying, moment by moment, than I ever thought was possible when I was young.

God has fulfilled his promise, not because I have fully and always entered into the fulfillment of this formula, because I have not. Many times I have failed. But despite all the failure, despite the times of weakness, I can bear testimony that the times I have walked in the strength of God have been superbly above all I could ask or think. Even with all the failure taken into account, my life is still an abundant fulfillment of this promise. "Now to him that is able to do exceeding abundantly above all that we ask or think [in any given situation]." If we are ready to give ourselves to the Word of God. to let it possess us, to understand it, and to obey it—if "that which you heard from the beginning abides in you," you also will abide in the Son and in the Father. The experience of that is eternal life!

14

The Teaching Spirit

One of the things that excites me about true Christianity is that it is not trying to produce religious plaster saints, but thoroughly human individuals who operate as God intended them to operate. The whole thrust of the Christian message is to the end that we experience life as God intended life to be. The instrument designed to do this is the Word of God.

But someone says, "This is where I have problems. I know the Bible is important. I know it is designed to produce in me what God desires. But my problem is, I have such difficulty understanding the Bible. I find there are a great many different interpretations of various passages, and so many contingencies upon which Scripture seems to rest, and so few areas of universal agreement that I have great difficulty with the Bible." The only answer to that is to see the full thought of John on this matter. He goes on in this passage to say that we have more than the Word of God. There is not only the outward testimony of the Word, but there is also an inner witness.

I am afraid little is said in Christian churches today about the great theme of the witness, the anointing, the *testimonium,* of the Spirit of God. Yet it is one of the most vital themes of Scripture, for it explains what makes the difference between dull and ineffective Bible study and compelling and fruitful Bible study. John says,

> I write this to you about those who would deceive you; but the anointing which you received from him abides in you, and you have no need that any one should teach you; as his anointing teaches you about everything, and is true, and is no lie, just as it has taught you, abide in him (1 John 2:26,27).

Notice that he introduces this theme by announcing the presence and purpose of an inner witness. "I write this to you about those who would deceive you," he says, "for you have received an anointing from him, which abides in you." In other words, this anointing is especially designed to meet the problem of uncertainty in the face of the many deceitful and deceptive concepts around us. How do you know what is the truth? How do you know which interpretation is right about a passage in the Word? Well, John says, you have an anointing which abides in you for that very purpose. This does not mean, of course, that Christians can never go astray, because they do. But it does mean that when they go astray, they do so either because they have been ignorant of the anointing, or are resistant to the teaching of the Holy Spirit within. And if they do go astray, they can only go so far, for this anointing, John says, "abides in you."

We have already seen that this anointing is the Holy Spirit himself, whom you received when you believed in Jesus Christ. Both the Word of God and the Spirit of God are received at conversion. We receive the Word of God from those who brought it to us, and we receive the Spirit of God from the Lord Jesus when, in response to the Word of God, we receive Christ into our life. If you are a Christian, you have both "the word which you heard from the beginning," as John calls it, and "the anointing which abides in you." With regard to the Word, remember, we are told to "let" the Word of God

abide in us, which requires a continual coming to the
Word. But with regard to the Spirit, John says, "he
abides"; he is there already if you have received Christ.
There is no need to ask for more of him to come in, as
many people are misled to believe today. He is all there!
He is a person, and a person comes in as a unit. When I
come into a room, I do not send my legs in first, and then
my head. I come in altogether. That is the way a person
comes in. When the Holy Spirit comes into a Christian's
life he comes in altogether, as a unit. He is all there and
he abides there. But it is necessary, as we will see from
this passage, for us to abide in him.

No Need for Teachers?

The apostle goes on to announce not only the presence
of this inner witness, but also to suggest the function and
the fullness of his witness to us.

> . . . you have no need that any one should teach you; as
> his anointing teaches you about everything, and is true,
> and is no lie (2:27).

What strange words: "You have no need that any one
should teach you," that is, you have no need for human
teachers. This seems, at first glance, to contradict other
passages of Scripture. We know there are teachers
provided by the Holy Spirit. There is a gift of teaching.
There are pastor-teachers sent forth by the Holy Spirit
into the body of Christ, to teach men the truth. Even the
apostles were teachers. John was a human teacher; Paul
was a human teacher. Peter, James, and the other writers
of Scripture were all human teachers. How then could
John say, "You do not have any need of a human
teacher"?

The explanation lies in the level at which this kind of
teaching takes place. In literature it is common to use the
eye and the ear as metaphors for an inner comprehension

of the mind. There are actually three levels of seeing and hearing possible to a human being. First, the eyes and the ears are physical organs designed to see and to hear. But the soul has organs of sight and of hearing as well. We speak of "seeing" something, by which we mean that we have understood it, or grasped it, intellectually. Or we "hear" something, by which we mean that we have heeded it, we have responded to it. Thus we have heard with the mind and the emotions, the soul. We may sense something is wrong about a thing we hear. We don't know quite what it is but we know it is there, and we say, "It doesn't sound right to me." We do not mean that there is something wrong with the decibels reaching our ears, we mean there is something wrong with the logic of it.

You experience this negatively when you hear or read a foreign language you have never learned. You hear the words or see the letters, but you do not know what they mean. You see them, but you do not see them; you hear them, but you do not hear them.

Perhaps you have experienced this when, as a stranger, you have unwittingly come into a family crisis. While you carry on a conversation, you sense there is something else going on. Certain words are said with hidden meanings, and you become aware that you are involved in a situation you do not understand. You hear, but you do not hear.

All this is on the level of the mind and the emotions, but there are also organs of the spirit. There are eyes and ears of the spirit by which we may gain certain flashes of insight and thus come to a full understanding of a truth in relationship to other truths. We see the whole thing clearly without the necessity of reasoning it all out. These are the eyes and ears of the spirit. In Matthew 13 where our Lord is giving the parables of the kingdom, he says to the disciples, "This is why I speak to them in parables, because seeing they do not see, and hearing they do not hear, nor do they understand" (Matt. 13:13). Do you see the three levels there? Seeing (with their physical eyes) they do not see (with their mental eyes), and hearing (with their physical ears) they do not hear (with their mental ears), nor do they understand (at the level of the spirit).

In verse 16 he says to his disciples, "But blessed are your eyes, for they see, and your ears, for they hear." But he does not go on to say, "Blessed are you, for you understand," for they did not understand. As they listened to these parables they did not know what he meant by them. They had not yet received the Holy Spirit, and they did not understand his full meaning although they knew intellectually what he was talking about. The crowd did not even get that far. They heard the words, but let them flow right on through, and that was all there was to it. The disciples had gone a step further, but they did not fully understand.

The Eyes of Your Heart

In Paul's great letter to the church at Ephesus, he prays for his readers concerning this very thing. In chapter 1 he says,

> I do not cease to give thanks for you, remembering you in my prayers, that the God of our Lord Jesus Christ, the Father of glory, *may give you a spirit of wisdom and of revelation* in the knowledge of him, *having the eyes of your hearts enlightened,* that you may know what is the hope to which he has called you, what are the riches of his glorious inheritance in the saints, and what is the immeasurable greatness of his power (Eph. 1:16–19, italics mine).

The Holy Spirit, operating in the human spirit, is required for us to understand, to grasp the immensity of these tremendous things, to be thrilled and gripped with the excitement of what God has set before us.

This then is where we do not have any need of human

teachers. Only the Spirit of God can touch the human spirit and give insight to it. That is why at this level no human being can help you, although the Holy Spirit will often base his teaching upon the word which the human teacher brings. You have a clear example of that in Matthew 16 when our Lord asked his disciples, "Who do men say that the Son of man is?" They named various ones, and then he said, "But who do you say that I am?" Simon Peter replied, "You are the Christ, the Son of the living God." Peter had been observing the Lord, but he was puzzled by him as all these disciples were. But when Jesus asked that question, "Who do you say that I am?", suddenly it all came clear to Peter. He saw it in a flash, in a sudden grasp of truth, and he said, "Why, you're the Christ, the Son of the living God." The Lord Jesus said to him, "Peter, blessed are you!" (Because God had done something for him.) "You didn't learn that by flesh and blood. You didn't reason that out; you didn't amass all the evidence and come to a reasonable conclusion as to who I am—but my Father has revealed it to you." That is the anointing, the teaching of the Spirit.

There are two very clear instances of this in Luke 24. After the resurrection, when our Lord joined the two disciples on the road to Emmaus, he found them troubled and disturbed. He said to them, " 'O foolish men, and slow of heart to believe all that the prophets have spoken! Was it not necessary that the Christ should suffer these things and enter into his glory?' And beginning with Moses and all the prophets, he interpreted to them [or he opened to them] in all the scriptures the things concerning himself" (Luke 24:25–27). They had not seen these truths before. They had read these Scriptures many times but they had never seen that they referred to the Messiah, to the Christ. They still did not know who this stranger was, but now they knew that the Scriptures described a suffering Messiah. Then in verse 32, after he had revealed himself to them and disappeared, they said to each other, "Did not our hearts burn within us while he talked to us on the road, while he opened to us the scriptures?" They had heard what he was saying but they did not grasp it until he opened their eyes, the eyes of their hearts, and the minute he did, their hearts began to burn. They were captivated by what they saw, caught up by it, entranced by these magnificent truths. That is what the anointing does. The Spirit of God takes the Word of God and opens it to us.

Again in verse 44 of this same chapter, our Lord appears to the disciples and says to them, "These are my words which I spoke to you, while I was still with you, that everything written about me in the law of Moses and the prophets and the psalms must be fulfilled." They had read these many times. But then, "he opened their minds to understand the scriptures" (v. 45).

A Deep Persuasion

Now I think we can see what this anointing, of which John speaks, is. It is an illumination of the mind and the heart, and a deep persuasion from the Holy Spirit. It involves intense powers of persuasion; it is a compelling thing, but it is not an impartation of knowledge. It is not a case of the Holy Spirit giving information which is not recorded in the Bible; it is a taking of the Scriptures and confirming them. It is an interior witness, confirming an exterior fact.

In the Book of Acts, as Paul is on his way to Jerusalem, he said to the people on his last journey, "The Holy Spirit testifies to me in every city that imprisonment and afflictions await me" (Acts 20:33). Was this some special secret information that the Spirit of God was giving him? No, as others spoke of the possibility of this, the Spirit bore witness within him that what they said was true. It had the ring of truth; there was an inner confirmation that this was what was awaiting him, as it surely proved to be.

Perhaps you have often had the experience of reading a

passage of Scripture a hundred times, having studied it and perhaps even taught it, but the 101st time it suddenly comes alive with a wealth of meaning that you never saw before, and it simply glows with significance. That is the teaching of the Spirit. This is why the Bible never becomes a dead book. I do not think I have ever preached a series of sermons on a book of the Bible but when I had finished it, I wanted to start back at the beginning and go through again. I had learned so much, and I knew I would learn that much more going through it again. That is the marvelous ministry of the Holy Spirit to teach us.

This teaching is not limited to Christians. I rather think all the great discoveries of science have come about through the work of the Holy Spirit. Men can hear a chance remark, insignificant in the context of the conversation they are holding, when a word from another person strikes a fire in their hearts to give them a key to the clear grasp of a situation. That is the Spirit of God at work in men. But for the understanding of divine truth, especially that which concerns man's relationship to God, only the believer can enter into this realm. This anointing *abides* in the believer: it is always ready to work.

The Deep Things of God

Notice what John says about the scope of the teaching. "His anointing teaches you about everything, and is true, and is no lie." That means that there is no subject of human knowledge that is excluded from this experience of the teaching of the Holy Spirit. But because it is primarily centered, in the believer, upon the most central subject of all: our relationship as men to God as God—it therefore touches everything in our life. The apostle Paul says there is a wisdom which is imparted to us which concerns "the deep things of God" (1 Cor. 2:10, ASV). Think on that phrase, the deep things of God! These amazing themes, these profundities of life, these mysteries of life hidden in Christ, are revealed as the Spirit teaches you from the Word, so that you grasp the basic issues of living and grow in grace. You learn that at the heart of creation, of all human significance, is planted the cross, the resurrection, and the enthronement of Jesus Christ.

John ends with this admonition to us that reveals both the narrowness and the necessity of this witness of the Spirit.

> . . . just as it has taught you, abide in him (2:27).

The emphasis here is on the word *you,* "as he has taught *you,*" not what he has taught the other fellow. After the resurrection, Jesus said to Peter, "Feed my sheep." Peter turned and looked at John and said, "Lord, what do you want this man to do?" Do you remember what Jesus said? "That is none of your business. You follow me. What I teach this man to do is for him to know. What I have said for you to do, that is for you to do."

First-hand Truth

This is an intensely personal thing. What you have learned from the word of the Spirit, through the intermediary of human teachers, is to be the ground of your actions. Your activity must always be based on the conviction of what has come home to *you.* In other words, you walk by faith in the Word of God, as God has taught it to you—not what you have learned by tradition. Tradition has, historically, been one of the most deadly foes of the church and has held people back from advancement in their spiritual life.

Neither are your actions to be based on what you have learned through some church hierarchy. Anytime you condition men to take their truth secondhand, through some other individual, some line of men standing in succession above them, you have conditioned them to respond immediately to falsehood when it starts from the top. That is why hierarchies go astray so quickly and so easily. No, in the Christian life, all truth is intensely personal and comes directly to you from the Holy Spirit.

Is that not wonderful? That means you do not need to have a scholar interpreting the Word of God for you. You can be grateful for scholars; you can read their very helpful comments and the Lord will use them to teach you something, but you are not dependent upon them. You have no need that any man teach you at that level, for the Holy Spirit can instruct you. We must be open, of course, to hear all that others have to say. Charles Spurgeon once said, "I do not understand those men who have such a high opinion of what the Holy Spirit says to them, and such a low opinion of what he says to anyone else." We must remember that the Spirit of God does speak through other men, as well as through us.

But finally, we must act only on what the Lord has said to us. That is what made it possible for Martin Luther to stand before the Roman Catholic hierarchy, with all the assembled dignitaries of state and church arrayed in opposition to him, one lone man, and say, "Here I stand! I can do no other, God help me." He was listening to the voice of the Spirit to him.

This obedience is absolutely necessary because it is only on this basis that you can "abide in him," and that is the source of fruitfulness. You cannot go another's route; you cannot live another's spiritual life for him, or force him to go your route, either. You are to open the Word, pore over it, listen to the Holy Spirit in it, listen to others as the Holy Spirit has taught them, and then, faced with this entire array of external testimony, obey that which the Spirit confirms to your heart as the truth. John says when you do that, you will abide in him.

15

The Coming Day

In this section of John's letter we have learned many
things. We have learned that error appears in cycles of
deceit throughout history. That is why, proverbially,
history repeats itself. We learned that error arises first
within the church, through church leaders, and then
moves out to infect the world. Religious error never
originates with worldly, secular thinkers, but within the
church.

Then we saw that error always aims at one definitive
point. It is an attack, ultimately, upon the person of Jesus
Christ—upon the deity of the Son of God. The full
impact of heresy always comes out at that point, as an
attempt to destroy the great fundamental teaching of the
deity of Jesus Christ.

We have also learned in this section that no lie is of the
truth; there is no such thing as gray areas in moral or
doctrinal truth. Finally, we saw that the believer's defense against the deceitfulness of the age in which we live
lies in two special things: in his obedience to (1) the Word
of truth, the apostolic word, the word which we have
"heard from the beginning," as taught to the heart by (2)
an abiding Spirit. The Word and the Spirit: these are
always the defenses of the Christian. But these must be
held in balance. The Word without the Spirit is dead

orthodoxy—lifeless, unappealing, completely repulsive to most people. The Spirit without the Word is wildfire, fanaticism, mysticism. But the two held in balance keep us to the central truth of God as revealed in his Son. John closes this section with a verse that looks on to the end, when each Christian stands at last face to face with Jesus Christ.

> And now, little children, abide in him, so that when he appears we may have confidence and not shrink from him in shame at his coming (1 John 2:28).

What is it that lies ahead for each believer? The answer clearly is a face-to-face encounter with the Lord Jesus. John uses two phrases to describe this, "when he appears," and "at his coming." "Appears" is the word for manifestation, when he is openly evident. The word he uses for "coming" is the word *parousia* which is Greek for "presence," thus, the presence of the Lord Jesus.

The Hope of Believers

This is the most frequently mentioned truth in all of the New Testament. This great hope for the reappearance of Jesus Christ underlies every other truth in the New Testament. It is found on almost every page. In the face of this, it is passing strange that it is one of the neglected doctrines of our day. There are people who are totally unaware that the Bible teaches the return of Christ to this earth for his church. Yet this has been the hope of believers in every age, and has sustained Christians in the darkest hours of the persecution of the church.

The truth appears in various ways in the Bible. In certain passages, the coming of our Lord appears as an event yet to come, occurring in a moment of time. In 1 Thessalonians, Paul says,

> For the Lord himself will descend from heaven with a cry of command, with the archangel's call, and with the sound

of the trumpet of God. And the dead in Christ will rise first; then we who are alive, who are left, shall be caught up together with them in the clouds to meet the Lord in the air; and so we shall always be with the Lord. Therefore comfort one another with these words (1 Thess. 4:16–18).

Wonderful comfort is given in these words, especially when you stand at the edge of a grave where you have laid away the body of a loved one. I have used these verses many times on such occasions and found them to speak great comfort to the heart.

But there are other passages that view this encounter with Christ from the standpoint of the experience of the believer as he steps out of time into eternity, at death. For instance, Paul speaks of being "away from the body and at home with the Lord" (2 Cor. 5:8). Compare that with the passage in 1 Thessalonians, "so we shall always be with the Lord." Paul says this occurs, in the experience of the believer, at death. In writing to Timothy, he speaks of his own death in this way, "Henceforth there is laid up for me the crown of righteousness, which the Lord, the righteous judge, will award to me on that Day ["Day" here is not used in reference to a point of time but as a characterization of an event], and not only to me but also to all who have loved his appearing" (2 Tim. 4:8). Here he uses the same term that John uses in the phrase "when he appears."

To summarize, then, in the experience of the believer this encounter with Jesus Christ occurs at death. In the calendars of men, in time, it is yet an unknown point in the future. On that day, the Eternal One will step again into time and reassert himself, manifest himself openly in the affairs of men. That event may occur today, it may occur this week, it may be next year, it may be fifty or a hundred years from now. Who knows? But at any rate, this meeting with Christ, from the standpoint of every believer in Jesus Christ, is no farther away from any of us than the day of our death—and it may be even closer than that!

This is the Day in which, as John says, he will be "manifested." In chapter 3 John says, ". . . when he appears we shall be like him, for *we shall see him as he is*" (1 John 3:2). He will no longer be hidden behind the scenes, no longer invisible to our physical eyes, but now openly evident, manifest, visible, face-to-face. We will stand in his presence, John says. As the disciples, in the Upper Room after the resurrection, found that suddenly the Lord Jesus was with them, so, suddenly we will be with him. As then, so with us. With the marks of crucifixion yet upon his body, perhaps he will invite us to touch him, as he did with Thomas, to feel and to see that this is the very one who once was crucified upon a cross outside Jerusalem, and rose again from the dead. With the marks of crucifixion yet upon him he will be readily identifiable to us. What a wonderful day that will be!

Possibility of Shame

But let us move on to ask another question about the verse John sets before us. What are the alternatives awaiting Christians on that day? Well, clearly, there are two, and only two: to have "confidence before him," or "to shrink from him in shame." A false teaching which has arisen within Christian circles suggests that the day of our appearing before the Lord will be a day of only the giving of rewards. There are to be no regrets, no shame, no negative notes at all; it is all sweetness and light. It is hard to understand how such teaching arises, in the face of a Scripture like this where John warns that it is all too possible to shrink in shame before him at his coming.

Paul, speaking of the same event says, "we must all appear before the judgment seat of Christ, so that each one may receive *good or evil,* according to what he has done in the body" (2 Cor. 5:10). Two possibilities: good or evil; one producing boldness and confidence and one producing a sense of shame. We learn from the Scriptures that this is to be the day when reality is made evident, when things will be seen as they really are. We are aware that illusion blinds our understanding as we view things today. Even looking back in our lives we can see that events were not quite what we thought they were when we were living through them. But a day is coming, the Lord Jesus says, when that which is hidden will be revealed, where everything covered will be uncovered, and that which has been spoken in secret will be shouted from the housetops. It is the day of reality, the day when the secrets of men are judged by the Lord Jesus.

See how Paul describes this in 1 Corinthians. Speaking of the foundation which is Jesus Christ himself, Paul says:

> Now if any one builds on the foundation with gold, silver, precious stones, wood, hay, straw [two classifications of activity]—each man's work will become manifest; for the Day will disclose it, because it will be revealed with fire, and the fire will test what sort of work each one has done. If the work which any man has built on the foundation survives, *he will receive a reward.* If any man's work is burned up, *he will suffer loss,* though he himself will be saved, but only as through fire (3:12–15, italics mine).

And then in chapter 4 of that same book, he says, in verse 5,

> Therefore do not pronounce judgment before the time, before the Lord comes, who will bring to light *the things now hidden in darkness* and will disclose the purposes of the heart. Then every man will receive his commendation from God.

As someone has well put it, "What we weave in time, we shall wear through eternity." Every motive is to be revealed, every secret thought to be uncovered before all, every activity laid bare. In the light of that fact, what will you be? Will you be bold and confident, or will you shrink in shame before him? That is the question John sets before us.

One Spot Is All It Takes

Perhaps you are saying, "I hope it will be some of both; there will be some boldness, and some shame." But think about that for a moment, and you will see that it is impossible fór it to be both. There is nothing in Scripture that suggests that there will be both; it is either one or the other, as John implies here.

It is characteristic of us that if there is one element of shame in our character it looms up before our eyes and overpowers all the areas of confidence. Haven't you noticed that in your own experience? You have a gravy spot on your tie, or a run in your stocking, and it does not make any difference how impeccable the rest of your dress is. You know that every eye is fastened on that gravy spot or that run. You feel unfit to be with others because of one spot, regardless of the rest. So, if we are going to be bold and confident before our Lord at his coming, it must be that we should be absolutely without shame. If there is one thing wrong, we will shrink in shame at his coming.

Now look at this matter of shame for a moment with me. What will make us ashamed? Well, what makes you ashamed now? In thinking through this, I took a piece of paper and headed it, "Things Which Make Me Ashamed." Then I began to think through my own experience, my own life. The first thing I put down was "Indecent Actions." Someone has said, "Everyone knows that of himself which he would not dare tell his dearest friend." Indecent things, shameful things, hidden things, cruel deeds, vengeful, spiteful actions. As we think back on them they make us ashamed.

Then I wrote down "Hurtful Attitudes." How many times have I been ashamed at the attitude I have had toward another? Even though I did not express it in words, I felt it. How many times have I been ashamed of my pride, of my jealous, hateful thoughts, of my loveless, callous unconcern for another who was obviously in need of help from me? How many times has my thankless ingratitude made my face flush with shame? I thought back upon how I have taken things from man and from God and never had a thought of gratitude. Then I wrote down, "Neglected Opportunities." Who of us does not feel this? Who has not had, at one time or another, a bad case of the "If onlies"? "If only I had done this"; "If only I had said that"; "If only . . ."

What is shame? Is it not a sense of unfitness, of defilement, a sense even of self-contempt, because we feel we are not worthy? Therefore its manifestation is a desire to hide. John suggests this in the Greek word he uses, which is rightly translated "shrink in shame," to hide. In the Garden of Eden, Adam and Eve, after the Fall, hid from the Lord God as he walked in the Garden in the coolness of the day. God called out "Adam, where are you?" Adam at last acknowledged the call, and the Lord said "Why did you hide?" And Adam said, "Because we found we were naked." That is symbolic, suggestive of the fact that they had nothing besides themselves, nothing to show for being alive. They hid because they were unfruitful, unproductive, with no purpose beyond themselves.

Nothing Fruitful

As I thought back through the things that make me ashamed, I realized that there is a common element in all of these factors: a sense of waste. That is why I am ashamed of my indecent actions, my hurtful attitudes, my neglected opportunities. Nothing fruitful, nothing productive, ever comes from them. The thing that John makes us face up to in this passage is that, if we do not learn the right basis for living, it is horribly possible for us to fill every day with activity, to achieve what passes for success, but in the only accounting that has any value at all, that accounting before God, to come to the end of our lives and find it all fruitless, wasted, without purpose.

Is that not the charge the Lord makes against one of the churches in the letters to the seven churches of Revelation? In chapter 3 he says to the church at Laodicea, "I know your works: you are neither cold nor hot. Would that you were cold or hot! So, because you are lukewarm, and neither cold nor hot, I will spew you out of my mouth." What was the cause of this condition? "You say, I am rich, I have prospered, and I need nothing; not knowing that you are wretched, pitiable, poor, blind, *and naked.* Therefore I counsel you to buy from me gold refined by fire, that you may be rich, and white garments to clothe you and *to keep the shame of your nakedness from being seen,* and salve to anoint your eyes, that you may see" (Rev. 3:15–18, italics mine). It is nakedness that causes shame, and that possibility is set before each of us. The one thing that is absolutely certain about your existence and mine, as a believer, without any doubt whatsoever, is that one of these days we will stand before the presence of the Lord Jesus.

Grounds for Confidence

But I do not want to close on that note, for this verse is not intended to be negative. It is given to show us how to avoid this condition. Its whole purpose is to declare the clear possibility of standing in his presence unashamed, to have boldness, to have confidence before him. Well, then, what can make us bold? What gives boldness now in your life? To answer that for myself I took another sheet and headed it, "Things That Make Me Bold." First, I am bold or confident when I know what I am doing, when I have complete familiarity with a process. When I first began to shave I was not very skilled with a razor (electric razors were not very much in vogue at that time), and I used to cut myself so frequently that I looked like a sieve. I leaked at half a dozen points after every shave. But the longer I shaved the more familiar I became with the process until finally I was bold and confident. I could shave quickly without cutting myself. Watch a driver who is just learning to drive. How cautious he is! He grips the wheel tightly and does everything very deliberately. But watch a driver who has become accustomed to driving. How bold he is; we have a skyrocketing accident rate to prove how bold such drivers can get! But there is a feeling of confidence that comes when you know the process.

Then I discovered that I am bold and confident when I know that the results are guaranteed; some factor gives me confidence that it is going to work out all right. Such confidence in a sure result makes anyone bold. I was riding in a plane not long ago, and a mother and her five-year-old boy sat in the seat opposite me. She informed the stewardess that this was their first flight, and this was evident because she was very nervous. She kept looking out the window, adjusting her seat belt, and biting her fingernails. But not the little lad. He was relaxed and confident, utterly untroubled. Why? Because he trusted adults. His mother had brought him into this situation, and he knew that she would not have done it if there had been any danger, so he was trustful and utterly bold. He knew it would all work out—and it did. They arrived safely, and the mother could have saved herself all the worry.

I discovered that I am also bold when I have an undisclosed resource, what is called, familiarly, an ace up the sleeve. When I have something I can count on that the other fellow does not know about, it makes me bold. It does the same for you, too, does it not? Now look at what John proposes as the way to avoid shame and to have confidence in the day of the Lord Jesus, when we meet him face to face.

> And now, little children, *abide in him* [there it is in three words], so that when he appears we may have confidence and not shrink from him in shame at his coming (1 John 2:28).

It is all in those three words. Abide in him. That sums up all that he has previously said about hearing the Word, believing it, obeying it, and trusting it. This is the same thing exactly as what is called in other places "the walk in the Spirit," or "fellowship with Christ," or "the fullness of the Holy Spirit," or "the victorious life." Do not be confused by these various terms. This truth is so magnificent, so broad, so wide, it takes many terms to describe the full sweep of it, but they are all referring to the same thing.

Get It Over with Now

Abide in him, he says. Basically that means to give up all confidence in yourself and step out each moment in full dependence on him who dwells within you for everything you do or say, anywhere, any time. Abide in him, so that your actions are no longer a result of you, mobilizing all your resources to do something for him; but it is he, utilizing all his abundant resources, doing everything through you.

Abiding in him involves three specific actions: It means that you accept his evaluation of the past. You prepare to change the ideas that you learned from your childhood through tradition or secular education and have accepted as true, but which are contradicted by what the Scriptures say. Most of us take it for granted that what we were taught as we grew up is the truth, and we judge everything by what we learned, even the Word of God. We cling to these ideas, choosing to believe them rather than to believe what God has revealed to be the truth. This results in wide areas of weakness and ineffectiveness, which we must someday face in all their waste and unproductiveness, in the presence of Jesus Christ. It is these that will make us shrink in shame before him at his coming. But if we face his evaluation of the past, and change our ideas, then the thing is over with now. There is a wonderful verse in 1 Corinthians 11:31, "But if we

The Coming Day / 179

judged ourselves truly, we should not be judged." It can all be over, settled *now*.

Then, abiding in him means we are to accept his provision for the present. In writing to the Philippians Paul says, "Work out your own salvation." That means, work out the solutions to your problems. He is not talking about redemption but about the everyday problems of life. Work them out "with fear and trembling," with a consciousness that the deceitfulness of the enemy is so subtle that it can slip up on you without notice, and you need to be very careful not to start relying upon yourself again. "Work out your own salvation with fear and trembling; *for God is at work in you,* both to will [he is in the choosing, in the making of decisions, in the choices] and to work for his good pleasure [to do what is pleasing to him]" (Phil. 2:12,13, italics mine). That is the process: now accept it, operate in that manner for God knows what he is doing. What is it that makes you bold? You are bold when you know what you are doing. Well, Jesus Christ knows exactly what he is doing in you. He was never at a loss for what to do in any situation, and he never will be at a loss for what to do in any situation into which he puts you. He does not always tell you in advance what he is going to do. You just have to say, "Lord, here you are. You put me into this, now you have some purpose in it—work it out. I'm confident that you know what you are doing."

Also, we are bold when we know that the results are guaranteed. Have you not noticed that this is exactly what the Word of God promises? In 2 Corinthians Paul says, "But thanks be to God, who in Christ always leads us in triumph" (2:14). He never fails. He guarantees the results. You are fighting a battle that is already won when you rest upon the activity, the wisdom, the responsibility of an indwelling God. It is done—the battle is won. It still must be fought and you are to fight it, but the results are guaranteed. They will come out as God has said they will. He always leads us to triumph in Christ.

Furthermore, we are bold when we have an undisclosed resource, an ace up our sleeve. And is that not exactly what is provided for every Christian who understands the programming of God? We do not rely on our own human weakness. "We have no confidence in the flesh," Paul says. We do not think we have the intellectual acumen to figure out all the problems; we are not trying to mobilize all the resources of our powerful personalities to put something over. But we step into every situation, no matter what it may be, at home, at work, or wherever, in the quiet realization that the Son of God indwells us to do this thing through us. Others, looking at us, say, "What a self-assured individual; how well he gets things done, how poised, how calm he (she) is in a situation." They do not know the secret we know: that it is not ourselves, it is Christ. "I have been crucified with Christ," says Paul; "it is no longer I who live, but *Christ who lives in me;* and the life I now live in the flesh I live by faith in the Son of God, who loved me and gave himself for me" (Gal. 2:20, italics mine).

Fully Pleasing to Him

Then, abiding in him means to trust his assessment of the future. What is the result going to be? It is that we are perfectly acceptable to God—well-pleasing in his sight! The record of the Gospels is that Jesus Christ never did a thing to displease the Father. For thirty-three and a half years on earth, not once did he ever do anything that displeased God. How could he, since it was the Father, in him, who did everything? The miracles occupy only a tiny portion of those thirty-three and a half years; the rest of them were filled with the ordinary events of life, such as you and I have to go through—getting up in the morning, living with people, eating, preparing food, sweeping, cleaning, all the multitudinous details of life—but not once did he ever do one thing that was displeasing to the Father.

That is still true of what he does today—what he does

in you. His activity in you is already acceptable to the Father. Not once will he ever do in you that which is displeasing to the Father, not once. Therefore, if you are facing those times in your life which are not lived out of his activity, and these are cleansed and put away, the only possible conclusion to this is that you can stand at last in his presence without shame. All the wastefulness of the past and present is judged and everything else is fulfilled by Christ; therefore, all is pleasing to God. There will be no shame. That is what Paul is yearning for in his letter to the Philippians. He makes it clear that his desire is to live a life which has no waste moments in it, no times when he is reckoning on himself, no seasons when he is acting out of the energy of his own brilliant personality, or from the background of his training as a Hebrew leader, not a single moment. He says, "I am constantly pressing on, pushing on, for the prize—that wonderful prize—when I shall stand in his presence and shall realize that everything worthwhile that has been done in my life since I have come to know him has been done in the activity of his life in me, and everything else has already been settled before I get there."

Have you ever noticed how Jude closes his letter?

Now to him who is able to keep you from falling and *to present you without blemish* before the presence of his glory with rejoicing . . . (Jude 24, italics mine).

Is that not it? John says, "Abide in him, so that when he appears we may have confidence and not shrink from him in shame at his coming." It may be that you need to settle certain things with the Lord right this moment. Think of the things that make you ashamed; the attitudes you harbor toward someone else, the habits you cling to that are unsightly, unseemly, unwholesome, the long-standing disagreements that you have had with others which make you avoid them. These are the things that need to be settled now. Abide in him, *now,* so that you will not have to shrink in shame before him at his coming.

Book Three

Maintaining Righteousness

16

Recognizing the Unrecognized

Up to this point in the first epistle of John, we have traced two major themes: the necessity of maintaining fellowship with the Son of God, the shared life, followed by the theme of maintaining truth in the midst of an exceedingly deceitful world. Now John takes up a new theme, the matter of maintaining righteousness.

If you know that he is righteous, you may be sure that every one who does right is born of him (1 John 2:29).

It is most unfortunate that the chapter break occurs after this verse and not before. If you compare this with verse 7 of chapter 3, you will see that verse 29 belongs with chapter 3 rather than with chapter 2.

In this section John has been thinking of Jesus Christ. He has reminded us that an hour is coming when each Christian will see him face-to-face. He is thinking of the joy of seeing him again without that incomplete understanding we experience now. It is not that Christians do not have personal contact with Christ now, because we definitely do. It is that which keeps our faces alight, our hearts aflame, and our lives filled with joy. As Peter describes it, ours is now an experience of not seeing and yet loving. But John speaks of a day when we shall see him face-to-face. Suddenly he sees how the knowledge of Christ which we now have, incomplete as it may be, is the key to a problem that every Christian faces at one time or another—the problem of recognizing other Christians, of how to distinguish between the phony and the true, the mere professor and the real possessor of Christian life, between the one who is genuinely born again and the religious activist. John says the key is, "every one who does right is born of him."

Surely there is someone who will say, "Aha, that's what I've been waiting for. I have thought all along that this whole business of doctrine and belief was secondary, that the real test is a life. The man who is helpful, honest, and kind and does the right thing is the man who is acceptable." If you are thinking that way, you are a victim of the folly of incomplete truth. Unfortunately, many people read the Scriptures that way. They extract a portion of a verse, one particular phrase, and canonize it, making that the whole Scripture and discarding the rest.

If You Know

Notice here that John introduces this phrase with a qualification: He says, "If you know that he is righteous, then (and only then) will you know that every one who does right is born of him." If you cannot fulfill the qualification you are in no condition to make the judgment. But if you know that he (Christ) is righteous, then you have the key.

In this little verse the apostle uses two different words for "know." The first one, "if you *know*," has to do with absolute truth. If you know (in a clear and unqualified way, if you understand in the fullest degree) "that he is righteous, then you will know" (by means of experience or observation) "that every one who does right is born of him." The key to this passage is this qualification. Do you know, as absolute truth, understanding it clearly, that Christ is righteous?

What does "righteous" mean, anyway? We can read Scripture frequently and yet never really grasp some of these major words. Righteousness is God behaving as God. It is whatever God does. God, obviously, is the standard for all human behavior, and for the behavior of any creature in the universe. God is always consistent with himself: he always acts like God; he cannot act in any other way. Therefore, whatever he does is righteous. That is the standard, so that righteousness is God behaving as God. Now let's read the verse again. "If you know how God behaves, then you will know that whoever behaves like God is born of him." He will bear the family mark. Whoever behaves like God is obviously born of God, for it takes God's life to behave like God.

Love That Satisfies Justice

We can break this down even further. In specifics, what does God do that marks him as righteous? The answer is given to us in the revelation that has come through Jesus Christ. Jesus came to manifest the Father, to show us how God behaves, how he acts. What he does is to act out of love in such a way as to satisfy justice. Love that satisfies justice is righteousness.

If you are hungry, and I feel sorry for you, and steal $5.00 from the bank to buy you a meal, I have manifested love toward you, but I have not satisfied justice with regard to the bank. That would be love without justice, an unrighteous act. No matter how commendable the motive, it is love without justice. If you indulge your children, giving them everything they want, you show love to them, but you do not show justice. You are not treating them according to reality. That wickedness of yours will ultimately be imparted to them, appearing later on as a rebellious attitude in them.

On the other hand, if I steal $5.00 from the bank to satisfy my hunger and you put me in jail, without feeding me, then you have manifested justice, but no love. The classic case of that is the scene from Shakespeare's "Merchant of Venice" when Shylock demands his pound of flesh as his righteous due before the law. But he is showing no consideration of love. Therefore it is an unrighteous act, even though it is legally correct. Thus many of the acts we do to conform with the law are still unrighteous acts in the sight of God, because there is no love in them.

Love that satisfies justice is always unselfish, self-giving, willing to suffer inconvenience—even heartache and shame. It is concerned about the need of another, and yet concerned that the need be met without affecting still others adversely. Righteousness is not merely doing something helpful. A great many things done in the world today are helpful, and we tend to label them as righteous, but they are not. So much of our activity in helping one another arises directly out of our own self-interest. Many of us would be positively astounded if we could see the degree to which this is true. Such actions may be helpful, and surely we are grateful for all such manifestations. Human life would not be possible if people did not respond in helpfulness to one another—even for causes of self-interest. But they are not necessarily righteous deeds.

Further, righteousness is not something costly, although there are indeed those who give away fortunes, even their lives, for causes they believe in. We tend to label these as righteous deeds, but they are not necessarily so. The apostle Paul reminds us, "If I give my body to be burned and have not love, it profits me nothing." Such deeds are not righteous, because righteousness always consists of love that satisfies justice. Righteousness is giving, whether or not anything is received in return, and in such a way that no encouragement is given to evil. That is the way God behaves. There is a burning phrase that has stuck in my mind ever since I read it in the Gospel of Luke, where our Lord describes the Father as "kind to the selfish and the ungrateful." That is righteousness. Now if you know how God behaves, then you will know what righteousness is when you see it, and you will know that everyone who does that is born of him. That is the mark.

To prove this, John goes right on in chapter 3, verse 1 to give us an illustration. Remember, these two verses should be linked together:

> See what love the Father has given us, that we should be called children of God;

Here is an astonishing thing, he says. It is not the fact that God loves, but *how* God loves. What manner of love is this! Literally, the Greek for "what manner" is "of what country." It is an exclamation of astonishment, of surprise. What kind of country is this, what foreign land is this, that is represented in love like that! It is so different. It is the strangeness of God's love that is in view here. It is strange, John says, in that it makes us the children of God.

How God Saw Us

Perhaps some of you are thinking, "Well, you may be surprised at this, but I'm not. I consider it quite logical. Why shouldn't I be a child of God, like anyone else?" But Romans 5 reveals to us how God saw us when he found us. Four words describe us in that passage: "While we were yet *helpless*," unable to make any contribution to the redemption we desperately needed, "at the right time Christ died for the *ungodly*," for us (Rom. 5:6).

But it does not stop there; it says further, "While we were yet *sinners* Christ died for us" (v. 8). While we were sinners—proud, overbearing in our attitude toward God, treating him with condescension and indifference, tiresome (that is what sin does, it makes us tiresome individuals)—Christ died for us. Even this does not exhaust his description; he goes on in verse 10 to say, "If while we were *enemies* we were reconciled to God by the death of his Son. . . ." Not only were we helpless, not only sinners, proud and prickly in our attitude, but also we were absolutely opposed to God, enemies of his grace, resisting every attempt he made to reach us.

That is why John cries: What amazing love! God flings the bloodstained mantle of his love over us and calls us his children. And he not only calls us this, but he actually makes us so. "And so we are!" Is that not amazing? You Christian people, do you ever think of yourselves that way? Do you ever think of yourselves as having been in this terrible condition when God found you, and that you would still be like that if God had not found you? What pride is it that makes us think of ourselves as some kind of fortunate catch that God has made? How happy he ought to feel that we have consented to join his side! But no! "See what manner of love the Father has given us, that we should be called children of God," that we prickly, tiresome, difficult people should be made children of God!

Only by Faith

Now God does not call all men his children, as some people do. Paul wrote to the Galatians, "in Christ Jesus you are all sons of God, through faith" (Gal. 3:26). The only one God ever calls his child is the one who has exercised faith in Jesus Christ. God is not "the Father of all mankind." This is an absolutely unbiblical phrase. It has no justification whatever in the Scriptures; in fact, it is positively denied. He is the Creator of all mankind. We all share with every other human being on the face of this earth a common heritage in humanity. We are all members of one race. This is an important truth; but we are not all the children of God. We are children of God only "by faith in Jesus Christ."

All men *can* be the children of God; redemption is provided for all. There is plenty of grace in Christ.

Wherever someone responds to the grace of God reaching out toward him, that one, by faith, becomes a child of God. God's love has reached the world, has encompassed the race. That is the extent of God's love, consistent with his justice. God desires that his enemies should become his children, and his children should become mature sons. That is his righteousness, and this is the unmistakable mark of one who becomes a child of God; he too begins to exercise righteousness. He begins to exhibit love in line with justice. Such a one becomes concerned and prompted to act contrary to his self-interest, yet consistent with the law, in the commitment of love. That is the mark.

Let me say that if you do not see that in someone else it does not necessarily mean he is not a Christian. It may mean, as it does with many of us at times, that at the moment he is not acting in a manner consistent with the nature God has given to him. But the point John is making is that if you do see this unmistakable mark of love acting in accordance with justice, then you need have no doubts whatsoever. The person is born of God. He may be confused in certain areas of truth, he may not agree with you about the mode of baptism, he may not have light on the dispensations, but if you see him acting righteously, then you know he is one of God's own.

Bucket of Cold Water

But do not expect the world at large to recognize this. They will not understand and may even strongly resent the fact that another has become a child of God. Every new convert discovers this when, in the flush of his new-found enthusiasm for Christ, he goes back to his family and friends to tell them he has now become a child of God. He expects them to glow with enthusiastic rapport, but he meets with coldness and an "Oh-is-that-so? I'll-watch-and-see" attitude. He feels the first bucket of cold water thrown upon his faith.

John explains why this happens in the second half of the first verse: "The reason why the world does not know us is that it did not know him" (1 John 3:1). We Christians manifest the nature of God only occasionally. We ought to be doing it more and more as we grow in grace, so that it becomes more consistently visible. But there are times when we do not, and even when we do it is sometimes rather indistinct. But when Jesus walked for thirty-three and a half years among men, living among them in the intimacy of daily life, there was never a moment that he did not clearly and continuously manifest righteousness, that nature and character of God. Never could there be a clearer human revelation of what God is like than there was in the Son of God. Even then, they failed to recognize him; they did not know who he was. As the Negro spiritual sings, "Poor little Jesus boy, they didn't know who you was."

They did not know, when he stood before them, that here was God behaving as God, in man. They saw only the externals. They saw him as a peasant's son, a carpenter, a tub-thumping rabble-rouser, or, at best, a good man experiencing incredible bad luck. Paul, writing to the Corinthians, said, "if they had [known him], they would not have crucified the Lord of glory" (1 Cor. 2:8). If they had any idea who it was that was standing before them—if they could have discerned the glory of his character, seen behind the externals to the inward beauty he was exhibiting, they never would have nailed him to a cross.

But they did not see. And why not? Because they shut their ears to what he said. They would not believe him and therefore they could not see him. It is always amazing to me how the "seeing is believing" proverb ever got credence among men. It is exactly the reverse; believing is seeing—not only religiously, but in every field in life. Believing is seeing; but because they shut their ears and their eyes to his words and his deeds, they would not believe; therefore they could not see. They did not know him, so they took him out and nailed him to a cross.

Now if they did not know him in spite of the perfect manifestation of righteousness which he was giving, then surely we cannot expect the world to recognize us as sons of God, or to treat us with the deference that a child of God might expect to receive. All the writers of Scripture tell us not to be surprised if the world discounts your Christian testimony, laughs in your face, and makes scornful, even contemptuous, remarks about what you believe. Do not be surprised; they did the same to the Lord. The principle by which we find power, rest, joy and strength is utter foolishness in the eyes of the world. Paul says so: "The word of the cross is folly to those who are perishing . . ." (1 Cor. 1:18). The word of the cross is the principle which repudiates self-interest, the principle which renounces any advantage you may gain out of a situation in order to gain advantage for God. It is the principle which risks income, position, and sometimes even life itself in order to be true, honest, clean, and committed. That principle, the world says, is foolish. "You'll never get ahead, not in this company, if you act like that." "Save that for church. It won't work in business; it's foolish." Is that not what they say? Yet to us who are being saved, if we have the guts to act on what God has said—not only at church but in the world, at home, at school, anywhere else in life—it is the power of God. It achieves what God has come to do in human life. It is power.

Power for Patience

Why do you need power? Do you think of it in terms of miracles, dazzling displays, and wonderful deeds that you could do to capture the attention of others? Is that why you want power? Look at Colossians 1:11 where Paul prays for power for believers: "May you be strengthened with all power [tremendous, isn't it?], according to his glorious might [isn't that exciting! for what?], *for all endurance and patience with joy."* Endurance! That means putting up with the conditions in which you live. And patience—waiting quietly for something to happen. And joy, in the midst of it all. That takes power, does it not? It is impossible to live like that in the midst of the conditions of life if you do not have the power of God. It takes far more power than any of us can possibly produce in ourselves. It takes God's power. The word of the cross, the principle of the denial of self and self-interest, *is* the power of God, to us who are being saved.

The question John leaves with us in this whole section is: What is the quality of your life? What kind of life are you displaying before others? Do they recognize you as a child of God? The world will not, necessarily—but do other Christians? Do you have the mark? The whole problem with this troubled, tortured, bedeviled world, with its twisted concepts and its evident confusion, can be traced right back to the Christian church. Christians have failed to manifest the righteousness of God. They are salt without savor, in the midst of society. Therefore, it ill behooves the church to point the finger of scorn or shame or blame at the world for the condition it is in. It is our fault; we are to blame. If we were living on this level, if we were laying hold of what is so abundantly provided for us in Christ, if, in our homes, we were living like this, there would be no more bickerings and quarrelings, fightings, coldness and frigidity between husband and wife, or parents and children. We would be a demonstration of the righteousness of God.

17

What Shall We Be?

Beloved, we are God's children now; it does not yet appear what we shall be, but we know that when he appears we shall be like him, for we shall see him as he is. And every one who thus hopes in him purifies himself as he is pure (1 John 3:2,3).

The emphatic word in that first sentence is the word "now." It appears first in the Greek structure, and the first word is often the most emphasized word in a Greek sentence. *"Now* we are the children of God." Eternal life belongs to us *now.* We are not waiting until we die to get it but we are born again *right now.* We have the life of Jesus Christ in us *now.* We are sons and daughters of God *now.* We are the heirs of all God's glory and promises *now.* But although these things are true, we do not look any different than others. Today, as in the days of our Lord, God's life is "veiled in flesh" and it is not always manifest within us.

Paul speaks of this in the great eighth chapter of Romans, where he says that the whole creation is looking forward to the day when the sons of God will be revealed. He uses two colorful words there. He says the whole creation "waits expectantly." The word *waits* is a

Greek word that means "to stand on tiptoe" and *expectantly* means "to crane the neck with eagerness." The whole creation is standing on tiptoe, craning the neck with eager anticipation of the day when the great secret now hidden among mankind will be revealed, and the sons of God will become manifest.

The world is unconsciously looking forward to that day. The conditions it will bring about upon the earth are so remarkable, so transcendently glorious that all the fine-sounding words that have been uttered in political campaigns about the improvements to be made in society will seem puerile and pitiful alongside the conditions that will prevail then. This is always the hope of the believer in Jesus Christ. He knows that the world is not heading to a blind end; it is going to an appointed meeting, and is right on schedule. The day is coming when the sons of God will be manifest.

No Specifics

But the mystery now deepens. John says that the world does not know who we are now—nor do we know what we shall be! What is it like actually to be with the Lord? What is it like to have Christ return and to experience with him the program God has in mind for his own? What is it like for our friends who have gone to be with the Lord? What are they experiencing? What are they like now? Those questions are shrouded in mystery to us. "It does not yet appear what we shall be." I do not mean they are clouded by uncertainty; the general answers are very certain. But it is not clear as to the precise nature of the conditions which are to be. It is interesting that the Scripture uses only negative expressions along this line. There is no positive description of what life beyond this world is like; it is all expressed in negatives. There will be no tears, no more sorrow, no night, no death, no separation, no weakness, no pain—but that is all negative. What will it be like? We can only guess at the opposites to these negatives. "It does not yet appear what we shall be."

There is that strange passage in the closing chapter of 2 Corinthians where the apostle Paul speaks of the experience of being caught up into the third heaven, with the Lord. He did not know whether he was in the body or out of the body; he could not tell. He heard things and saw things which, he said, were not lawful to utter. I think the real meaning of that phrase is that they were simply indescribable in terms of our present experience. It does not yet appear what we shall be—as far as the positive understanding of the conditions of life beyond this.

Furthermore, it does not yet appear how our present circumstances relate to what we shall be. Certainly we do not understand how what we are going through right now is producing what is coming, yet that is what the Scriptures declare. In 2 Corinthians the apostle Paul cries, "For this slight momentary affliction [is that not an amazing description, when you read the list of things he went through: stoning, prison, shipwreck, hungering and thirsting, and all the other things? But he groups it all together and labels it "this slight affliction"] is preparing for us an eternal weight of glory beyond all comparison." I am forever fascinated by that phrase "weight of glory" (2 Cor. 4:17). I would like to know what that means. We speak of a weight of responsibility, by which we mean a burden to be borne, but this is a weight of glory, a responsibility so tremendous, perhaps, so vast in its implications and yet so glorious in its experience, that it is like a great weight which is fully met and answered by the strength we shall have.

Paul says this weight of glory is being produced by what we are going through right now. Does that not cast a great deal of light on our experience today? How many of us have questions about what is happening to us, especially when pain and suffering strikes? We know there is some lesson in them (we have learned that much about God), but we think all the lessons are intended to be put to use down here, right now. Sometimes when we go through sorrow, difficulty, or pain and suffering we say, "Lord, teach me a lesson from this." We learn certain lessons and think they are all learned, yet the pain goes on. That is when our faith is really put to the test. That is when our hearts cry, "Why?" But that is exactly why John says it does not yet appear what we shall be, and Paul adds, this light affliction is producing something. It is all working out something that will not be manifest now, in this life, but later. It is producing a weight of glory that is yet to appear.

Some years ago I heard of an artist who was painting a picture he felt would be his masterpiece. He was working away on it in his studio, painting the background color, when a friend came in. The artist stepped back and said, "Oh, look at it! It's my masterpiece. What do you think of it?" The friend said, "Well, it doesn't look like much to me, just a mass of color." And the artist said, "Oh, I forget. You're seeing it as it is, but I see it as it will be." Surely God looks at us that way, but it does not yet appear to *us* what we shall be.

Three-ring Certainty

John frankly acknowledges that there is still much we do not understand. But notice, he quickly moves on to a note of certainty:

> . . . but we know that when he appears we shall be like him, for we shall see him as he is (3:2).

We do not know everything, but we do know three definite facts about the future. *Certainty number one: We know that he will appear.* This is an absolutely inescapable fact in God's program for mankind; he will appear. He appeared once; he will appear the second time. Of this there is absolutely no doubt. All history is moving to this goal. Even the apparent confusion that exists today is but creating the conditions predicted in the Scriptures, and working out the great purposes of God. Remember that his coming, as far as your experience is concerned, is no further away than your own death, and you do not know how soon that will come.

Certainty number two: We know that we shall be like him. I urge you to read that very carefully now, and note the context out of which it comes. It is linked with our present limited knowledge. Note that it does not say, "when he appears we shall *become* like him." A misconception has arisen among some Christians who regard this verse as teaching that, when Jesus Christ appears, we shall all suddenly become like him, in a moment, in a twinkling of an eye. Certainly, as regards the body, this is so. Our bodies become like his. Paul writes to the Philippians, "We await a Savior, the Lord Jesus Christ, who will change our lowly body to be like his glorious body" (Phil. 3:20,21). All the groanings and weakness which we experience each day will be forgotten when our bodies are changed to be like his. That happens, as Paul tells us in 1 Corinthians 15, in a moment, "in the twinkling of an eye," when this mortal puts on immortality, and "death is swallowed up in victory" (vv. 52–54).

But the body is only the shell of the inner life. We do not suddenly change our total character and personality when we see Jesus Christ, and there is no Scripture that says so. Rather, as John is saying here, what we have been becoming through the years of our life will suddenly be revealed when he appears. And what we have been becoming is, little by little, stage by stage, like him. The full extent to which we have become like him will be revealed when we see him, and not before.

How Much Like Christ?

The question, of course, that comes shouting out at us from all this is, How much of my life is becoming like him right now? What percent of the time am I, as a Christian, like Jesus Christ? How much of my time, now, am I projecting the image of his life in me, rather than the image of the flesh in me? That is the crucial question, because that is what will be revealed when we see him. Everything else will be burned, as Paul says in 1 Corinthians 3, since it is but wood, hay, and stubble. The gold, the silver, and the precious stones are the aspects and parts of our lives in which we have consented to be like him. But those times when we resist him, those areas in which we shut him out and assume that we have what it takes to live as God wants us to live in our own strength and energy, are all wood, hay, and stubble and will be burned, and we will suffer loss.

The point is that the change into his likeness must happen now. We are becoming like him right now. Look at 2 Corinthians 3:18:

And we all, with unveiled face [with the blindness taken from our eyes by the Holy Spirit who teaches us all things], beholding the glory of the Lord, *are being changed into his likeness* [right now, as we see the Lord revealed to us from the word by the Spirit, and in the experience of fellowship with one another, we are being changed into his likeness] from one degree of glory to another; for this comes from the Lord who is the Spirit.

Thus in the day when we see him, when he appears, then we will be like him to the extent that we have learned to be like him now. That is what makes this "light affliction" Paul speaks of so tremendously important, because it is working for us, producing a likeness to him. As we see him in our circumstances, and we learn to accept them, prickly and thorny as they may be, as coming from him, sent by him to work in us that which he desires; as we learn to do this without grumbling, without complaint or rejection, we discover that we are becoming like him. All these things are God's instruments to shape us and mold us into his likeness. When we grumble and gripe, or complain and try to run away, we are rejecting the instruments God has sent to make us into his likeness. So we face the possibility of becoming much less like him than we could be.

Certainty number three is also mentioned in this verse, *"we shall see him as he is."* "But," you say, "according to what this verse says, this is the *reason* we become like him; when we see him as he is, then we all become like him." That is exactly what has given rise to what I have previously called a misconception in the Christian life, this idea that everyone is suddenly to become fully like Jesus when we see him as he is. No, we are already becoming like him even when we see him as in a mirror, faintly—darkly, as Paul puts it. It does not take a full-orbed view of Christ to make us like him; that is happening even now. But this little word "for" in this verse is a Greek particle that can also be translated "that." The best commentators admit that it is uncertain whether this should be translated, "we shall be like him *because* we shall see him as he is" or whether it should be, as I think, "we shall be like him *that* we might see him as he is," *in order* to see him as he is. That is why we are being changed into his likeness now, in order that when he appears we shall see him as he is. We shall be able to understand him, to enter into communion with him, to fellowship with him.

What Your Dog Doesn't Know

As we well know from our own experience, you must be like something in order to understand it, to enjoy fellowship with it. That is why your dog cannot enter into your sorrows or your joys. You come home bro-kenhearted, and sit down. The dog senses something is wrong. He whines and sits looking up at you with his brown eyes expressive of concern, but he cannot under-stand. He is puzzled, he does not know what is wrong, he cannot enter in, he cannot comfort you. He does not and cannot understand what you are going through. Again, you are happy, and he knows you are happy. He wags his tail, but he does not know what it is all about. He cannot know because he is a dog, and you are a human; therefore, he cannot enter into your experience.

But we can, for that is what the apostle says about us. No man can understand the things of God except the Spirit of God, he only can understand. No man can enter into fellowship with God by himself. We cannot possibly understand this mighty, wonderful, transcendent Being, this great fountain of love and grace and truth. We can never know him until we become like him. But that is what is happening now. Do you understand? That is what is happening to you, through your circumstances, now.

If you see it that way, then you will see why John adds this third verse here.

And every one who thus hopes in him [Christ] purifies himself as he is pure.

If the degree to which you become like him is the degree to which you will see him as he is, then what a powerful motivation this is to become like him now: to accept your circumstances, to stop quarreling with what God sends to you, and begin in everything to give thanks, allowing these strange instruments of God's grace to do their work in your life.

Paul says, "suffering produces endurance, and endurance produces character" (Rom. 5:3,4). Suffering produces endurance—that means it makes you ready to wait and watch and pray for God to work things out. And endurance produces character, as you experience God working things out. Again and again you see that the situations which caused you to fear, or made you uncertain, as you patiently waited and looked to God, doing what he indicated you could do at the moment but otherwise resting quietly, began to work out in wonderful ways. And character produces hope. Not hope in the worldly sense of uncertainty, of chance, but hope in the biblical sense: hope of certainty, absolute assurance. A few experiences like this and you know absolutely that God is adequate, that he is able to work everything out. You know that every testing is another opportunity for God to demonstrate his great ability to work things out. Thus hope "makes not ashamed"; it gives confidence, a sense of unbeatable confidence which keeps you poised and assured under any circumstance.

Use the Soap

All that is what happens now, as God begins to work through our circumstances to make us like him. So John says that everyone who has this kind of hope purifies himself, even as Christ is pure. "But," you say, "purify myself! That's the one thing I can't do!" Well, that is true. God knows that. He knows you cannot purify yourself, yet he says to purify yourself here. What does he mean? Well, you purify yourself when you use the means he has provided for purification.

You mothers know how this works. Your little boy has been playing in the streets and is covered with dirt. He comes in and you send him into the bathroom to purify himself. Like all boys, he turns on the water, runs his hands through it, turns the water off, wipes his hands on the towel and comes out. You look him over and say, "But you're not clean."

"Well," he says, "I washed myself."

"But look at the dirt on your hands and on your arms and on your face and behind your ears. You're not clean at all."

Then every wise mother asks, "Did you use soap?" Of course he didn't, so she sends him back to use the soap. What is soap? It is a purifying agent, a cleansing agent. It will do the job if it is employed. So when he comes back the second time he has washed with soap and the soap has cleansed him, purified him. Now he says, "Look, Mom, I've cleaned myself up."

It is true he did it, but he did it by using the means

provided. The provision for our cleansing is the Word of God and the Spirit of God. "The blood of Jesus Christ, God's Son, cleanses us from all sin." "If we confess our sins, he is faithful and just to forgive us and to cleanse us from all unrighteousness." This means we must begin to take seriously this matter of a break of fellowship with Christ because of an impatient spirit, or an ugly word, or a lustful idea or thought which we have dwelt on. We must realize that the stain of it does not disappear by the passage of time. It has interfered with our fellowship with the Son of God, and we must do something about it. We cannot simply forget it; we must do something about it. We must purify ourselves, using the provision he has provided, that we might be clean.

What a wonderful practical tie there is between this truth of the coming of the Lord and our appearing before him, and the living of our daily life! "Every one who thus hopes in him purifies himself as he is pure." Let me illustrate that by the life of Martha Snell Nicholson who, for more than thirty-five years, was an invalid, bound to her bed, and yet whose spirit was so transcendently triumphant through those many weary years that she wrote some of the finest Christian poetry which has ever been written. A number of years before she died she wrote about her hope of the coming of the Lord. This is what she says:

> The best part is the blessed hope of his soon coming. How I ever lived before I grasped that wonderful truth, I do not know. How anyone lives without it these trying days I cannot imagine. Each morning I think, with a leap of the heart, "He may come today." And each evening, "When I awake I may be in glory." Each day must be lived as though it were to be my last, and there is so much to be done to purify myself and to set my house in order. I am on tiptoe with expectancy. There are no more grey days— for they're all touched with color; no more dark days—for the radiance of His coming is on the horizon; no more dull days, with glory just around the corner; and no more

lonely days, with His footstep coming ever nearer, and the thought that soon, soon, I shall see His blessed face and be forever through with pain and tears.

That was written from a bed of pain and anguish. Yet is it not significant that this very same person could write the following powerful expression of the desire she felt to purify herself in view of that transcendent event?

When I stand at the judgment seat of Christ
And He shows me His plan for me.
The plan of my life as it might have been
Had He had His way, and I see.

How I blocked Him here, and I checked Him there,
And I would not yield my will—
Will there be grief in my Saviour's eyes,
Grief, though He loves me still?

He would have me rich, and I stand there poor,
Stripped of all but His grace,
While memory runs like a hunted thing
Down the paths I cannot retrace.

Then my desolate heart will well-nigh break
With the tears that I cannot shed;
I shall cover my face with my empty hands,
I shall bow my uncrowned head . . .

Lord of the years that are left to me,
I give them to Thy hand;
Take me and break me, mould me to
The pattern Thou hast planned!

18

The Greatest Revolution

The two verses we come to now give us the most penetrating analysis to be found anywhere in the Bible of the reason for human distress and darkness. They also declare God's answer to this human distress in one mighty sentence. Thus they describe the message which for 1900 years has laid hold of hearts, of both young and old, and compelled them to go out across the street and across the seas in the name of Jesus Christ.

> Every one who commits sin is guilty of lawlessness; sin is lawlessness. You know that he appeared to take away sins, and in him there is no sin (1 John 3:4,5).

I would suggest to you that verse four is a more profound identification of the source of human heartache and misery than all the psychology books that have ever been written. "Every one who commits sin is guilty of lawlessness; sin is lawlessness." There is a spirit of revolt abroad. These are revolutionary times, in the truest sense of the words. There is a widespread, universal refusal to acknowledge authority in our day. There is a determination to please self at all costs, to do "what I want," regardless of what anyone else wants. Therefore, the major characteristic of our day is the word of this ancient text—lawlessness! Lawlessness, both as a principle and as an activity, that is, a lawless *attitude* within every heart, resulting in lawless *acts* by every person. That is the biblical picture of humanity.

Who, Me?

Do you challenge that? Let me say it again: a lawless attitude within *every* heart, resulting in lawless acts by *every* person. Do you deny that? Are you mentally saying to yourself, "But I'm not lawless. It's all right for you to talk about others this way, but don't talk about me. I'm a law-abiding, respectable person. I'm not lawless"? I am not referring now to violations of the law of man—such as traffic ordinances—nor does the Scripture. I suspect, however, that many of us would hesitate to be examined too closely even in this area. But I am speaking of law in its widest sense, law as an expression of the nature of things. After all, that is what laws are, expressions of reality.

We speak of the law of gravity. Why do we call it a law? Gravity is the attraction of one bit of matter to another, and we call it a law because it is inescapably there. It is real; it has to be reckoned with. There is no avoiding it; it is realistic. We speak of the laws of electricity, and we mean the way electricity operates, the way it works. We say these functions are laws because they invariably work in certain ways. We refer to laws of being, by which we mean that there are certain predictable responses we inevitably make because of the nature of things.

Now if law in its widest sense is simply an expression of the nature of reality, then lawlessness describes unrealistic behavior, behavior that ignores such laws. Lawlessness is to become a law unto oneself, to make up one's own rules for life and to disregard those that already exist.

Now would you like to count up your lawless acts,

those times when you have said, "Well, I don't care what happens, I'm going to do what I want anyhow"? What about the occasions when you have misled others to believe you think one way when actually you think another? The times when you have told yourself, "Never again!" but you have gone right back and done it again. "Oh," you say, "I thought lawlessness was hijacking airplanes, or bombing bank buildings." Well, that is only one form of lawlessness.

Respectable Lawlessness

Lawlessness universally expresses itself in two general ways: in open defiance, and apparent respectability. The attitude of open defiance is obvious in its manifestations—people of every age unashamedly rejecting the restraints of authority. But lawlessness is equally expressed through apparent respectability. This needs greatly to be said, because we, who reject the open arrogant defiance of some, tend to draw our self-righteous skirts about us and regard ourselves as lawful individuals simply because there are aspects of law which we recognize and to which we submit ourselves. But the deadly principle of lawlessness is as much at work in the respectable crowd as it is in the defiant group, as Paul makes clear in the first and second chapters of Romans. There he examines both sides and says they are equally guilty. That this charge is true is obvious because of certain manifestations of lawlessness in the respectable group as well as among the defiant. Essentially these are threefold: hatred, darkness, and death. Hatred, the violation of love; darkness, the extinguishing of light; and death, the destruction of life.

Now look at this twentieth-century world, with its love of scientific technological advancement, its fascination with the exploration of space, and its manifestation of confusion, uncertainty, and darkness on every side. Look first at the respectable world. Is there not hatred there? Is it not evident in prejudice and haughtiness, in cattiness, in exclusive clubs, in selfish cliques, in indifference to the needs of other human beings? It is manifest also in quarreling parents and resentful children, in bitter feuds within the home, in scheming acts of revenge against other individuals and groups, in broken homes, in the skyrocketing divorce rate, in neglected children, in cruelty that breaks out in a most frightening manner from time to time. At the root of it all is this principle of lawlessness.

There is also darkness, the extinguishing of light. Is that not evident everywhere in the world, even in your own life? It is manifest in confusion, in uncertainty, in double-mindedness, in vacillation, in the frequency with which we change direction according to what is expedient. It is evident in anxiety, fears, tensions, neuroses, obsessions, and the fantastic wave of mental illness sweeping the world today. The root of it again is lawlessness, the refusal to recognize reality.

Again there is violent death, which is so disturbing to the respectable world in which we live. It is supremely evident in war. There is not a thoughtful Christian individual who can look at war and see it as anything but the utter madness of men. But lawlessness is seen as well in the violence that fills our streets, in murders, persecutions, and suicides. Death is evident in the blank hopelessness that spreads like a pall of gloom across great segments of our society; in the despair and emptiness that fills human hearts.

Warring Camps

Is this survey realistic? Am I describing life as it is? Oh, I know there are other things in life. I know there is joy; I know there are moments of gladness, peace, and quietness. There are the good aspects of life. I know I am looking at the dark side right now, but that dark side is there, is it not? The world is divided into two great warring camps. The antagonism and enmity between these two camps breaks out at all levels of society today. There is the radical, defiant group and the respectable, apparently law-abiding group. The radicals are looking at the respectables and saying, "You're all a bunch of hypocrites. You don't live like you talk. You smother us, you're trying to extinguish all freedom, you want to make us conform to narrow channels of your own choosing, and we refuse to do so." They point the finger at the respectables and say, "The trouble with the world is you: your narrow, bigoted attitudes, your stuffy formalism." On the other hand, the respectables are looking at the radicals and saying, "The real trouble is, you are all lawless. You have no respect for tradition or convention. You do not see the necessity for order and peace. You are trying to create trouble and foment revolution and riot, you are working to upset society wherever you go. The trouble with life is you!" But the Scripture says both sides are equally afflicted with this virus of lawlessness: "Every one who commits sin is guilty of lawlessness, because sin is lawlessness."

Well then, what is the answer? What is the preeminent need of our race? What is the solution to these pressures and difficulties? It is rather obvious, is it not? Take away the lawless spirit, eliminate this basic cause of human disaster and distress. We must change the nature of man. Man himself is his own major problem. General Carlos Romulo, for many years the Philippine Ambassador to the United States, stated the case precisely: "We have harnessed the atom, but we will never make war obsolete until we find a force to bridle the passions of men." He is exactly right. Why do we waste time with surface manifestations, outbreaks of evil that are merely symptoms of an underlying disease? We must strike at the disease, do something directly about the thing that is wrong, eliminate the basic cause.

Beyond Our Reach

But though the answer is obvious, it is hopelessly out of our reach. It is, of course, precisely what we have been trying to do, without success. We have tried education, but the problems mount on every side. Education has failed. It does not touch the root of the problem. It merely covers everything over with a veneer that in many ways makes the underlying disease more dangerous.

We have tried psychological treatment. We thought if we could raise up a host of men and women trained to understand the human mind and heart, and if the people would come and talk to them to find out what makes humanity tick, then these things could all be straightened out. But why is it that the problems are greatly augmented now, thirty years or more after psychological treatment became widely available? This method is failing. The flood of lawlessness mounts on every side. Psychology does not touch the cause.

We have tried legislation and police enforcement, and these serve at times to contain the problem within certain limits. But again, these forces are failing. They cannot cope with the problems, which are too vast, too deep-seated, too widespread. Legislation fails. We have tried what I call "Bo Peepism," that is, "leave them alone and they'll come home, wagging their tails behind them." It too fails, more rapidly, perhaps, than any other plan. When you leave people utterly alone, evil seems to multiply tremendously. But because we do not know what else to do, periodically we run through the whole scheme again and try all the solutions once more, in a desperate effort to make something work.

Is there any hope? Are we doomed simply to destroy ourselves as a race? The apostle John says no, we are not doomed to destroy ourselves, and yes, there is hope. He puts it all in this one sentence,

You know that he appeared to take away sins, and in him
there is no sin (1 John 3:5).

There is stated the great purpose of the coming of Jesus
Christ into the world. He appeared, he was manifested,
to take away sins. Linked with that is the great possibility
revealed by it, "in him there is no sin." As John has
defined sin, "He appeared to take away lawlessness, and
in him there is no lawlessness." That is the glorious
gospel of hope. Some complain of this, saying, "That is
so narrow, so limited. Surely there must be many ways to
save humanity." But such complaint is like complaining
that there is only one thing to breathe—air. Well, all we
need is one thing to breathe. And we only need one way
out of this human dilemma, this racial problem. There is
only one way because there is only One who has ever
appeared in human history who can take away sins. That
can be established categorically, dramatically, documen-
tarily.

He does not do it by an act of magic. He does not wave
a wand or utter some religious abracadabra and the thing
is done—poof, suddenly you are free from sin, lawlessness is gone, you will never have any problem with it
again. How does he do it? He does it by the impartation
of life in the place of death, light in place of darkness,
and love in place of hatred. And when you receive Jesus
Christ, that is only the beginning; the whole Christian life
follows. As we have been learning, it is a process of
growth, a sequence of gradual development, but the
results are inevitably the same: there is the taking away of
sin, there is the elimination of lawlessness, there is the
restoration to the human heart of order and peace.

The Hardest Cases

That is not merely an empty claim. That has been the
demonstration of over 1900 years of human history.

Again and again in every generation, the hardest cases have responded to this amazing remedy: homosexuals, alcoholics, drug addicts, sex addicts, acid heads, murderers, thieves, everyone. Even more difficult cases have surrendered: the proud intellectual, the bitter, the cynical, the angry young men, the jaded old people. And always there have been the despairing, the wounded in spirit, the helpless, the pathetic, the lost, broken derelicts who drift through life. Jesus touches everyone: Chinese, Indians, Negroes, Hottentots, Russians, Eskimos. No matter where or when man has lived it is always the same story, always the same deliverance, always the same results: the healing of lawlessness. The miracle occurs when men come to know Jesus Christ and receive him into their lives. Then the sickness begins to heal.

It is this healing miracle that has made human life possible for 1900 years. On any given Sunday morning there are out on the golf courses men and women who have no interest at all in coming to church. There are others on the beaches, and others lounging quietly at home in bed reading the Sunday newspapers. They are enjoying themselves. They do not realize that they are able to do so only because the gospel of Jesus Christ has penetrated this culture and society enough to permit human life to exist and make possible such moments of enjoyment. Even those who are opposed to the gospel are able to enjoy themselves only because this salt has been at work in society, arresting the awful evil of human lawlessness which otherwise would have quickly and rapidly destroyed every vestige of human life. Without this restraint the times would be so terrible that not one of us would have a moment's peace to live free from persecution, violence, threat, or fear. The gospel of Jesus Christ is what makes human society possible.

Will Durant, the famous historian who wrote the monumental book, *The Story of Civilization,* has this to say about Jesus Christ:

The revolution that Jesus sought was a far deeper one, without which reforms could only be superficial and transitory. If He could cleanse the human heart of selfish desire, cruelty, and lust, Utopia would come of itself, and all those institutions that rise out of human greed and violence and the consequent need for law, would disappear. Since this would be the profoundest of all revolutions, beside which all others would be merely *coup d'etats* of class ousting class and exploiting in its turn, Christ was, in this spiritual sense, the greatest revolutionist in history.

Jesus went to the heart of the problem, and he deals with it right at the heart yet today. "In him there is no lawlessness." If you learn to walk and live and work in him, as Christianity makes possible, then you will know the same peace, the same ordered, restful activity that was "in him" 1900 years ago.

Is there any message more important than this? Can there possibly be any more challenging cause, any more effective calling than to have a part and share in this? What more significant thing can you ever do with your life than to have a part in this magnificent enterprise that changes the human heart at its deepest level? Do you not feel the call of the trumpet in that? What a tremendous cause. What a triumphant claim. What a magnificent ministry.

Further, when you think that this has been backed by 1900 years of demonstration, during which men and women have actually, literally been set free, delivered from this virus of lawlessness and have been restored to peace, blessing, order, freedom, and liberty, then I ask you, what could be greater than this? What message is more needed in this world of ours than this? Shall we, the Christian church, turn away from declaration of this message to some lesser thing? Shall we give ourselves to the mere salving of symptoms, or shall we give ourselves more fully to this message that sets men free?

19

The Mystery of Righteousness

If there is no lawlessness in Christ, then what *is* in him? Love is the very being of God, the essence of his nature, and thus of the nature of Christ. John says God *is* love. Yet that life which is love is also light. It illuminates, it clarifies, it dispels darkness, it breaks through our confusion and our lack of understanding and makes us see things as they are. We read of the Lord Jesus, "In him was life, and the life was the light of men" (John 1:4). So, with this threefold gift of love, light, and life, when Christ enters a human heart he destroys lawlessness.

Now the great question is, How do we lay hold of this threefold gift in actual daily practice? How does the gift of love from Christ destroy and push out the lawlessness of our lives? In what way does it happen? John now beautifully summarizes it for us in verses 6 and 7 of chapter 3:

No one who abides in him sins; no one who sins has either seen him or known him. Little children, let no one deceive you. He who does right is righteous, as he [Christ] is righteous.

Here is the mystery of righteousness. John does not call it that, but Paul refers to it as "the mystery of Godlikeness, or godliness," the way a person begins to live like God, to become Godlike though remaining a man, in his attitudes, his outlook, his actions, and his reactions. If you read the Old Testament you know that certain men of olden times discovered this secret. They became, to a great extent, God-like. Abraham, Joseph, Moses, King David, and others became stabilized, outgoing, love-oriented; they became men in every true sense of the word.

That Sacred Mystery

The secret was hidden to most, although it has always been the same; the secret of God-likeness is forever this: "Christ in you." But no one understood that in Old Testament days. They could not because it had not yet become historically evident. But now the mystery has been made clear. Paul calls this "the mystery hidden for ages and generations but now made manifest to his saints" (Col. 1:26). Let me share with you the full passage in which that occurs, as it is found in Phillips' translation.

> I am a minister of the Church by divine commission . . . that I might fully declare God's word—that sacred mystery which up till now has been hidden in every age and every generation, but which is now as clear as daylight to those who love God. They are those to whom God has planned to give a vision of the wonder and splendour of his secret plan for the nations.

Did you get that? God has a secret plan for the nations. That is at once the explanation of, and the remedy for, all the evil that exists in the human race. Now he goes on,

> And the secret is simply this: Christ *in you!* Yes, Christ *in you,* bringing with him the hope of all the glorious things to come.

Now those are not just so many beautiful words. That is a very practical proposition which God is working out through human history, and is making available to men. Peter says the same thing in his second letter (the Living Bible translation):

> For as you know him better, he [Christ] will give you, through his great power, everything you need for living a truly good life: he even shares his own glory and his own goodness with us! And by that same mighty power he has given us all the other rich and wonderful blessings he promised; for instance, the promise to save us from the lust and rottenness all around us, and to give us his own character (1:3,4).

That is the good news. John puts it bluntly and plainly, "No one who abides in him sins." Or, to use the interchangeable term for sin which he has just given us, "No one who abides in him lives lawlessly." Perhaps some will say, "Now, wait a minute! Isn't this a contradiction? In the first chapter, verse 8, John says, 'If we say we have no sin, we deceive ourselves, and the truth is not in us.' And now in chapter 3 he says, 'No one who abides in him [Christ] sins.' How is this? And isn't it even more positively put in verse 9 of chapter 3, 'No one born of God commits sin; for God's nature abides in him, and *he cannot sin* because he is born of God'?" Surely this is a bit of a problem. In verse 6 he says a Christian does not sin; in verse 9 he says he cannot sin, because he is born of God. Yet, again in chapter 1, he says if we say we do not sin, we are liars; and in chapter 2, verse 1, "if any one does sin, we have an advocate with the Father, Jesus Christ the righteous."

Admittedly, we have come to one of the most difficult passages of Scripture. Yet it is a very important one, and it is not a contradiction. The man who writes this is no fool—he is an intelligent person. He does not say something on one page that contradicts what he says on another page. He is an inspired apostle, and writes with wisdom, intelligence, and understanding. The problem does not lie in the text; the problem, if any, lies with us: I propose therefore that we take some time with this passage because of its importance, that we might understand the working of the mystery of evil in human life and, likewise, the mystery of righteousness which counteracts it.

We shall examine this problem in much greater detail when we get to verse 9, but for the present I will point out that it is really settled by the tense of the verb the apostle employs here. "No one who abides in him *sins.*" He uses the present continuous tense for the word, "sins," to mean that no one who abides in him keeps on sinning or lives in lawlessness. If John had wanted to refer to a single act of sin, he could have employed the aorist tense which would have conveyed, without any question, "No one who abides in him can commit even one single act of sin." He did not say that, but used this continuous tense instead. So he is saying, "Any one who abides in Christ does not go on living in sin." He cannot live lawlessly; he does not keep on sinning.

Two Aspects of Relationship

But let us not miss the wood because we are so intent upon the trees. How do you avoid living lawlessly? How does one come to this place of not living sinfully? Well, as he puts it, it is all in this one word, "abides." "No one who *abides* in him sins." Remember that in chapter 2 he had said, "And now, little children, *abide in him,* so that when he appears we may have confidence and not shrink from him in shame at his coming." The key is abiding. We have already seen that the relationship of a believer to Jesus Christ involves him in two aspects. Abiding in Christ is an advance on simply being "in Christ." Our Lord himself spoke of these two aspects of a disciple's relationship to him in these words, "you in me, and I in you." Those two aspects are very important. "I in you" is to be in Christ. It is to believe, to receive Jesus Christ. It is to be joined in a union with him that results in new birth, the impartation of his life and love to us, by an act of faith. It is to receive him, to act upon his invitation to come into your life. When you do, you are "in Christ." You are in union with him. "I in you," that is the first aspect.

But that is not the aspect John is describing here. That union does not necessarily result in being freed from the bondage of sin. It makes freedom possible, but in itself it does not result in deliverance. That is why, as we have seen, it is quite possible to be "in Christ" and go on living for a time in sin, lawlessly. But it is the second relationship, "you in me," Christ in us, experienced by an attitude of faith, in which he makes his home in our hearts, that frees us from sin's reign. We allow him to live through us, we expect him to do so, in every moment of our experience. It is this that is called "abiding," and it is this that results in freeing us from the bondage and the power of sin, so that we can live godly, God-like, lives.

As you read through the Scriptures you discover certain things that are produced by this abiding relationship. In the great fifteenth chapter of John's gospel, Jesus said these words: "He who abides in me, and I in him, *he it is that bears much fruit*" (v. 5). So, abounding fruit comes from this relationship of abiding. Abiding is abounding. The fruit is the fruit of the Spirit, "love, joy, peace, longsuffering, gentleness, goodness, faith, meekness, temperance" (Gal. 5:22,23, KJV). These are the marks of one who abides.

Later on in that same chapter of John, in verse 7, he says, "If you abide in me, and my words abide in you, *ask whatever you will,* and it shall be done for you." Here, effectual prayer is a result, not of being "in Christ," but of "abiding in Christ." Are your prayers being answered? Are you seeing God at work in your experience? Are the things you ask for that are clearly in line with his great program for men coming to pass in the lives of individuals for whom you pray? This is the promise, "If you abide in me, and my words abide in you, ask whatever you will [within that relationship], and it shall be done for you."

Now John says "No one who abides in him sins," lives lawlessly. He is able to live in a God-like manner. Therefore this relationship of abiding is very important. Well, you say, just what is it? This is what bothers me. I've heard all these great promises before—and God knows I want them—but it eludes me.

Let us ask the Lord again for clarification on this. Once again, in the fifteenth chapter of John's Gospel, Jesus says these words, "If you keep my commandments, you will abide in my love" (v. 10). That is putting it plainly, is it not? "If you obey me, you will abide in me. And he that abides in me bears much fruit, he that abides in me can ask whatever he will and it will be done, he that abides in me will not sin. If you keep my commandments, you will abide in my love." Of course that obedience is by faith. This is not an exhortation to give ourselves to a groveling, dogged obedience, saying, "Here's a rule and I've got to do it." No, it is an expectant obedience, an obedience that acts, expecting him to come through to make it a joy. That is the whole secret. It is by faith.

Abide/Obey

How does this work in practice? Since Christ is in you (if you are a believer, you are in him and he is in you) then you need but set yourself to do what he says, expecting him to act. The minute you start doing that, the power to carry it through will be there, to make you able to do it and to make it a joy. It is like the times when those Israelites were told to cross the Red Sea and the river Jordan. Each time the command of God was to go through the water. It looked like suicide, utter foolishness. The worst thing they could do would be to plunge headlong into the depths of the waters. But as the children of Israel stepped down and their feet touched the water, the waters parted and they went through. When they acted on what they were told to do, before they could see that anything was happening, the miracle occurred.

This was, of course, far more than a spectacular miracle. It was a parable, designed to teach us how God acts. When we hear his command to us, whether we feel it will work or not, the whole idea is to obey. Act on it! Do what he says! When we do, we discover that the minute we begin to act, the power of God acts also. What we are hoping to accomplish will be accomplished. It works out as God said. We discover that God is at work within us. That is what Jesus means when he says, "If you keep my commandments, you will abide in my love" (John 15:10). This is also what Paul is saying to the Philippians. "Work out your own salvation with fear and trembling; *for God is at work in you,* both to will and to work for his good pleasure [the thing that pleases him]" (Phil. 2:12,13).

Do you find it difficult to love someone, for instance? This is one of the most nagging, persistent problems of life. When someone treats us cruelly, or indifferently, our natural reaction, stemming from our tie with Adam, is immediately to strike back, to avenge ourselves, to cut them off, or to say something caustic. But that is not the command of the Lord. His word is crystal clear. "Vengeance is mine . . . says the Lord" (Rom. 12:19). Do not avenge yourself. He says, "Love your enemies. Do good to those who hate you and despitefully use you. Pray for your enemies. Love one another."

But you do not feel like doing that; in fact, that is the last thing you feel like doing. You are like those priests who did not feel like putting their feet in that cold, dirty water of the Jordan River. But God had said to do it. And when the soles of their feet touched the water, it parted, and the people went on through. So also, when you set yourself to act as love would act toward this person—if you obey God, in other words, and expect him to act, he will. The feeling of love will follow your act instead of preceding it, and you will discover that your whole relationship, your whole attitude to the individual is different. You will see him no longer as an obstacle in your pathway, but as a person with a problem—a problem like the problems you have had—who needs understanding and acceptance.

Are you tempted to lust? Are you tempted, in this sex-saturated society, to give way to lusts and desires of the flesh that you know are wrong? There is plenty of it around today, and in "respectable" circles, too. But the Word of God is, "Shun youthful passions and aim at righteousness, faith, love, and peace" (2 Tim. 2:22). It is not that sex is wrong. Sex is wonderful. Sex is what God made it to be; it is his gift to humanity. But the improper use of it is wrong.

Well then, obey him! Turn from these passions and turn to him in expectant faith and you will find there is an immediate sense of release, a flood of cleansing, purifying love from him that makes your renunciation not an act of dismal determination, but an act of delight, of gladness and freedom. What a difference! Even an unregenerate man, a non-Christian, can set his will against doing something that is harmful or wrong or evil, but he will not have any particular joy in doing so. He will be acting from a grim determination to walk in this way, with no compensating light or gladness. The difference for a Christian is that when he so acts, Christ is there. We obey him, and thus we abide in his love. Every act of renunciation against these forces that would destroy us results in an accompanying sense of joy, causing us to glory in God's grace.

Content with Evil?

If you have him, you can do these things. If you cannot do them, it is because you do not have him. That is why

John goes on to add here, "no one who sins has either seen him or known him." That is, so strong is our link with him, and so powerful are the cleansing tides of his life in us, that if we say we have Christ in us and do not show some evidence of it in increasing degree, then we have been deceiving ourselves. We have never seen him or known him. If you can live content with evil, without a struggle, deliberately doing what the Word of God declares is not right; if you can go on thus and it does not particularly bother you, then you have no right to call yourself a Christian. You have not seen him; you have not known him. Jesus Christ came into the world and into your life to destroy lawlessness. No one who lives lawlessly has either seen him or known him.

So he concludes in verse 7, "Little children, let no one deceive you." The true sign is this: "He who does right is righteous." Remember, righteousness is love behaving justly. He who acts that way (and that kind of love always involves self-sacrifice) does so because he is linked to the Righteous One. There is no other way to act righteously. "He who does right is righteous, as he is righteous."

It is interesting that in the Greek, the pronoun "He" is literally "that one." It appears also in verse 5: "You know that 'that one' appeared to take away sins." And verse 7, "Little children, let no one deceive you. He who does right is righteous, as 'that one' is righteous." It is almost as though John sees Christ standing there. He who does right is righteous because "that one" is righteous, and he is living in him. Because he is living in him, righteousness must be breaking out from time to time in that individual's life. It has to be there. When a person discovers this and learns to abide in him, all the time expecting "that one" to be working in him, then he soon learns he cannot do anything without him. But he discovers that with him, he can do anything he is asked to do. That is why Paul says, "I can do all things in him [Christ] who strengthens me" (Phil. 4:13).

20

The Mystery of Evil

Today we are facing a flood of immorality fed by an unseen fountain that is gushing out moral filth faster than it can ever be cleaned up. It is most frustrating to those attempting to deal with these problems to discover that the power behind all this is apparently an unseen power, disembodied, invisible. You cannot legislate against it; it is above and beyond law, beyond human control! This modern enigma corresponds exactly to what John is declaring in chapter 3, verse 8. He says plainly:

> He who commits sin is of the devil; for the devil has sinned from the beginning. The reason the Son of God appeared was to destroy the works of the devil.

The apostle declares that behind all that we are facing today is a malevolent being who continually subverts every human effort to counteract his activities, pouring out a continuous flood of evil into the stream of human life. This is why we can never permanently solve the problem. We are forever running into repeated manifestations of the working of this superhuman force in life.

Notice that this verse is part of a larger passage in which the apostle deals with the whole problem of evil.

These are really two parallel passages, running side by side in verses 4–7 and 8–10. Their parallelism is evident in three ways. First, each has a word to say about sin. In verse 4 the apostle says, "Every one who commits sin is guilty of lawlessness; sin is lawlessness." Then in verse 8 (the first verse of the second parallel passage) he says, "He who commits sin is of the devil. . . ." One verse describes the nature of sin, lawlessness; the other declares the origin of sin, the devil.

Then, in each passage there is a word about Christ and his appearing. In verse 5, "You know that he appeared to take away sins [lawlessness], and in him there is no sin [lawlessness]." In verse 8, "The reason the Son of God appeared was to destroy the works of the devil."

Finally, there is a logical conclusion resulting from these statements. In verse 6, "No one who abides in him sins . . ." as a result of the fact that Christ has come to take away sins. And in verse 9, "No one born of God commits sin . . ." as a result of the fact that God's nature abides in him, and the Son of God has come to destroy the works of the devil.

These two passages are dealing with the mystery of evil which has confronted the human race from the very beginning. There is no adequate explanation for the hideous tangle of human problems, such as exists today, if we fail to see the malevolent genius of the devil behind these things. As Paul put it, "We are not contending against flesh and blood, but against the principalities, against the powers, against the world rulers of this present darkness, against the spiritual hosts of wickedness in the heavenly places" (Eph. 6:12). All the apostles agree that we can never adequately explain what life is about—especially the problem of human evil—if we do not come to grips with and recognize the existence of these unseen forces.

In this verse in John we must particularly note two phrases. One is, "the devil has sinned from the beginning" or, literally, "the devil *is sinning* from the beginning." The second phrase occurs in the latter part of the verse: "the works of the devil." It is important that we distinguish between the sin of the devil and the works of the devil, because they are quite different.

Fallen Angel

The sin of the devil is, as John says, "from the beginning." It dates from the time when he first became the devil. God never created a devil, nor did he ever create a fallen man or even any fallen angels. But chiefly, he never created *the* fallen angel, the devil. He created a being of beauty, glory, intelligence, and responsibility, but, as in the case of man, he gave him a free will. It was the activity of that free will, opposed to his Creator, that changed the angel God created into the devil. The Lord Jesus is himself the authority who tells us that the devil "abode not in the truth," he did not continue to stand in the truth. There was a time when the devil was "in the truth" but he was not the devil then. Most scholars feel that we have a description of the fall of this angel in Isaiah 14, where a being is described whom Isaiah calls "the Day Star" or, from the Hebrew "Lucifer."

> How you are fallen from heaven,
>   O Day Star, son of Dawn!
> How you are cut down to the ground,
>   you who laid the nations low!
> You said in your heart,
>   "I will ascend to heaven;
> above the stars of God
>   I will set my throne on high;
> I will sit on the mount of assembly in the far north;
> I will ascend above the heights of the clouds,
>   I will make myself like the Most High"(Isa. 14:12–14).

Five times the devil said, "I will." Here was a glorious being who was not content with the glory he had. In his own view he was not glorious enough, and he determined to be more glorious. Free will became in the devil, "I will," and that "I will," five times repeated, regarded God as an obstacle to the devil's plans and no longer a necessity in the devil's life. He set himself to become the equal of God, to become "like the Most High." Thus he set himself above all the law and will of God and became a law unto himself. That is what lawlessness is, acting as though you are a law unto yourself without regard for any other law, any other person, or any other authority. But whenever we adopt the attitude, "I will do what I want, I am a law unto myself," we have repeated the sin of the devil.

That is why John says everyone who commits sin is "of the devil," because he is repeating, in his own limited area of experience, the sin of the devil. He is living like the devil, for the devil continues to live just as he began to live at the moment of his fall—independent of God and therefore opposed to God. This is the nature of sin wherever it appears in human life, whether in a Christian or non-Christian. He who commits sin is of the devil because he is permitting the devil to reproduce in him the devil's character, for the devil continues to live in the lawless attitude into which he fell when he sinned from the beginning.

The works of the devil are the natural results of the sin of the devil. They are what inevitably follow. Sin is an attitude within the heart. It is an attitude of lawless disregard of the authority of God. But the works of the devil are the activities that result from that attitude. In Romans 8 the apostle Paul uses a similar description, the mind of the flesh, which, he says, is hostile to God, enmity against God. That is an attitude within. That is the feeling, "I'll run my own life. I don't need any God to tell me what to do. I don't need any God to support me or help me or tide me over difficulties, I can take care of my own affairs. I'll run my own life." That is the mind of the flesh, and it is hostile to God. But in Galatians 5 Paul speaks of "the works of the flesh": immorality, impurity, enmity, strife, jealousy, selfishness, envy, carousing, drunkenness, and other things. These are the things that result from having the mind of the flesh.

Murdering, Lying, Stealing

In John 8:44, the Lord Jesus partially describes the works of the devil for us. He says they are murder and lying.

> He was a murderer from the beginning, and has nothing to do with the truth, because there is no truth in him. When he lies, he speaks according to his own nature, for he is a liar and the father of lies.

In John 10 he gives us yet another work of the devil. Concerning the false shepherd, whom he calls the thief, he says "the thief comes only to steal and kill and destroy" (John 10:10). These are the works of the devil: murdering, lying, and stealing. These inevitably follow the sin of the devil. Whenever there is a rebellious attitude in a human heart toward the authority and will of God, or that will reflected in the government of man, the works of the devil will follow.

This is the way the devil attacks and misleads mankind: Morally, he *steals* away the blessings God intended for man—peace, quietness, courage, love, and joy. The devil never offers anything positive. All the things the devil apparently offers to mankind are but illusions, glimmering mists that disappear when you grab them, leaving you with nothing but cobwebs and ashes.

Physically, the devil attacks mankind by destroying through disease (all disease ultimately stems from the activity of the devil) and death. That does not deny the existence of bacteria or the reality of germs, but these are the tools of the devil in attacking the body of man. Also, by means of disaster, war, crime, and violence, the devil is active in human society. He delights to ravage, to twist and smash and mangle, as our newspapers reveal to us every day.

Intellectually, the devil attacks man by lying to him. He deceives him, tells him falsehoods, makes him act on principles that are wrong, directly contrary to fact. He teaches us to believe certain widespread proverbs that everybody accepts as true. "Watch out for yourself." "You'll never get ahead unless you think of yourself." "Number One first, and the devil take the hindmost." We all act on these precepts at times, because we believe the devil. Thus he brings confusion and darkness, and extinguishes the light that is in man. All this is why intelligent, happy young people, moving into adulthood, are caught up in vicious, savage patterns of delusion and destruction. They believe the lies of the devil about sex and drugs and other things, and they allow him, through these, to steal their strength and their joy and their youth. These are the works of the devil.

They were evident in the very beginning of the race, when Cain *murdered* his brother in order to *steal* his place of acceptance before God, and *lied* to God about what he had done. "Where is your brother?" God asked. "I don't know," Cain replied. But he did know.

Remember how King David, after he had walked with God for years and was a man after God's own heart, chose to give way to the sin of the devil and to act lawlessly. He became a law unto himself and decided to get what he wanted apart from what God wanted. When he did, he *stole* from Uriah the Hittite his most precious possession, his wife. Then, to cover it up, he *murdered* him with nothing more lethal than a pen dipped in ink. Then he *lied* about it, covering it all over, until God sent Nathan the prophet to unveil the whole hideous story and bring it out into the open.

In the early church, Ananias and Sapphira sought to *rob* God of what they said belonged to God. They said they had given to him, but they had not. Because they wanted to gain prestige among the Christians which they did not really possess, they *lied* to the Holy Spirit, as Peter accused them. And they would have *destroyed* the fellowship of the early church, wrecking it for their own ends.

The business of the devil is to tempt you in any way he can to adopt a sinful attitude of rebellion and willful independence. When you do that, the inevitable result is that the works of the devil will be *your* works. You discover that you will lie, you will steal, and you will destroy to whatever extent and degree you feel you can get away with. If not outwardly, openly, and brazenly, then it will be inwardly, subtly, and respectably. But there is no way to escape.

We think we can. We are continually deluding ourselves by thinking we can control these reactions. But as Jesus said in the Gospel of John, chapter 8, "Truly, truly, I say to you, every one who commits sin is a slave to sin" (v. 34). You no longer have the power to determine how far it is going to go. It will go beyond your own desire, and you will end up doing things you never dreamed of doing. We are always carried on beyond ourselves. We do not master sin; it masters us. It is only a matter of time before the results of it become evident and the works of the devil are there.

Dissolved Problems

What is the answer to all this? There is only one answer, which John gives us here: "The Son of God appeared to destroy the works of the devil" (3:8). Christ came to set us free from this bondage, to deliver us from this inevitable chain reaction. He came, literally, to unloose, to untie the works of the devil, as though these were actual chains about us. Dr. Paul Tournier says in one of his books that when we come into the experience of the grace of G d the problems we were facing in life are not always solved; what happens to them is that they are dissolved. They simply disappear; they fade away like the morning mist. We do not find specific solutions to them so much as we find them simply disappearing, as God's grace enfolds and surrounds us. This is exactly what John is saying. The Son of God has come to untie, to loosen the bonds of the devil, the works of the devil in human life, to dissolve them and thus to set us free.

How does the devil manage to put us in bondage? He does it by substituting his own way for the method God intended for living. The devil always imitates. He never comes up with anything original for he cannot. He is forever imitating God with cheap and shabby imitations of the real thing. He imitates the Trinity, Father, Son, and Holy Spirit, by substituting a false trinity—the world, the flesh, and the devil. These great powers in human affairs are an imitation of God's true character as Father, Son, and Holy Spirit.

The devil also imitates the method of God. Stuart Briscoe put it very clearly when he said that the way God intends man to live is as follows: The death of Christ is the *prelude* to all Christian experience. When the Son of God died, he laid the groundwork for everything that happens in the Christian life. The resurrection of Christ is the *pattern* of all Christian experience. Just as the Son of God arose from the dead, so we are to be constantly rising from the death around us into a new vitality, a new adventure of living, day by day. To be in Christ, to be a Christian, is the *province* of all Christian experience. You never can experience real living unless you are in Christ. And Christ in us is the *power* of all Christian experience. God intended man to live in a moment-by-moment dependence upon the power of Christ within.

But the devil imitates this plan of God's, substituting his own formula. The fall of Satan becomes the *prelude* to all sinful experience. The life of Satan, his present existence, is the *pattern* for sin, as we have seen. The devil is sinning as he did from the beginning, John says. That forms the pattern for all sin. The world of human society is the *province* of all sinful experience—society governed and mastered by sinful, devilish principles, unwittingly doing what the devil wants. That is the world. But within us is this strange thing called the flesh, which is the *power* of all sinful experience.

There is the devil's limitation of the work of the Son of God. The Son of God came to set the false aside and to restore us to the true. He came and died upon a bloody cross, and rose again in power, in order that in your life he might undo the works of the devil. You can be free from these things, and mastered, not by the devil, but by the Son of God.

21

When the Spirit Says No

We come now to one of the most difficult verses in Scripture:

No one born of God commits sin; for God's nature abides in him, and he cannot sin because he is born of God (1 John 3:9).

From time to time I run into people who say they have gone beyond the ability to sin. They have arrived at what they call "sinless perfection." Obviously, these would be very difficult people to live with, but they are around. If, in trying to deal with them from the Scriptures, you should quote a verse like 1 John 1:8, "If we say we have no sin, we deceive ourselves, and the truth is not in us," they rely upon the tactic, "if they persecute you in one verse, flee into another," and turn to this verse in 1 John 3. There, they say triumphantly; God's Word itself says that it is possible, even necessary, for a real Christian to come to the place where he cannot sin.

Through the centuries there have been many differing interpretations of this verse, all of which boil down essentially to seven views. First, there is the view I have just mentioned; this verse teaches that a Christian cannot commit even one single act of sin. These people almost

233

always speak of a crisis experience in the Christian's life which they usually call "sanctification." A Christian passes through a time of crisis, faces himself and his whole sin nature, and the whole thing is settled. The sin nature is taken away, and from that time on the Christian cannot sin. It is a kind of religious "sheep dip" experience, where one goes through and comes out cleansed on the other side, with no further possibility of sinning. I have already dealt with this in essence. John says in this same Epistle, certainly with no intent to contradict himself, "If we say we have no sin, we deceive ourselves. . . ." Those who hold this view are clearly self-deceived.

Double Standard

A second view suggests that the word "sin" should be narrowed down to certain specific things—gross sins, such as murder, adultery, cruelty, and other violations of love. What the apostle is saying here is that it is impossible for Christians to commit certain kinds of sins. Most Catholic commentators take this verse to support the distinction between mortal and venial sins, i.e., certain sins which are mere peccadillos that can be forgiven, and others which are impossible to forgive. That view holds that there are certain kinds of sins which no real Christian can commit. But the answer to that is that all the sins listed in any catalogue of mortal sins have been committed by the believers mentioned in the Bible. It is clear from the Scriptures that believers *can* commit these sins. No double standard for sins, as is suggested by this division of mortal and venial sins, exists in the Scriptures.

A third related view of this passage is that it refers to certain willful sins. It teaches that a Christian cannot commit willful or deliberate sins. He may drift into sin, he may through weakness or carelessness fall into sin, but he never deliberately violates the will of God. But what about David in the Old Testament who willfully and deliberately committed the twin sins of murder and adultery? And who of us would dare claim that we have never willfully, deliberately sinned?

Sin by Other Names

A fourth view says that sin in a believer is not regarded as such by God, that what may be done by an unbeliever and called sin is not so called when done by a believer. If an unbeliever tells a lie, that is a sin; but if a believer does it, that is a mistake or, at most, a manifestation of weakness—but it is not a sin. That view is so presumptuous and so ridiculous as hardly to warrant an answer. It is enough to point out that early in this passage John defines sin for us. He says it is lawlessness, becoming a law unto oneself. Any act of it, whether committed by a Christian or a non-Christian is exactly the same—it is sin.

There is yet a fifth view of this passage which declares that John is describing an ideal condition, not a realistic one, that ideally this should be true. This, of course, changes the meaning of the passage to make it say that a Christian *should* not sin, rather than that he cannot. But that is to water down the force of the word which John uses. What he says, plainly and without equivocation, is that a Christian cannot sin because he is born of God. So this view does not settle the matter.

A sixth view, widely held by many people, is that John is contrasting two natures within the believer: one which is received from Adam, the natural life which always sins; and the other, the new nature received from God which never sins. This seems to be a plausible explanation of this verse, and for some time it had great appeal to me. It is true, of course, that the old nature within a believer does sin, and the new life which God has implanted can never sin. However natures are not in view here by a whole person. It may be possible to distinguish between a conflict in desires within us (who is not aware of that?—a civil war going on in the presence of temptation where we feel ourselves pulled first in one direction and then in another), but it is quite another thing to try to distinguish acts as belonging to one nature or another. A person acts as a whole being. A decision must be made between conflicting desires, and the result is an act. That act is the act of the whole person, not merely of one side of his being.

That view reminds one of the burglar who was arrested and brought before a judge. His defense consisted of pointing out to the judge that his whole body was not involved in the burglary, but only his arm and hand. Though he would freely admit that the arm and the hand had taken something that did not belong to him, nevertheless, it was unfair of the judge to punish his whole body. The judge wisely solved the problem by sentencing the arm and hand to thirty days in jail, leaving it up to the rest of the body whether or not it chose to accompany them!

It is true that the apostle Paul says in Romans 7, "It is no longer I that do it, but sin which dwells within me" (v. 17). This might lead us to think that Paul is making this kind of distinction, saying, "I no longer sin. It is just something within me, that is not me anymore, which does this kind of thing." But the apostle is clearly not denying a personal involvement in sin, but rather he is denying the conscious intent to sin. He is saying that even when he thinks he is avoiding sin, even when he is earnestly trying to do what God wants out of the energy and power of his flesh, he finds himself confronted yet with the results of sin—weakness, barrenness, and despair. The whole struggle in Romans 7 is that baffling, frustrating experience of a person who is sincerely trying to do God's will but finds his life still in the doldrums of guilt, despair, depression, and weakness which can only come as a result of sin. That is why he calls out, "Wretched man that I am! Who will deliver me from this body of death?" (v. 24).

No Longer Natural

The seventh view of this verse, and the one I espouse because it fits the context, is that a Christian cannot persist in habitual, continual sin, because he is born of God. He cannot sin without a struggle or a sense of grief so powerful that ultimately he will be brought to repentance and a forsaking of sin. What he is declaring to us, then, is that sin is no longer natural to the believer. Though for a time he may slip into it rather easily, nevertheless it is now contrary to his nature. His heart is set toward God, and his life is a truceless antagonism against sin. "No one born of God commits sin; for God's nature abides in him," he declares. He cannot persist; he cannot go on continuously living in what he knows to be sin. As I have already pointed out, this is made clear in the tense of the compound verb, "to commit sin" which is in the present, continuous tense, "to go on committing sin."

This usage fits the context of the verse. Twice John has told us that the Son of God has appeared to take away sin, and to dissolve the works of the devil, the results of sin. He comes into our lives by faith for this very purpose. Since he is a sovereign, supreme being, in whose hands all power in heaven and on earth resides, he moves irresistibly to this end within us. Therefore it is quite to be expected that John would say it is not possible for anyone who has been born of God to go on endlessly living in sin, and content to do so.

This means that if we have been born again, soon after our conversion (often very soon) there comes a time when the Spirit of God, who has filled us with joy, blessing, peace, assurance, and other glorious things in Christ, begins to put his finger upon certain specific things and says, "These must go." Our usual reaction is to say, "But they're such little things, they really don't matter. Let's not talk about these trivial things, these peccadillos; let's go on in this happy relationship together." But they are not minor. They are the things that have been keeping us in bondage. They are the reason for our restlessness, our distress, our depression, and our heartache.

Because God loves us he will not put up with them, so he perseveres, despite our struggling; he is absolutely inflexible, even ruthless. We twist about in a dozen different ways and try to get around his insistence, but at every turn, there he stands with his arms folded, saying, "What are you going to do about this?" Have you ever had that experience? Have you known what it means for the Spirit of God to say No? Other scriptures confirm this interpretation of verse 9. There is Philippians 1:6: "And I am sure that he who began a good work in you will bring it to completion at the day of Jesus Christ." He will not grow discouraged; he is not going to quit. He has started to free you from sin, and he is going to do it. He will not force your will, but he will bring you into circumstances that will make you listen, and at last he will do the job.

There is that passage in Romans 8 which says, "For those whom he foreknew he also predestined to be conformed to the image of his Son [that is the goal he has in mind; that is what he starts out to achieve in you], in order that he [the Son] might be the first-born among many brethren." Then he goes on, "And those whom he predestined he also called; and those whom he called he also justified; and those whom he justified he also glorified" (8:29,30). You see, he is determined to do what he began.

Again Paul says, "For the desires of the flesh are against the Spirit, and the desires of the Spirit are against the flesh; for these are opposed to each other, *to prevent you from doing what you would*" (Gal. 5:17, italics mine). There is the Spirit of God standing across your path, like the angel stood across the pathway of Balaam the prophet as he sought to do what God had commanded him not to do. Everywhere he turned the angel stood across his path, and the only one intelligent enough to see him was the donkey Balaam rode. Thus God stands across our path. We cannot do the things that we would. There have been times in my experience as a Christian when I have felt the full force of some temptation, and I could have fulfilled it—I had every opportunity to do it and felt a full desire to do so, but I couldn't. Something held me back; I just could not do it, despite all my desire. That is the Spirit saying No.

No Reverse

Now notice what John says is the reason for all this: "God's nature (or God's seed) abides in him, and he cannot sin because he is born of God." When we are born again something very radical has happened to us. There is a deep, inward transformation which changes us from the bottom up. Because of that change the process can never be reversed. God's seed abides in us, and we cannot persist in habitual sin because there is a root within, a life that is constantly surging up, that simply will not permit this thing to go on forever.

We do not have two natures; we have only one—and it is now linked to Christ, joined to Christ. As Paul says, "Christ, *who is our life*" will one day appear. As Christians we do not have any other life than his life. He is our life. We are "married" to him who is risen from the dead (Rom. 7:2–4). We do not have any other life but his. True, there is another nature within us, but it is not ours any more—it is a false life. The difference between these two natures is that, for the believer, one is true and the other is false. One is the true life that is his by virtue of being joined to Christ; the other is false. Temporarily we can act in response to that false life, but like everything else false, it has no permanency about it. A Christian can commit single acts of sin, even repeatedly, for awhile; but he cannot go on, cannot habitually, persistently, contentedly live in sin.

We are joined to Christ. Because of this tie which can no longer be broken by us, the Spirit of God is continually pressing us on to enter this "abiding" state we have been discussing. We are joined to Christ by regeneration, but our attitude can sometimes be very resistant and difficult. The Spirit of God is constantly teaching us to relax and to "abide" in him—to learn to be quietly, trustfully dependent upon the life we have received within us to express itself through our actions, our words, and our deeds. That is abiding. As we have seen in verse 6, "No one who abides in him sins. . . ." This is why the Spirit of God is forever putting us into circumstances which temporarily force us—and that word is not too strong—to abide in Christ. That is why even the newest believer in Jesus Christ, though he may not understand much at all about the theology of abiding in Christ, will nevertheless sometimes experience it, because he is put into circumstances that force him to do so, even if only for a limited period of time. Such is God's way of teaching us that dependence is the intended basis of life; it is Standard Operating Procedure. If we walk in the Spirit, Paul says in Galatians, we will not fulfill the lusts of the flesh. So to help us break the habit of sin, God forces us into circumstances in which we *must* walk in the Spirit.

Lord, Save Me!

From this we can make two brief observations. First, this is the explanation for many of the pressures and trials we go through—not for all of them, but for many. When we get into a circumstance where we don't know what to do, after we have exhausted every other possibility, there is only one place left to go—to God, to Christ. When, in a kind of quiet desperation, we turn to him and say, "Lord, I've had it; I don't know what else to do but trust you," he says, "That's exactly the point I was hoping you'd see. That's what I've been trying to get you to do all along, to trust me, to depend on me to work through you." In that desperate moment, even though it be for but a moment, we are abiding in Christ, and the pattern and power of sin are broken.

You can see this in the story of Peter walking on the water. As the fearful disciples looked out from their boat in the midst of the storm, they saw Jesus walking on the waves. They thought he was a ghost and they were frightened, but Jesus said, "Be not afraid, it is I." Then Peter boldly said, "Lord, if it be you, bid me come to you on the water." The Lord immediately said, "Come." Without thinking through all that was involved, Peter climbed out of the boat and started across on the water, doing fine—until he began to think about what he was doing. When he suddenly realized that he was out away from the boat, unsupported, on the surface of the waves, and he saw them billowing up on either side and heard the wind blowing, he took his eyes off the Lord and down he went. About the time he began to blubber he looked up and saw the Lord and said, "Lord, save me." It is said to be one of the shortest prayers in the Bible! The Lord reached out his hand and lifted him up, and the two of them walked back together on the water.

That is the Christian life. The Lord will put you in places where you have to say, "Lord, save me." He does this continually. I remember one sharing time at a Bible Study Fellowship Conference. One woman stood up, and with her voice breaking with emotion, tears very close to the surface, she said, "I want to tell you that a year ago I was arrested for nearly beating my two-and-a-half-year-old son to death. It so frightened me that I would be capable of doing a thing like that in anger that I began to listen to what the Lord was saying to me, and I came to Christ." Then her voice did break, and with tears flooding down her cheeks, she said, "And you know, the greatest joy that I have in Bible Study Fellowship is that they've made me the attendant at the nursery. I've got eleven children and next year, they tell me, it will be doubled." She was so happy she could hardly contain herself.

A Sheep and a Pig

The second observation we can make from this is that the inability to persist in sin is primary proof of the new life in Jesus Christ. If you are claiming to be a Christian, but you are not turning from sin; if you are going on week after week, month after month, year after year in a condition and relationship that you know is wrong, then you are not a Christian. Despite your experience, despite your claim, despite your attendance in church or anything else, you have never been born again! This is the proof of it. Is that not what John says? "No one who sins has either seen him or known him." No one who persists in sin, no one who habitually remains in a rebellious, lawless attitude toward God, has ever seen him or known him.

It is possible for both a sheep and a pig to fall into a mudhole, but the difference in their nature becomes immediately evident in their reaction. The pig is perfectly happy. He rolls over on his back, singing "Home Sweet Home." But the sheep is miserable and earnestly desires to get out. So, John says, no one born of God can persist in habitual sin, for God's seed abides in him, and he cannot go on sinning continuously, because he is born of God.

1 John 3:10

22

One or the Other

In this section on the subject of maintaining righteousness the apostle has briefly put the whole matter into one verse: "If you know that he is righteous, you may be sure that every one who does right is born of him" (1 John 2:29). He says that the secret of doing right is to possess and experience within oneself the life of the Righteous One. There is only One who is righteous, or who has ever been righteous, the Lord Jesus himself. His life must be lived again in us in order for us to be righteous.

In the verses that follow, we have seen the effect of Christ's life in three dimensions. As to the future we are given a hope that purifies us. We look to a coming event that is more certain than anything happening in our world today, the return of Jesus Christ. As to the past, we learn that the Son of God came into our hearts to remove lawlessness, the spirit of rejection of authority. That takes care of the past rebellion of our life. And as to the present, he has come to deliver us from the works of the devil: from murdering, lying, and stealing. The fact that we are more and more turning from harmful practices is a sure sign that we belong to God. John makes this issue of identity even clearer in verse 10 of chapter 3:

243

> By this it may be seen who are the children of God, and who are the children of the devil: whoever does not do right is not of God, nor he who does not love his brother.

Could anything be plainer than that? All humanity, in the sight of God, is divided into two classes. Someone has said that people divide themselves into two classes, the righteous and the unrighteous, and the classifying is always done by the righteous! Unfortunately, that may be true. There are certainly not three classes, as we often fondly imagine. We would like to think there are the children of the devil, and the children of God, and then there is a vast group in between who are morally neutral, neither devilish nor divine. If pressed on the point, most people would probably classify themselves in the middle somewhere. But God says no.

Characteristically throughout this letter, John draws the extremes of black and white, but these are not simply his ideas. These reflect an actual situation. Truth is truth and error is error. John says there are no gray areas of truth, no shades or degrees of truth. So it is in this matter of mankind. We are either children of God, or children of the devil, one or the other. There are not three classes.

Nor is there only one class. Many today would have us believe that all men everywhere are, by virtue of their natural birth, children of God. But the Bible never sustains that idea for even a moment. These words of John echo the words of the Lord Jesus himself when he said to certain Pharisees of his day, "you are of your father the devil, and your will is to do your father's desires" (John 8:44). This phrase, "children of the devil," does not mean that they are created by the devil but it means that they reflect the nature and characteristics of the devil. They are tied, in some remarkably mysterious way, to his life. In the opposite direction, a child of God is someone who is tied to the life of God.

The Devil's Children

But according to the record of the Scriptures, because of the Fall of man in the Garden, mankind today is no longer containing and expressing the life of God, but is expressing the perverted, twisted life of the devil. There is a great deal of misunderstanding about this matter of the children of the devil. Perhaps most think of the children of the devil as violent, malicious, openly immoral people—those whom we would ordinarily call wicked people. It is true that the devil expresses his life in violence, in immorality, in lawlessness, defiance, and hostility. People who habitually reflect that attitude unquestionably are the children of the devil. The Bible tells us the devil goes about "as a roaring lion," expressing himself as a lion does, in violent power.

That is not the only way the devil acts, however. The Bible also says that the devil is "an angel of light." He can be suave, cultured, kindly, moral, and respectable, even sweet. It is possible for a human to reflect these characteristics and be equally as devilish as someone given over to open violence. As we have already seen, this but reflects our Lord's own teachings along this line. He said to religious, moral, respected, and respectable men of his day, "You are of your father, the devil." They were appalled. They said, "What do you mean? We are not born of fornication. Our father is Abraham." He said, "If Abraham were your father, then you would love me and you would hear me. But you are of your father the devil, and you will be doing the works of your father."

As we view humanity from the biblical point of view we see that, without exception, every one of us was born into the family of the devil, because we are part of the fallen race of Adam. We are children of the Adam who sold himself to the devil, and all his children are like him in that respect. The tendency toward sin, that twisted perversion, is passed along to us from our forefathers along with the color of our eyes, the eventual height of our bodies, and all other physical features. We are born with a bent toward evil. You only need to live with a few babies to see this demonstrated. How utterly self-centered a baby is! Everything exists for him, in his thinking. The whole world is there but to serve his particular need, and that, in essence, is the expression of the life of the devil.

It is only by new birth that we become members of the family of God, children of God. That is why Jesus said to the cultured, respected leader of his own day, Nicodemus, who came to him by night, "Except you be born again, you cannot enter into the kingdom of God." All your knowledge, your education, your morality, or your religion is of no value here. Unless you are born again you are still part and parcel of the family and the kingdom of Satan. The whole thrust of the gospel is always in this direction. It is to deliver men from the kingdom of Satan and to bring them into the kingdom of God, into the kingdom of Christ, the Son of his love.

The Healing Has Begun

There is also much misunderstanding about the phrase "the children of God." Many people who hear Christians using this phrase say, "What hypocrites you are! What do you mean, 'children of God'? What makes you think you're any better than anybody else? Why do you put on such airs and act as though you are saints and we are sinners?" They seem to feel that if a person says that he is a child of God, that he is thereby claiming to be perfect and without sin. But no thoughtful, Bible-taught, Spirit-led Christian ever takes that position. To be a child of God does not mean that we are perfect. It does not mean we have learned all that is involved in being a child of God, nor that we have begun to experience it ourselves.

What it does mean is that the healing process has begun. God has begun a transforming work and the evidences of it should be obvious right from the beginning. Not that it is all completed, but it has begun.

As you walk down a street you will often see a building with scaffolding around it, and looking through the scaffolding you can see that things are in a state of incompletion. A sign out in front says the building is "Under Construction." You would not write an angry letter to the contractor or the architect and say, "What's the matter with you! What do you mean, claiming to be under construction? Why, I walked by there and there's no glass, there is nothing finished about it at all!" He would reply, "Why, of course not. We never claimed it to be finished; it is simply under construction." This is what Christians are claiming when they call themselves children of God.

As we have also seen, once one becomes a child of God by faith in Jesus Christ and is really born of God, it is an irreversible process. We cannot be unborn. God, having begun a good work in us, will perform it until the day of Jesus Christ. Once that wonderful change has taken place, God himself undertakes to bring us along, and he will do his job. We cannot lose this new life.

Ah, but there is the rub! Many people sincerely think they are children of God because they have repeated a certain set of words or prayed a certain prayer, or gone forward in a meeting, or performed some other activity or ritual, when actually they are not and never have been born again. They are self-deceived. What has happened is that the flesh, which is subtle and as Jeremiah put it, "irreversibly wicked," unspeakably bad, has determined to remain in the seat of power (as it always does). It has simply turned religious or moral; perhaps it has cleaned up a few unsavory aspects of life and thus deceived the heart of the individual.

Temporary Relief

Such people have been content with a surface change, or with a mere relief of feelings. Perhaps such a person was greatly distressed about some condition in his life, and someone talked to him about Christ. It looked like a way out, so he said, "Well, yes, I will receive Christ," and he went through the performance of asking Jesus to come into his life. But all he was really looking for was relief. He got relief, there was a temporary improvement in the problem, and he thought this was conversion, this was regeneration. But the person never came to the place where, absolutely helpless, sensing that he could do nothing in himself any more, he cast himself upon the sustaining grace of God. That is what conversion is. It is a feeling of "I can't do anything to help myself. There's no improvement that I can bring out. I'm licked. I've got this problem within me, with which I've come face to face, and which I can do nothing to solve." Then the eye of faith sees the work of Jesus Christ upon the cross as doing for him what he could never do for himself, and he is born again. God's Spirit regenerates him, and he moves into the kingdom of God.

Righteousness and Love

Well, you ask, how do you know that you've been born again? How can you really tell that this has happened? This is what verse 10 is all about. All the apostles tell us this, but no one puts it any more clearly than John. In the latter part of the tenth verse he says, "whoever does not do right is not of God, nor he who does not love his brother." In other words, the unmistakable sign, the "unimitatable" sign, is a twofold mark: if he has not begun to turn from evil, and if he has not begun to love his brother, then he is only deceiving himself. The twofold mark is righteousness and love, intertwined.

Rebellion against authority must begin to cease, and hostility and indifference toward others must begin to end.

There are some who think they are Christians but who have never been born again. They have held resentments for years and done nothing about them. There are some who have professed to be Christians, who have yet been going on consistently doing things that the Word of God clearly says are wrong.

Let me be even more specific. Certain people say, "I know premarital sex is wrong, but I want to do it because everybody else is doing it. Because I know God is forgiving and loving, I'm going to do it and then come back and ask for forgiveness afterward." If this is what you are saying, and you are acting on that basis, then let me say with all the authority of the Scripture: there is no clearer sign than this that you are yet a child of the devil! Despite all your profession, despite all your religious confession or your experience, if you can say, "I'm going to do this thing that's wrong and depend upon the grace of God to forgive me afterward," you are of the devil; you are not a child of God. The lie of the devil is there. You can hear echoes of what he said to Eve in the Garden of Eden. He first asked, "Has God said this? Is that the kind of a God you've got? Is he so harsh and demanding that he will exclude you from this delightful thing?" Then in utter inconsistency (and the devil is always inconsistent), he immediately reversed himself and said, "God is too loving. He will never execute this sentence of death. He is such a gracious, forgiving God, he will never take it out on you." That is the devil's lie.

God's Resounding No

In Romans 6 the apostle Paul puts this issue very bluntly. Having reviewed all that God has done in Jesus Christ, he says,

> What shall we say then? Are we to continue in sin that
> grace may abound? (Rom. 6:1).

That is, should we go right on sinning, depending upon
God's forgiving grace to take care of the situation? That
is a rhetorical question, which is followed by one of the
strongest negatives in the Greek New Testament. It is
translated in various ways. In one version it is, "By no
means!" Another says, "God forbid!" Still another says,
"May it never be!" But literally, what the apostle says is,
"It cannot be!" You cannot say that and be a child of
God. He goes on to reinforce this by asking,

> How can we who died to sin [in Christ] still live in it?
> (Rom. 6:2).

It simply cannot be. There was no genuine transference
from the power of Satan to the power of the Son of God,
if that be the case. You are kidding yourself.

Now you may be tempted; all of us have been tempted
at times to think this. But to actually do something,
deliberately challenging God to be gracious in spite of
our sin, is absolute proof that the individual is a child of
the devil and has never been born again. Jude takes this
up in his letter, in the fourth verse where he says,

> For admission [to the church] has been secretly gained by
> some who long ago were designated for this con-
> demnation, ungodly persons . . .

To be ungodly does not mean to be wicked or violent,
it simply means to disregard God, to pay no attention to
what he says, to go on and act the way you want
regardless of what God says. That is ungodliness.

> ungodly persons who pervert the grace of our God into
> licentiousness . . .

Ungodly persons utilize the forgiving grace and mercy of

God to excuse their indulgence in licentious, sensual things:

> . . . and deny our only Master and Lord, Jesus Christ.

These verses search us, do they not? They probe right down to the depths of our lives. They do not let us get by with things at all. If someone is thinking this way, then the thing he needs to do, the only thing he can do, is to come as a common, unredeemed sinner to Jesus Christ. Aware at last of the deceitfulness of his heart, he must fling himself upon Jesus Christ and receive from him the gift of life and be born again.

I have seen young people and older people alike, who thought for years they were Christians and drifted along with a surface manifestation of the Christian life, but within there was rebellion, and deliberate actions of deceit and hypocrisy. But at last, God in grace and faithfulness, made them see that they were merely deceiving their own hearts, and that they had never been born again. That was the moment of truth. God's grace reached them, and they saw that they were still victims of the deluding power of the devil, still following the course of this world, still walking according to the lusts of the flesh, doing and fulfilling the desires of the heart and the mind, but never yet transferred to the kingdom of the Son of God's love.

Are you there? Have you been attending church for years, but never been born again? You have never known what it is to have your inward desires changed. If you have been living like this, will you do business with God right now?

Book Four

Maintaining Love

23

The Path of Love

On a trip to the Holy Land some years ago, we spent a week in Jerusalem. Our hotel was located right on the Mount of Olives, commanding a most spectacular and dramatic view of the entire Old City. On the first morning I was up early to go out into the brilliant sunshine and look over the city. From my vantage point on the Mount of Olives, I could see all the historic spots of Christian interest. My mind went back to the time when our Lord sat there and looked out over that stubborn, recalcitrant city. Tears came welling up into his eyes from a bursting heart, and he cried, "O Jerusalem, Jerusalem, killing the prophets and stoning those who are sent to you! How often would I have gathered your children together as a hen gathers her brood under her wings, and you would not!" (Matt. 23:37).

The most compelling emotion I experienced at that moment was the awareness, drifting to me across twenty centuries, of the compassion and love of the Lord Jesus Christ. The love of Jesus Christ! The apostle Paul wrote to his Corinthian converts about love and made it clear that the love of Christ is the one force which has succeeded again and again in breaking through the hard crust of human hate and suspicion. Time and time again it

255

has melted the cruel, arrested the rebellious, and changed the implacable.

Why Fight?

Years ago in Virginia I met an old man who was the rector of an Episcopal church. He had been converted in D. L. Moody's meetings in Cambridge, England. When Moody came to the center of English culture and education in Cambridge, the students were very much in rebellion against him. They felt he was a backwoodsy American who could not even speak the English language properly—and he couldn't! They were affronted by the idea that this coarse American should be asked to speak to the cultured students of Cambridge.

The man I met was one of those students who had been opposed to Moody. A band of them had agreed that when the meeting began they would break it up with catcalls, hooting, and mockery, and refuse to allow Moody to continue with his message. But when the meeting began, Moody's associate, Ira Sankey, sang a beautiful number that greatly moved the hearts of those students. As soon as the song ended, Moody strode to the front of the platform and, in his characteristically blunt fashion, began, "Young gentlemen, don't ever let anybody tell you that God don't love you, for he do!"

They were so startled by this ungrammatical beginning that they all paid attention. This student said that as he left the meeting that phrase ran again and again through his mind and he thought to himself, *Why do I fight a God who loves me? Why should I be in rebellion against such a God?* Later that day he sought out D. L. Moody and the evangelist led him to Christ. As the man told me that story he looked back across the years to recall the time when he first came to realize the amazing love of God.

That is the new theme to which we now come in the Epistle of John. John has been talking about maintaining fellowship, maintaining truth, and maintaining righteousness. Now he comes to the theme of maintaining love. It begins in chapter 3, verses 11–18.

> For this is the message which you have heard from the beginning, that we should love one another, and not be like Cain who was of the evil one and murdered his brother. And why did he murder him? Because his own deeds were evil and his brother's righteous. Do not wonder, brethren, that the world hates you. We know that we have passed out of death into life, because we love the brethren. He who does not love abides in death. Any one who hates his brother is a murderer, and you know that no murderer has eternal life abiding in him. By this we know love, that he laid down his life for us; and we ought to lay down our lives for the brethren. But if any one has the world's goods and sees his brother in need, yet closes his heart against him, how does God's love abide in him? Little children, let us not love in word or speech but in deed and in truth.

A familiar pattern in John's Epistle is that of presenting various contrasts: light and darkness, death and life, truth and error, God and the devil. Now he ties together these contrasting themes, love and hate. He presents them exactly as they occur in life—not in watertight compartments, isolated from each other, but intertwined together. For the purpose of study, however, we will separate them, beginning with John's tracing of the path of love. Notice where John begins his word about love. He suggests to us, in verse 11, that the origin of love is at the conversion of a Christian.

> For this is the message which you have heard from the beginning, that we should love one another . . .

John sees love as beginning with Christian commitment and conversion. It is produced, he suggests, by the message "which you have heard from the beginning."

Not Merely a Command

That is a familiar phrase. We have seen it several times in John. In chapter 2, he says, "If what you heard from the beginning abides in you, then you will abide in the Son and in the Father" (v. 24). The Epistle also opens on that note. "That which was from the beginning, which we have heard, which we have seen with our eyes, which we have looked upon and touched with our hands . . . we proclaim also to you." This is a reference to the beginning of a Christian life. These who received this first letter of John are reminded of the time when they first heard the gospel of Jesus Christ. From that very moment they received a new awareness of the requirement of God in human lives, that we should love one another. The implication is clear here that this is not merely a command, such as we have in the Ten Commandments. Rather, it is the realization of the *possibility* of loving one another, which originates with conversion.

I know there are many who are upset by the fact that Christians claim to have a monopoly on love, that real love only begins when you are a Christian, and that it is impossible for a non-Christian to show genuine love. There are those who say, "Isn't it true that atheists love their children as whole-heartedly and as genuinely as Christians do? Isn't that real love? Isn't the love of a boy for a girl, or a friend for a friend just as beautiful and tender, whether or not they are Christians?" The answer of course is, yes. Love is love. The Bible never claims that Christians have a monopoly on love. But it does claim that love of the highest quality, love in its truest aspect, begins to flow only in a Christian experience. There is a difference between the love of a Christian and the love of a non-Christian, and it is described in this very letter as the difference between death and life. In verse 14 John says, "We know that we have passed out of death into life, because we love the brethren. He who does not love remains in death."

Love Deflected

Well, what is this difference? We must of course recognize that all love is from God. God *is* love, John tells us. Love pours from God into human hearts like sunshine and rain upon the ground, upon the just and the unjust alike. No human being would love if he were not in some relationship, in some contact, with the God who is love. All love comes from God; the love of parents for children, the love of friends for friends, the love of sweethearts for each other—all is a gift of God to the human race, like sunshine and rain, food, shelter and raiment, and all the other things that make life beautiful, happy, and wholesome. But something happens to the love of God, this pure, unspotted love which comes from God's heart upon mankind. As the love of God comes into the twisted, distorted heart of fallen mankind, it also becomes twisted and distorted, deflected from its true goal. In fallen man, it becomes love directed only toward himself. Love, before Christ comes, is self-centered love.

There is nothing wrong with the love itself; it is the direction it takes, the object upon which it focuses, which distorts it. Love comes from God, true; but love in the fallen heart is always centered upon self. Therefore the love we show as non-Christians is really a love of ourselves. We love our children because they are extensions of us. We love father or mother because our life is related to theirs. We love our relatives (presumably) because they are ours. We love *our* dog, *our* cat, *our* horse. We love the friends who please us; we love those who help us. If you observe human life you will see how true this is. Love is always directed to those who do something to or for, or receive from, us. Therefore what we really love is the projection of ourselves in others.

Jesus recognized this in the Sermon on the Mount. He said to the Pharisees, "if you love those who love you, what reward do you have? Why, even those despised tax collectors do that." If you love those who are kind to you, you are no different than anyone else. But at Christian conversion a different kind of love arises. When a person is born again he passes, as John says, from death into life, and he begins to love those he never loved before and to love those he has loved before in a different way. One of the clearest marks of a genuine Christian conversion is that almost immediately the individual involved begins to express concern for someone else, usually someone whom he has had difficulty loving before.

Evidence of Life

That brings John to the second fact about love. First the origin of it, he says, is conversion. The pure, unadulterated love which God intended love to be, begins only at the new birth. Second, it is the evidence that a new life has been imparted.

> We know that we have passed out of death into life, *because we love the brethren.* He who does not love abides in death (v. 14).

It is easy to see why the apostle who wrote this has become known as the Apostle of Love. John says more about this great quality than any of the other writers, even though it was Paul who wrote that glorious paean on love in 1 Corinthians 13. But if you read the gospel records of John you will note that love is not natural to him. He and his brother James earned from Jesus the title "sons of thunder" because they were constantly wanting to blast back at those who opposed them. It was John and James who came to the Lord when a village refused to let them enter, and said, "Shall we not call fire down from heaven upon them?" It was John and James who were constantly quarreling with the other disciples. John's temperament was not one naturally of showing love, but when he was born again, when he submitted to the deity and lordship of Jesus Christ, this man began to show love. So completely did he submit to the lesson that he became known as the Apostle of Love.

Such love is thus the sign of the new life. It is a love which does not depend upon a reciprocal relationship, but loves anyhow, loving the unlovely, loving the unqualified, loving the ungrateful and the selfish and the difficult. To view people apart from the relationship of Christian love is to see them as either our friends or our foes, as either rivals or helpers, as those who can help us along to the object we want or as obstacles in our pathway. In other words, we do not look at people as being like ourselves, we look at them as either obstacles or helpers to us. We see them always as related to us. But when Christian love is born, a change takes place and we begin to see people as people, like ourselves—needing love, having problems, feeling fears and anxieties, and experiencing troubles. We are able to empathize, to sympathize, to enter in. This, then, is the character of true love, and it is always the evidence that a new life has come, the life born of God.

Perhaps you remember the story of Jacob De Shazer, one of the members of Colonel Doolittle's crew who bombed Tokyo early in World War II. He was captured by the Japanese and put in prison. He hated his Japanese captors and feared nothing they did to him; he was so violent in his hatred that they kept him in solitary confinement. But in a remarkable way he obtained a copy of the Bible and began to read it through. In the loneliness of his cell he began to realize the life that is in Jesus Christ, and an amazing change came over him. His hatred of the Japanese changed completely, and he began to show love toward his captors. They were utterly astonished by what had happened to him; instead of burning with wrath, he became the most docile of prisoners, eagerly cooperating with his captors, and praying for them.

Eventually the story of his change of heart was written

up in a little tract, and after the war it fell into the hands
of a young Japanese, Captain Mitsuo Fuchida, the man
who led the air raid against Pearl Harbor, and who gave
the command to drop the bombs on that fateful Decem-
ber 7. Mitsuo Fuchida was a hero in Japan after the war
because of that exploit and others, but his own heart was
empty. When he read the tract that told the story of De
Shazer's amazing change of heart, he was arrested and
puzzled by it. From somewhere he obtained a New
Testament and began to read it with growing interest and
amazement. At last he came to the story of the crucifixion. When he read the Lord's words from the cross,
"Father, forgive them for they know not what they do,"
his heart broke. He realized that this One who could love
his enemies and pray for those who persecuted him and
despitefully used him was manifesting a quality of life
that no natural human being could possibly show. Mitsuo
Fuchida became a Christian.

With Saints We Know

Since love like this is the sign of a converted heart, of
course the most obvious place for it to show is with our
brethren, with other Christians, for the hardest people to
love are those closest to us. As it says in the jingle,

> To dwell above
> With saints we love
> O, that will be glory;
> But to dwell below
> With saints we know
> Well, that's another story!

It is true that it is difficult to love those who are close to
us. The ordinary encounters we have with nasty baggage-
handlers and waiters do not bother us because they are
remote from us. But if the ones who are near to us
mistreat us, we find it difficult to show love. Can you love
those who are near to you? If you cannot, you remain in
death, for this is the mark of new life.

Now because there are many attempts to imitate this valuable quality, John goes on to trace for us the essence of love:

> By this we know love, that he [and it literally reads as though the Lord Jesus is standing right there, 'that one'] laid down his life for us; and we ought to lay down our lives for the brethren (1 John 3:16).

That is the essence of true love. It is a laying down of life, a giving up of self-interest; that is the quality that marks God's kind of love. "He laid down his life for us," John says. Once for all he poured out his soul in death, laid down his life for us. Because of that, we ought to be laying down (and here he uses the present continuous tense) our lives for each other, our brethren. Not in the same way he did, for we can seldom die for another, but we can live for one another. The laying down here means the giving up of self-interest, the voluntary surrender of the right to meet our own needs so that we can meet the needs of another. It is the giving up of self so that we might minister to another. That quality of genuine love will manifest itself, not in word, but in deed.

> If any one has the world's goods and sees his brother in need, yet closes his heart against him, how does God's love abide in him? (v. 17).

If we can see others in need—physically, emotionally, or spiritually—and pass them by unconcerned, then all our words and our fine talk about love are, as Paul says, nothing but a clanging cymbal, a loud noise, a mere banging upon metal.

> Little children, let us not love in word or speech but in deed and in truth (v. 18).

It is this easy talk about love while actually withdrawing from those in need which constitutes the phoniness that turns so many away from Christ. The great sickness of fundamentalism lies right here. We have uttered glowing words about God's love for us and our love for men, but we have built barriers around ourselves, and refused to let others see our inner lives. Because we have become isolated units, refusing to blend hearts together, we have lost the glory of body-life, through which Jesus Christ intends to manifest the glory of his Spirit at work. Since God only works through a body, it is absolutely essential that we take down those isolating barriers and stop pretending to be something we are not. We must be willing to admit our faults and our failures, and to pray together. When this special kind of love, which for Christ's sake puts up with difficulties and irritating qualities about another, is shown, it becomes the most powerful force in all the world. When it is seen it hits with amazing impact.

A Cadillac and Courtesy

I once heard a young Jewish convert give the amazing story of his life. Art was raised as an atheist, even though he was of Jewish descent. Early in his life he became a Marxist, a committed communist. He was always a troublemaker, at the center of every uprising that took place. At the close of World War II he happened to be in Germany with the American Army and personally saw the gas chambers at Dachau and Buchenwald. He came away from them shocked and sick at heart. He was filled with hatred, first toward the German race and then, realizing that this was not merely a national problem but a human problem, filled with a pervasive loathing for the whole human race. He came back to Berkeley and tried to give himself to education but more and more he realized that education was not the answer. Education could not change hearts; education could not and did not touch the basic problems of human beings.

Finally he gave it all up and resigned his position. His wife lost her mind and was put in a mental institution. Divorced, and without ties, he went out to wander up and down the face of the earth, hardly knowing where he was going. One rainy day in Greece he was hitchhiking, with a week's growth of beard on his face and a dirty rucksack on his back. Of course no one wanted to pick him up. He had stood in the rain for hours when at last a big Cadillac came by and stopped. To his amazement the man did not merely open the door and gesture for him to get in. He got out of his car, came around and began to pump his hand and to welcome him as though he were some kind of king. He took the dirty rucksack and threw it on the clean upholstery. Art said he winced when he saw that. Then the man invited him to get in the car and they drove on.

The man treated him as though he were a welcome guest. He was taken to a hotel, and the man rented him a room and cleaned him up and gave him some food. Finally he asked him what he was doing and where he was going. All the pent-up heartache, misery, and resentment of his life came pouring out of this young Jewish atheist. He told the other man the whole story, and the man sat and listened. When he was all through, he said, "You know what the world needs? Those who are willing to wash one another's feet." Art said, "I never heard anything so beautiful! Why do you say that?" And the man said, "Because that's what my Lord did." For the first time in this young atheist's life he heard a Christian witness, and that was the beginning of the end for him. He is now a Christian worker, devoting his life to Christ.

I do not need to tell the whole story of how this young man came to know Jesus Christ. The thing that arrested him and broke through all the years of hatred, all the pent-up resentment and bitterness of his heart and life was this one act which showed genuine courtesy and kindness in the name of Jesus Christ. "By this," Jesus said, "shall all men know that you are my disciples." That is the path of love. If life is there, that kind of love will be there. John's exhortation is to let it show: "Little children, let us not love in word or speech but in deed and in truth."

24

The Course of Hate

We have looked together at the path of love which John has traced for us, as to its origin, its essence, and its evidence. Now we will take the same passage but follow the course of hate. Twice in this century the world has been engulfed by a tremendous cataclysm of hate and evil, of darkness and death, in the sickening horrors of war. Yet the forces that produce these modern slaughters are no different and no more violent than those that were present in a meeting of two brothers in a field long, long ago. On that day, one brother suddenly took his axe, crushed his brother's skull with one swift blow, and crimsoned the earth with his brother's blood.

That is the scene John sets before us in the third chapter, beginning with verse 11. The axe of Cain has now become a hydrogen bomb, but the motivation that sets either on its deadly swing is always the same. If we understand the act in the field long ago, we will understand the reason for the wars and conflicts of our own day.

For this is the message which you heard from the beginning, that we should love one another, and not be like Cain who was of the evil one and murdered his brother. And why did he murder him? Because his own deeds were evil and his brother's righteous. Do not wonder, brethren, that the world hates you (1 John 3:11–13).

What is the origin of love and hate? Where did these two powerful forces come from? It is rather remarkable to note that neither force originates in man, in spite of what we usually think. We conceive of ourselves as having the ability to love, and the ability to hate. We think of ourselves as the originator of these attitudes. But this passage reveals that love springs only from God, from outside of man. John also makes it clear that hate originates outside man. Cain, he says, was "of the evil one," which is a reference to the devil. By this John indicates that the powerful force of hate is always devilish, hellish. Its presence in the human heart reveals the terrible fact that the individual who is expressing hate has fallen into the silent, remorseless grip of the devil.

We shall never understand these forces in life unless we understand them from this biblical point of view. It is in the coming of the Son of God that the fundamental, foundational realities of life are unveiled to us. If we disregard these revelations simply because they do not agree with the way we have usually thought, then we are blindly shutting our eyes to the truth. But if we heed them, we will have an understanding of life. Therefore it is very important that we understand that love and hate both originate outside of man. Love comes only from God; hate comes from the devil. Hate is really love, twisted, diverted from its intended course and centered upon a false object. The devil takes the life and the love of God and diverts it, twists it, and mutilates it—and love comes out as hate. Therefore anyone who hates is like Cain, in the grip of the devil; he is "of the evil one."

Quiet Takeover

That is rather sobering, but we must start with that significant fact. I am sure that Cain was unconscious of the fact that when he hated he was under the control of another mind, another purpose. He felt no different; he felt no premonition that something was taking over in his life. There was no sudden chill running up and down his backbone to make him aware that a sinister evil spirit was possessing him, just as we feel no different when we hate. Yet, when his heart began to burn with hatred for his brother, there was a quiet takeover, with no inward feeling to betray it.

We see the same thing in the Gospels. Remember that as the Lord gathered with his disciples in the Upper Room for the institution of the first Lord's Supper, after they had partaken of the Passover Feast, the Lord stood to break bread. John's Gospel says that as Judas sat at the table with the Lord, Satan entered into his heart. He did not feel any different, but there was an open door to his heart through which the spirit of evil entered, from which he could no longer escape by an act of his will. Soon he went out into the night to accomplish his treacherous betrayal.

The same thing occurs in the story of Ananias and Sapphira. Those early Christians became jealous of the spiritual privileges that Barnabas and others were enjoying so they decided to claim a dedication for themselves that they did not really possess. They wanted the reputation before other Christians that they, too, were fully dedicated, wholly committed Christians and had given all their property to God, as the others were doing. But they kept back a part of the proceeds without saying a thing to anyone. When they came before the apostle Peter, who was filled with the Holy Spirit, do you remember what his question was? "Why has *Satan* filled your heart to lie to the Holy Spirit?" It is possible even for Christians to come under the grip of the devil. This is the first great revelation that the Scriptures give us of the course of hate: It begins with that evil, sinister being whose whole life and ministry are opposed to God and who silently takes over the heart of anyone who consents to give way to envy or jealousy.

No Ultimate Control

As we know from the Scriptures, the natural man continually lives in this unrealized control by Satan. In the Epistle to the Ephesians Paul says, ". . . in which [we all] once walked, following the course of this world, following the prince of the power of the air" (2:2), thus under his control. This is why hate is always so close to the surface in the life of the natural man. Any rebuff, any crossing of the will brings it right out. A burning spirit of anger or of hatred bursts through to the surface immediately, because this is the nature of the evil spirit who is at work in "the children of disobedience."

Civilized man often recognizes much of the evil that comes from hatred. In our world today many thinkers and philosophers are genuinely concerned about human events and are aware that the fountain from which much of the world's unrest springs is hatred. They are concerned about the evil results that come from the exercise of this passion, and so they attempt to control it. But the natural man is unable to come up with any real answer to this burning evil in his life, nor can he control it. He can only attempt by education to limit the manifestations of hatred, or by moral restraint to keep it suppressed. Of course, all he succeeds in doing is merely to change the name on the door. Hate becomes, at best, indifference or avoidance of another person. The best that an unregenerate person can do in handling hatred toward someone is to say, "Well, I won't have anything more to do with him. Let him go his way and I'll go mine." That is the highest level to which an unregenerate man can rise. At worst, hatred becomes contempt, disdain, prejudice— evil names which are nothing but synonyms of hatred at work among men today. A skunk by any other name still smells. You can sprinkle the perfume of a finer word or a better label on hate, but it still remains the same ugly thing, and it still produces the same ugly results in human life.

Now let us look more deeply at what this powerful

force is. John reveals not only the origin of hate—it is from the devil, he says—but he also lets us know its essence, its nature. "Why," he asks, "did Cain murder his brother?" The answer is very startling. Was it because Abel was a bad person? Was it because he did something evil to Cain and Cain was but revenging himself? No, it was because Abel was good, that Cain murdered him! He was doing proper, rightful, helpful things. That is why Cain murdered his brother.

> Why did he murder him? Because his own deeds were evil and his brother's righteous (3:12).

Think of that! Cain murdered his brother because his brother was good, not because he was bad. What do you think Cain would have answered to the question, "Why did you murder your brother?" I have often wondered if Cain ever stopped to ask himself that. Some time later, after the whole thing was over, in some moment of self-examination, did he ever ask himself, "Why did I do that? Why did I murder my brother?" His answer undoubtedly would have been very much like the answers we give to justify our attitudes of hate and dislike of other people. Probably he would have answered on the emotional level: "Oh, I couldn't stand him any more. He was so pious, so smug. He was always showing me up, and I just couldn't stand it any more." Or perhaps he would have resorted to some form of self-defense: "Well, he was a threat to me, to my reputation. The world was simply not big enough for us both. It was either him or me, so I got rid of him."

Self-made Religion

But what are the facts of this story? In the Genesis account of their encounter in the field, we are told only a few things about them, but those few things are very crucial. Both brothers, being religious men, brought an offering to the Lord God. Abel brought a lamb, and Cain brought a gift of grain to God. In the Epistle to the Hebrews we are told that it was "by faith" that Abel made his offering to God, and faith is always an obedient response to a command or a promise of God. Abel offered his sacrifice in obedience to what God had asked. Cain did not offer his "by faith," which means he refused to offer what God had asked. He did that deadly thing which so many millions are doing today: he devised his own religion. He said, "I have my own way of serving God," and he came up with his own plan for an offering and brought the first fruits of the field. When it was rejected, he was angry. The account tells us "his countenance fell," that is, he began to pout and sulk. He was angry and sullen, stewing within himself because God had not accepted what he had brought.

Even then, according to the account, he is not judged by God. God does not lash out with a lightning bolt against him, but speaks a word of warning to him. God asks, "Why does your countenance fall? Why are you angry? Do you not know that a sin offering is lying at the door? You can go back and bring the right offering. I'm not going to wipe you off the face of the earth because of your disobedience. You can still repent; you can still change your mind. You can go back and bring the right one."

But even with that word of warning there is absolutely no change in the heart of Cain, and he continues to burn with anger against God. At that moment he falls into the snare of the devil, as so many times you and I have fallen into the same snare when we have allowed some fancied sense of injustice to burn without our hearts. Because we feel that we are not treated fairly we begin to blame God. At that moment the silent control begins. The invisible sinister force takes over, and we become "of the evil one." The result in Cain's case was the deadly swing of the axe and the gush of his brother's blood.

Attack against God

Let us ask again, why did Cain do this terrible deed? It was because he was angry with God. He refused to accept God's evaluation, God's judgment of what was right and wrong. Displeased at God's ordering of life, he was angry because God would not play according to his rules. In other words, he himself wanted to be God, and he was angry when God refused to let him exercise the sovereignty which only God can have. In his mind, twisted now by the devil, all of this seemed to focus upon his innocent brother. All of his anger at the invisible power of God, the invisible Person of God, became focused in a visible object, his brother. That is a revelation of the nature of hate. It is directed at a human object, but it is always an attack upon God, a rejection of the rule of God.

John says, "Do not wonder, brethren, that the world hates you." Hate is a deeper force than we usually think it to be. It is more than a mere psychological reaction of one human being to another. It releases sinister forces into the human bloodstream. It brings dark powers into control of human minds and hearts. Many years ago Joseph Parker said, "The man who preaches repentance sets himself against his age, and will be mercilessly battered by the age whose moral tone he changes. There is but one end for such a man. Off with his head! You had better not preach repentance until you've pledged your head to heaven." "Do not wonder," John says, "that the world hates you." The nature of hate is such that it is an attack against God himself. David learned this, after causing Uriah the Hittite to be killed. In Psalm 51, he cries out to God, "Against thee, thee only, have I sinned" (v.4).

Further, throughout this account John reveals that the outcome of hate is murder, and he adds a striking word in verse 15:

Any one who hates his brother is a murderer, and you know that no murderer has eternal life abiding in him.

The latter part of that makes clear that he is aiming this particularly at the Christian. Anyone who hates his brother is a murderer. Does your heart burn with hatred toward another? You just cannot stand him—or her? You wish he would go away and leave you alone; you do not want him around at all? Well then, if the circumstances are right, and the penalty could be avoided, you would murder him if you could! That is what this reveals. All that keeps you from it is a fear of reprisal from God or man. If some way you could get away with it, hatred would invariably flash out into murder—as it did in that first scene between Cain and Abel.

Wherever hate is, murder is always the immediate possibility and, in the eyes of God, it is as good as done. God reads the heart, he does not need to wait for the actions. These are not the words of the so-called harsh God of the Old Testament; this is what the Lord Jesus himself taught in the Sermon on the Mount.

You have heard that it was said to the men of old, "You shall not kill; and whoever kills shall be liable to judgment." But I say to you that every one who is angry with his brother shall be liable to judgment . . . and whoever says, "You fool!" shall be liable to the hell of fire (Matt. 5:21,22).

Anyone who hates is a murderer already, and only lacks the proper opportunity or he would accomplish the deed.

Temporary Slaves

What, then, is revealed when a Christian hates? Let us be honest and admit that it is all too frequently true that Christians show hatred toward each other and toward others outside of Christ. But John tells us, "You know that no murderer has eternal life abiding in him." That means that the eternal life which Christ has given is no longer in control of that individual; it is no longer "abiding" in him. This does not mean that the person ceases to be a Christian when he hates, but he ceases to act like a Christian. He is no longer being the Christian that he has become. Eternal life is no longer abiding in him and he has slipped back, temporarily, into the control of the devil. He is acting out of the evil one. You see something similar in verse 17, where the Christian who is indifferent to the needs of another no longer has God's love abiding in him. It is not that love is not available to him; but it does not abide in him. Thus the apostle brings us face to face with the reality of the situation of hate. If we hate someone, we have become the temporary slave of Satan. We are God's child doing the devil's work.

What is the answer to this? What is the way to control hatred? For the world in general, it is quite clear that there can be no answer, there can be no effective control of this force, apart from the regenerating work of the Lord Jesus Christ and the cross of Calvary. It takes the power of God to break the power of hate, and only God can do it. That is why there is no ultimate hope for the control of wars and strife and anarchy and trouble, apart from an acceptance, on the part of individuals everywhere, of the redeeming grace of God. That is why we Christians are quite right when we tell people they can never solve their world problems at the peace tables or the conference tables and negotiate an ultimate control of warfare. That can never happen. This force is ingrained too deeply into human life to submit to that kind of superficial treatment.

But how are Christians to handle this problem of hatred? What do you do about it? Do you resort to the folly of trying to suppress it? Do you push it down, cover it over, and bite your lip? You are still under the control of the evil one and, sooner or later, he will take you

farther than you want to go. The only control is to judge
this thing. Deal with it as God sees it. Call it what it is—
hatred—originating from the devil, a devilish thing at
work in your life and heart. Then confess it, agree with
God about it. Then you will receive the answering power
of love from the Son of God who dwells in your heart.
The Holy Spirit is always ready to pour out, in place of
hatred, words of love and appreciation, approval and
acceptance. There is no other answer. Until we live on
these terms, we have not begun to demonstrate the life
that is in Jesus Christ.

Oh, the power of love—wonderful power to attract and
to draw men irresistibly to contact and encounter with the
Living God. But that love can never be manifest where
there is a protection, an excusing, a justifying of the spirit
of hate. That is why the exhortation comes, "Little
children, let us not love in word or speech but in deed
and in truth." How we need that word today!

25

The Christian's Tranquilizer

We have been observing in this third chapter that John is contrasting the themes of love and hate. Hate is self-centeredness; love is self-giving. Hate originates with the devil; love comes only from God. Hate results in deception and destruction; love results in helping and healing. These are acts, and this process exemplifies the evolution of all action; first, passion is born—the attitude, the thought—and then the act follows. Love, when it has conceived, brings forth help and health. Hate, when it has conceived, brings forth deception and death.

In the rest of the chapter the apostle John stresses the importance of the *act* or *deed* of love. Love must issue at last in something you do or say. It must be more than simply a warm thought of the heart, or an intended or imagined act. But as John now will tell us, when love becomes a deed, it does three valuable and important things for us: 1) it reassures a doubting heart, 2) it gives boldness and effectiveness to prayer, and 3) it gives evidence of a Spirit-filled life. Those are the themes that John develops in the latter part of chapter 3, from verse 19 to the end. Now we come to the first of these:

By this we shall know that we are of the truth, and reassure our hearts before him whenever our hearts

condemn us; for God is greater than our hearts, and he
knows everything (1 John 3:19,20).

In that phrase, "whenever our hearts condemn us," the
apostle John recognizes that the problem we often face is
that of a condemning conscience. This is a rather fre-
quent and often involuntary experience among Christians. Who has not had trouble with a bad conscience or a
condemning heart? It is often because of an attack of the
evil one, though sometimes it can come about from
nothing more serious than having eaten too late the night
before. There are physical problems which affect us
spiritually, but all too often this is the result of an attack
of the evil one upon us, an attempt to try to dislodge us
from faith in Jesus Christ, to overthrow us and disarm us
and annul our effectiveness as Christians. And often this
attack succeeds.

Perhaps nothing is more common than this problem of
Christians who suffer from a bad conscience, from a
condemning heart. Sometimes these attacks come upon
us in the midst of our most spiritual moods, attacking us
when we least expect, with no apparent reason whatsoever. We can go to bed at night, happy and relaxed and
refreshed in the Lord, and wake up with a gnawing, guilty
spirit, a condemning heart. We can be enjoying the
fellowship of God's people and feeling at ease with the
Spirit of God, with everything well between us, and only
a few hours later be suffering from a sense of uneasiness,
a vague undetermined sense of guilt or condemnation.
This is the problem that John is facing and you will
recognize how common it is and how frequently it occurs.

A guilty conscience usually arises from at least one of
three conditions. The problem certainly occurs when we
have committed some gross or repeated sin, such as
falling into a bad temper, or indulging in some lustful
experience, or taking someone else's property, or stealing
another's reputation—things in our life that we know to
be wrong. As Christians, if we fall into these experiences,

we are bound immediately to suffer from a guilty conscience. The Spirit of God is quick to make us feel guilty about these things.

But this is *not* the condition that is in view in this paragraph. John has already handled this problem. If we have a guilty conscience because of the commitment of some evil act or sin, there is only one channel of return, only one way back. "Confess your sin," John says, for "God is faithful to forgive us our sins and to cleanse us from all unrighteousness." There is only one thing to do when we are conscious of having committed an act that is wrong, and which produces a sense of guilt or condemnation: Confess it! Agree with God about it, and the cleansing that God has already provided in Jesus Christ will abundantly wash away the sense of guilt. You well know that experience. But that is not what John is talking about here.

Ignored or Misunderstood

This passage has to do primarily with the other two conditions. First, there are times when we have a sense of guilt or condemnation because we have been ignored or misunderstood or mistreated. Who has not had this experience? Perhaps right now you have a sense of resentment and of failure because of something you have done to which no one has paid any attention. You have been working so hard and you have been ignored.

Or, perhaps you did something out of a perfectly honest and open motive, intending to bless and help someone else, but they misunderstood. Instead of being grateful they were angry with you and even denounced you, scolded you, or accused you of wrong or of a less acceptable motive. You feel condemned and guilty over that. Appalled by their reaction, crushed and hurt, you are tempted to believe some of these accusations. You say to yourself, "Maybe they're right, maybe I haven't been motivated rightly after all. How do I know that my heart was right? I thought it was, but perhaps others see more clearly than I. Maybe I'm not even a Christian at all." The enemy is quick to use this to bring condemnation, if he can. And thus your heart condemns you.

In the second case, it may occur when you have been long inactive as a Christian for one reason or another. You have not been doing much; perhaps you have not been able to. You have been disabled, laid aside, sick, or even on too long a vacation, and you have a sense of not accomplishing much. You have been resting a long time and have not done anything. Here again the enemy is quick to come in and try to twist this into a sense of condemnation. He says, "The trouble with you is, you don't care any more. The reason you don't care is because, basically, you're not even a Christian. You've grown indifferent. Look how useless you are, look how worthless you are to the cause of Christ. How can you call yourself a Christian and feel this way? You have such a lack of concern for the things of God and the work of God." You do not recognize this as the voice of the evil one, you feel it is your own heart speaking and you feel a sense of condemnation.

Silencing the Heart

Now what is the remedy? Well, look at what John says. We must "know that we are of the truth." That is the essential thing. We must reassure ourselves of the great fact of our relationship to Christ. This is the ground for believing and reassuring ourselves that we are indeed "justified by faith," standing in God's presence not by our own righteousness, but by the righteousness of the Son of God, accepted in the Beloved, "in Christ." As Paul tells us in Romans 8, "There is therefore now *no condemnation* to those that are in Christ." In Christ all that he is appears on our behalf and there is therefore no condemnation to us. Therefore, if we are going to silence the doubts of our hearts we must know that we are "of the truth." That is where we must begin.

The same need is expressed in Ephesians where the apostle Paul urges us to "put on the breastplate of righteousness" (6:14), by which the heart—the emotions which are so easily subject to discouragement, gloom, and despair—is guarded. Put on the breastplate of righteousness. Realize again that you are "of the truth," for it is by the mind's knowledge that the heart's doubts are silenced.

Now how do you do that? Notice his argument here: "By this," he says, "we know that we are of the truth." By what? Well, what he has just mentioned in verse 18: "Little children, let us not love in word or speech [only] but in deed and in truth." By *this* shall we reassure our hearts in the knowledge that we are of the truth. He is referring here to the deed or act of love. We are to deliberately, and with specific intent, do a kind and helpful deed, or speak a loving word to the one (or ones) who have injured us or caused us to be plunged into this morass of condemnation. This is what John is teaching here, just as Paul taught, and as all the apostles taught, following the words of the Lord Jesus himself, "Bless those that persecute you. Do good to those who do evil to you. Return good for evil."

That is radical, is it not? It is so revolutionary that we find it very difficult to do. We reject it, for the most part, which is why so much of our time is spent under a sense of condemnation. For, as John says, it is *this* that makes us know that we are of the truth: when the love and good intentions of our hearts actually work out into some response, some deed, some activity of love and concern for those who injure us.

Strike Back with Love

Now take the two conditions that we have set before you. When you are ignored or misunderstood, when you have done the right thing and somebody has taken it the wrong way, what is your reaction, what do you feel like doing? Well, I know how I feel, and I am sure you feel the same way, for all of us are made in the same mold— only some are moldier than others! You want to strike back, do you not? You want to say a caustic, nasty thing in return. You want to refuse any further contact with that individual. "All right, let him go. If that's the way he feels about it, I'll go my way and let him go his." Well now, what is John saying? He says to leave the whole matter in God's hands. Do not strike back. Forgive that individual and forget the thing that is causing you difficulty. Take it patiently. The Lord Jesus gave us the example, as Peter reminds us: "When he was reviled, he reviled not again but committed himself into the hands of him who judges righteously" (1 Pet. 2:23). When we do this, John says, there immediately comes a sense of peace, a sense of reassurance. The Spirit within quickens us with the knowledge that we are of the truth. We are indeed sons and daughters of the Father, "who is kind to the ungrateful and to the selfish." We are manifesting the character of the One to whom we truly belong.

In 1960, just before the outbreak of the war, it was my privilege to visit Viet Nam and to speak to a conference of pastors gathered from the length and breadth of that little country. We met with some 300 pastors down in the delta area, in the little village of Vinh Long. During the course of the conference one of the pastors came to the interpreter and asked if he would arrange a meeting with me. The meeting was set up and, through the interpreter, the pastor poured out a tale of distress of heart. He recounted how he had been woefully mistreated by his brethren in the ministry, how he had been cut out of an office that he had felt was properly his and had been set aside (rather roughly he felt) and replaced by another man. The thing was rankling in his spirit, and he was very disturbed. At this conference he wanted to have a full airing of the matter while all the men were gathered together. He said, "What do you think I ought to do? Don't you think I should take advantage of this meeting and see that the whole matter is brought out and have this other man thrown out so I can have my proper place?" I turned to the second chapter of Philippians and had the interpreter read to him in his own language those wonderful words.

> Have this mind among yourselves, which is yours in Christ Jesus, who, though he was in the form of God, did not count equality with God a thing to be grasped, but emptied himself, taking the form of a servant, being born in the likeness of men. And being found in human form he humbled himself and became obedient unto death, even death on a cross (Phil. 2:5–8).

I suggested that he forget the whole matter. He did not accept this then, but as the conference went on and the Holy Spirit began to work in wonderful ways, I could see that he was struggling with the matter. At the end of the conference, after a wonderful time of blessing, he came up to me and said through the interpreter, "You were right. God has been dealing with my heart. It was only to try to justify myself that I was thinking all these things. God has helped me to put the whole matter aside. What a sense of joy and peace is mine now."

Now that is exactly what John is talking about. By *this,* by this response of genuine self-giving love to another who has injured us we prove to ourselves that we are of the truth and thus reassure our condemning hearts. Dr. F. B. Meyer some time ago wrote this:

> We make a mistake in trying always to clear ourselves. We should be wiser to go straight on, humbly doing the next thing and leaving God to vindicate us. "He shall bring forth thy righteousness as the light and thy judgment as the noonday." There may come hours in our lives when we shall be misunderstood, slandered, falsely accused. At such times it is very difficult not to act on the policy of the

men around us in the world. They want to appeal to law and force and public opinion. But the believer takes his case into a higher court and lays it before his God.

That is exactly what John is suggesting to us.

Well, you ask, what about the third condition, when I feel guilty because I have been inactive or disabled? What does John say about that? The same thing! Do a deed of love, even if it is no more than to say a prayer for someone, or to write a letter, or to send a gift. Let that nature of love which is within you express itself in some form. Help another. Give of yourself.

No Retirement

I am personally convinced that this is one of the greatest causes for doubt and torment among Christians. Especially is it true among older Christians, those who have retired, who have served a long time and feel themselves entitled to a rest. Perhaps in many ways they are entitled to a rest, but we are never entitled to retire from the Christian faith and the proper expression of it. Older Christians often succumb to a sense of self-pity and give themselves over to self-interest. Everything they do is related to what they want and, as a consequence, there is little expression of concern for others or ministry to others. There is, therefore, no power to resist an accusing conscience. John is suggesting something very practical here. Call up a lonely friend. Write a cheerful letter. Call on another person. Read a story to a child, for Christ's sake. "By *this* we shall know that we are of the truth, and reassure our hearts before him whenever our hearts condemn us."

Now John offers an explanation of why this works. "Because," he says, "God is greater than our hearts, and he knows everything." God knows that self-giving love is not a natural thing for the human heart. It is not natural to respond in kindness to those who do evil to us. It is totally unnatural for one who is an unbeliever. To genuinely return good for evil is simply impossible to an unregenerate nature. Therefore, God knows that the accusations of our hearts are wrong. He knows everything. God is greater than our hearts. He knows that these lying accusations (that we are really not Christians, not really in Christ, not really of the truth) are wrong. You *are* of the truth, and therefore you *can* forgive another, and you *can* bless another heart, and you *can* minister in grace to another. You *can* do something to help someone else in need. Now do it. And when you do, that great underlying truth which God knows but which you have temporarily forgotten, will immediately become evident to you. You too will *know*. There will be things that you can point to in your life that are not merely professed or imagined or intended, but actual things that God has enabled you to do that are entirely unnatural to the Adamic life, that can reassure you that you are of the faith. "By this we shall know that we are of the truth and reassure our hearts before him."

I was struck by the words of John R. W. Stott in his commentary on this passage, from which I borrowed the title of this chapter. Dr. Stott says, "Stronger than any chemical tranquilizer is trust in our all-knowing God." I am sure these words have great practical value for God's people. What is a tranquilizer but an attempt, by chemical means, to achieve ease of spirit, peace of heart? Has not God made ample provision for this through the spiritual mechanism of reassuring our hearts before him by the expression of active love in our lives? All this passage is really saying to us is that most of the problems of anxiety, restlessness, and guilt would be tremendously alleviated, if not completely eliminated, by some deliberate, active expression of self-giving love.

26

Power in Prayer

Reassurance, we have just seen, is the first result of the practice of love. Two more results follow in this section, beginning with verse 21 to the end of the chapter.

> Beloved, if our hearts do not condemn us, we have confidence before God; and we receive from him whatever we ask, because we keep his commandments and do what pleases him. And this is his commandment, that we should believe in the name of his Son Jesus Christ and love one another, just as he has commanded us. All who keep his commandments abide in him, and he in them. And by this we know that he abides in us, by the Spirit which he has given us (1 John 3:21–24).

You will notice that this is the other side of the case. This is the situation when our hearts do *not* condemn us. Here is one who has solved the problem of a condemning heart, has resolved his situation before God, perhaps by the exercise of some gracious loving word or deed, and thus has received the assurance that he is "of the truth," that he is "in Christ." If your heart does *not* condemn you, then what happens? "We have confidence before God." As Paul says in his letter to the Philippians, "We . . . worship God in spirit, and glory in Christ Jesus, and put no confidence in the flesh" (Phil. 3:3). The person whose heart does not condemn him is not looking at himself at all; he is looking at the greatness, the majesty, the glory, and the power of God. He is glorying in the availability of the Lord Jesus Christ. To "glory in Christ Jesus" is to not glory in anything man can do or hopes to do, but to glory in what Christ can do in him. He thus has no confidence in the flesh whatever.

In practical terms, the result of putting no confidence in the flesh is that we will have confidence before God, and we will receive from him whatever we ask. The result is to experience a daily adventure of answered prayer, the excitement of actually seeing God working in your life and in the lives of those with whom you are in contact, the daily stimulation of asking and receiving from God. This is really the normal Christian life. This is what God intended us to experience every day.

Many people have almost lost all hope that Christianity can ever do or be what its glowing terms describe. The reason is that they have not entered into this kind of relationship, where each day, every day, they experience the glorious adventure of seeing a living God at work, answering prayer and giving to them things that they ask. But in this passage we have a beautiful picture of the normal life of a Christian. It is all centered in prayer, because prayer is the most characteristic and the most fundamental relationship that a Christian can experience. Prayer is the expression of dependence on a living God, and the whole Christian life is to be characterized by a continuous attitude and spirit of prayer. "Pray without ceasing," says the apostle Paul.

The Right to Come

Now look at the earmarks of true prayer which John brings out in this passage. First, there is the *spirit* of prayer. "We have confidence before God" (and the word is, literally, boldness); we have boldness before God. If you have boldness before someone, it implies that you are in a close relationship with them, that you have a clear right to come before them. There is no fear of rebuke but a good understanding between you. Thus, to have confidence or boldness before God implies that you have a clear understanding of your right to come before him.

Occasionally I have strangers come to me and ask a favor of me, in terms of counseling or advice. They usually approach me in a rather diffident manner, often calling me "Doctor" though I'm not even a nurse! They usually speak in a very polite tone, and some have even confessed to me later that they experienced some degree of trembling and fear. I wonder what my reputation was in their eyes! But there are certain people who have no fear of me at all—my children! They come to me with boldness—in fact even brazenness at times. I do not always grant their request, but they do not hesitate at all in coming to me because they feel they have the right to come.

That is what John is getting at here. Prayer should grow out of such an understanding of the truth God has declared in his Word, that we have no questions about our right to come. We do not come on our own merit or position before him, for we know that we have no such ground. We come on Christ's merit. We come in his place. We come "in his name," and thus we can have boldness, just as he had boldness before the Father. All through that wonderful three-year ministry of his, note how many times he declared how perfectly at home he was in his conversations with the Father. He said, "Father, I know that thou hearest me always, because I do always those things that are pleasing to you." Boldness, therefore, is the spirit out of which prayer grows.

Cattle on a Thousand Hills

But notice also the *purpose* of prayer, as John sets it forth here. "We have confidence before God; *and we receive from him . . ."* The purpose of prayer is that you and I might be on the receiving end of God's grace, God's goodness, and God's glory. We receive from him. God is a giving God; he delights to give. He has all the resources of a superabundant universe from which to pour out to us. The cattle on a thousand hills are his. His purpose and his plan are to give to us. Paul, in writing to the Corinthians says, "You know the grace of our Lord Jesus Christ, that though he was rich, yet for your sake he became poor, so that by his poverty you might become rich" (2 Cor. 8:9).

This is God's purpose, to make us rich. Not in material things, always, by any means, for that is not where true riches lie. Many a millionaire would give every cent of his money if he could have a little peace of heart or joy of spirit. But God loves to pour true riches into human life. The riches of abundant life—that is what Christ came to give. There is nothing more exciting than to see an invisible God do visible things which only he could do; meeting our needs, satisfying our hearts, and accomplishing our desires—doing, as Paul adds in Ephesians, "far more abundantly than all that we ask or think" (Eph. 3:20). Now that is not mere theological twaddle; those are words to which a faithful God has committed himself, for our supply. If we are poverty stricken it is only our own fault, for God has designed a wonderful process, prayer, by which we might receive from him.

Now look at the *scope* of prayer: "whatever we ask." Not *everything* we ask, because sometimes, James tells us, "we ask amiss, so as to consume it upon our own lusts." Prayer was never intended to be a means of acquiring a new Cadillac, or some other new toy the heart is set on. That lies outside the realm and purpose of prayer. But within the realm for which prayer is intended, there is no limit. "Whatever we ask." There is no limit to the nature, or the type of request. It can be physical, spiritual, material, or emotional. As long as it lies in the direction for which prayer is intended, it is "whatever you need, whatever you ask."

This is a great promise, is it not? One of the most amazing stories, among many that I know of, in regard to prayer, is the supply of four peculiarly-shaped bolts, designed for a certain piece of equipment, to some missionaries in a desert place in Guatemala. God supplied those unique bolts in a most amazing way amid circumstances where such supply could never appear even remotely possible. There are many such well-authenticated incidents of the supply of needs in other areas, such as changed attitudes, reversed decisions, and restrained violence. The record of Scripture and of Christian experience is full of remarkable answers to prayer whereby God has changed a complete situation on many levels of experience. "Whatever you ask." It is not only about "religious" things that you need to pray. You can pray about anything. As Paul puts it in Philippians, simply, "Let your requests be made known to God" (Phil. 4:6).

Now John suggests to us the *conditions* of prayer. God always gives his great prayer promises on the basis of certain clearly described conditions, and these need to be carefully regarded. As one of my favorite slogans puts it, "When all else fails, follow directions." This is certainly true in connection with prayer. Here are his directions: "because we keep his commandments and do what pleases him." Those are the conditions.

Many people misread that badly. They take it to mean, in effect, "if you go to church, read your Bible, and witness to your friends (these are the things they think are pleasing to God), he will answer your prayers." But that is not what it says, and that is not what it means. Activity, of any kind, is not necessarily pleasing to God. This is the mistake the Israelites made in the Old Testament. They thought that offering sacrifices and fulfilling the rituals demanded by the law of Moses were, in themselves, pleasing to God. But God sent the prophets to them to say, "Away with your vain oblations. Your sweet-smelling incense stinks in my nostrils." Why? Because their lives were not in accord with their religious activities. It is not *what* you do, it is *why* and *how* you do it, that interests God. A right motive and a right attitude are essential conditions to answered prayer.

That brings us to verse 23, where we have the *context* of prayer:

> And this is his commandment, that we should believe in the name of his Son Jesus Christ and love one another, just as he has commanded us.

John wants us clearly to understand that it is not activities which are pleasing to God; it is attitudes. It is not the Ten Commandments that are in view here; it is the one great commandment which lies behind all ten—"the first and great commandment," Jesus called it. "You shall love the Lord your God with all your heart, and with all your soul, and with all your strength, and with all your mind; and your neighbor as yourself" (Luke 10:27). The only way to love God acceptably is to believe in the name of his Son Jesus Christ. That is why John puts it this way. Jesus once said to certain Jews, "This is the work of God, that you believe in him whom he has sent" (John 6:29). That is the place to start. We cannot do anything until we have done that. We cannot love God until we believe on the name of his Son Jesus Christ; then we can love one another, as he has commanded us.

Whatever Love Demands

John is not talking about the act of faith by which you became a Christian. That is included, but what John has in view here are those repeated acts by which you count on Christ's power and authority to do whatever love for your neighbor demands of you. These two are blended together: "Believe in the name of his Son . . . and love one another." It is all one commandment. John is saying that the condition by which prayer is answered, and answered abundantly, is that we make repeated, decisive acts of fulfilling the demands of love toward another, depending upon the power of Jesus Christ within us to perform it. That is "believing on the name of the Son of God," counting on his authority, on his power.

Notice that there are both direction and decision in this process. There is the direction toward which prayer always moves: love for another. That is the context of prayer; that defines what is meant by the term, "whatever we ask." Whatever we need to fulfill this demand to love one another we can have. We are not to ask for things outside that, but if we really set ourselves to love another then we can have whatever we need to fulfill it. That is the direction.

The decision is the action you take to accomplish this, counting on Jesus Christ to come through and make it possible. God never moves your will to make a decision. You must do that. But when you decide to do what he tells you to do in his demand to love another, he then comes through with the power to make it possible. The result is that everything you do is pleasing to God. If it is all moving in this direction it does not make any difference whether it is little or big, whether it is costly or not, whether it is a glass of water given in the name of the Lord, or thousands of dollars invested in some enterprise. Even though it is but a kind word spoken to a hungry heart, it is pleasing to him. It is not the activity; it is the attitude, the motive that prompts it, that makes all the difference. It is "by faith," counting on the living God within you to make it possible.

She Hated the Man

This was all illustrated to me recently when a couple from out of town came into my study. As they sat down, I noticed that the woman was particularly troubled. She was so distressed that she could hardly keep the tears from running down her cheeks. The man began to explain the circumstances. They had a son-in-law who was involved in a very difficult moral problem, and who was also repugnant to this dear woman, absolutely repulsive; she could not stand to be near him. She loved her daughter, and she hated the man for what he was doing to her daughter. She was eaten up with rankling resentment and bitterness against him. Every thought of him burned in her mind and heart, and she could not put him out of her thoughts. All this was destroying her. She could not sleep at nights; she could not eat. She was always tense, anxious, striking out at others in her home, and caustic and sharp in her words.

As we talked, all this came pouring out. She was not trying to be defensive and justify it; she just poured it all out. She said, "This is the case, and I don't know what to do about it. I can't stand this fellow." I said to her, finally, "You know this is not what the Lord wants of you, don't you? He tells us that we are to love one another. You are to love this fellow who is so repulsive to you."

She said, "I know that's what the Bible says, but I just can't do it." I said, "But that's the place to start, you see. You're saying that you can't, but really you can, because God says you can. You feel you can't because, of course, out of your own strength and effort you can't. But God can, because God does. God loves him already. He sees him, not as you see him, as an obstacle to your family's happiness; he sees this man as a man in the grip of an evil habit, an evil thing that is wrecking and ruining his life, but for which he is not wholly responsible. God's heart goes out in compassion and pity to him, and he desires to deliver him. That kind of God lives in you, and he can love that man through you, if you will let him. All he is waiting for is your will set in line with his. If you will say, 'I want to. If you will make me want to, I'll do it, Lord,' that is what he is waiting for."

She said, "Well, God knows I want to love him, if I could." I said, "You tell him that, will you?" Together we bowed there, and she poured out her inability to love.

She confessed her sin. She admitted that she had refused to love her son-in-law, and didn't want to do it. But she saw that this was contrary to the will of God and, she asked God to love him through her. Even as we finished praying, the peace of God was beginning to possess her heart again. The weary, strained, tense lines were fading away from her face. God was fulfilling what he had promised to do. She went on to a new relationship, growing out of her changed attitude, that eventually worked the problem out to a happy conclusion.

Notice now how verse 24 completes this whole picture:

> All who keep his commandments abide in him, and he in them. And by this we know that he abides in us, by the Spirit which he has given us.

Jesus said, "If any man loves me he will keep my word, and my Father and I will come into him and make our home in him." Here John completes the whole picture. The activity of love, he says, results in (1) a reassured heart, (2) power in prayer, and anyone who begins to live on that level makes it evident that (3) he is living a Spirit-filled life, the life that God intended. God abides in him, and he abides in God, and this is the mark of it.

When John says "By this," he is referring to all that precedes. "By this," that is, by this reassurance of heart, by this evidence of answered prayer, by this flowing out of love to another in active deeds and thoughts—by this we know that he abides in us and it all comes by means of the Spirit of God who indwells us.

Now do you see what John is after? You cannot bottle up the Holy Spirit in your life for your own enjoyment. He must flow *through* you. If you try to keep him to yourself your whole experience will stagnate and become mediocre, dull, sterile, and lifeless. But if you let him flow through you, ministering to others in his name, by his power, then your own life will become refreshed and fragrant and fruitful—by the Spirit of God who dwells in

294 / Maintaining Love

you. Everybody else, looking at you, will see that you have discovered the secret of victorious Christian living, of the abundant life made available in Jesus Christ. Do you want that? Well, God is no respecter of persons. This is available for anyone, everyone, young or old, rich or poor, it does not make any difference; this abundant life is available in Jesus Christ.

27

When Unbelief Is Right

Anyone who knows anything at all about Christianity knows that it puts great stress upon believing. Not believing myths and legends, as many seem to think, but believing facts. Faith is not a way of convincing yourself that something is true when you know it is not, as someone has defined it. Faith is believing something that is true.

To be a Christian you must be a believer, but it is equally true that every Christian is also called to be an unbeliever. There is a time when unbelief is the only right thing. The very same Scriptures which encourage us to believe likewise urge us not to believe. In fact they not only urge us, they command us not to believe. This is no contradiction, any more than to say that in order to live it is necessary both to inhale and to exhale. These are contradictory things: you cannot inhale and exhale at the same time, but both are absolutely necessary to maintain life.

It is the same with this matter of belief and unbelief. You cannot believe truth without rejecting error. You cannot love righteousness unless you are ready to hate sin. You cannot accept Christ without rejecting self. "If any man would come after me," Jesus says, "let him deny himself and take up his cross and follow me." You cannot follow good unless you are ready to flee from evil. So it is not surprising, therefore, that the Scriptures tell us we are not to believe, as well as to believe. This is what John declares in verses 1–3 of chapter 4:

> Beloved, do not believe every spirit, but test the spirits to see whether they are of God; for many false prophets have gone out into the world. By this you know the Spirit of God: every spirit which confesses that Jesus Christ has come in the flesh is of God, and every spirit which does not confess Jesus is not of God. This is the spirit of antichrist, of which you heard that it was coming, and now it is in the world already (1 John 4:1–3).

This section, you will notice, comes as a parenthesis in the discourse on love. It grows out of the last verse of chapter 3:

> All who keep his commandments abide in him, and he in them. And by this we know that he abides in us, by the Spirit which he has given us (1 John 3:24).

The presence of the Holy Spirit in our lives, manifesting the qualities of truth and love, reassures us that we are in Christ and "of the truth." It is that presence of the Holy Spirit which makes all the difference. But John says not to believe every spirit. There is one true Spirit, but there are also other spirits as well, false spirits, deceiving spirits, that have gone out into the world.

The Oldest Trick

It is significant that this warning comes in the midst of John's discourse about love, because false spirits tend to make a great deal of the subject of love. Every cult, every deviant group, every false movement makes its appeal in the name of love. No word in our language is capable of being stretched in so many directions as this word, *love*. Yet so many people seem utterly gullible about it. If someone comes talking about love, then they say they must be of God, they must be "of the truth." But the oldest trick in Satan's bag is to appear to offer the fulfillment of love and desire.

Is that not what we see in the Garden of Eden? The devil comes to Eve and says, "Is it really true that God is so harsh, so difficult, so unloving toward you that he has forbidden you to eat the fruit of a tree? Why, I think more of you than that. I'd never do anything like that to you. Could God actually say a thing like that and be a God of love?" This is the implication of his argument. "Why," says the devil, "if you eat of this fruit you will discover wonderful things. You will become as gods. You will enter a wonderful world that you've never dreamed of before. You will discover the thing you were made for, from which God is trying to keep you. As your friend, as your counselor, I suggest you hold back no longer. Take of the fruit and eat it." Does that not sound familiar? That is exactly the line that cults, isms, and schisms are using everywhere today. "If you really want to *live,* try what we have in stock."

But the Scriptures warn us that the mark of childish immaturity is to be caught up and taken in by that kind of approach, "to be tossed about by every wind of doctrine," every new teaching that comes along. It is childish to gullibly swallow every slick line and go along with it. A mark of maturity, therefore, is unbelief, as well as belief.

John indicates that this is a widespread problem. "Many false prophets," he says, "have gone out into the world." In Matthew's Gospel the Lord Jesus warned of this. "Beware of false prophets" (Matt. 7:15). They are wolves in sheep's clothing, outwardly appearing to be loving, tender, and concerned, but inwardly desiring only to wreck and ruin.

There are *many* false prophets, says John, underlying for us the fact that we live in a world of deceit. We live, in many respects, in a hostile environment in which falsehoods are widely accepted, and we are greatly pressured to conform to these things. In John's day, in the first century, there were teachers going about doing certain signs, perhaps giving predictions of things to come, or manifesting tongues, miracles, and other such things. Of these John writes and says, "Do not believe these spirits—until you have tested them."

Behind False Prophets

First test them. Don't be a sucker; don't believe everyone who comes along. It is important to note that there is here a very clear recognition of what the Bible teaches all the way through: behind the false prophet or false teacher is an evil spirit. Men simply do not speak out of their own intellectual attainments. Quite unconsciously they are being guided—really misguided—by an evil spirit, a "spirit of error," John calls it, an antichristian spirit which is behind these false prophets and teachers.

There is a true Spirit, the Holy Spirit of truth, the Spirit of love, and just as he speaks through men so evil spirits also speak through men. When you hear people talking about religious things or values, do not gullibly swallow everything they say, especially if they appear to be setting forth something about love. Especially test that line; recognize that behind the individual may be a spirit of error.

We moderns are in much greater danger than the ancients, for in the world of John and Paul's day there was a widespread recognition of the existence of invisible spirits, the invisible realities behind the scenes of life. The ancient world recognized these as gods and goddesses, and bowed down to them. Though they seriously misunderstood and twisted these realities, making them into mythological and legendary figures, nevertheless there was a widespread recognition that man does not exist in the universe by himself; there are superior beings who influence the thinking and attitudes of men everywhere. This kind of teaching was therefore much easier to accept in the first century than it is in our day. In the twentieth century we pride ourselves upon the fact that we have grown beyond this; we have come of age. Man is often intellectually unable to accept this kind of thing today. As a result we expose ourselves without any defense at all to the control of these evil spirits.

But if we are going to follow the words of Jesus Christ we must accept his explanation of the power behind evil in the world. He makes clear that it comes from a host of evil spirits. Paul says also, "We are not contending against flesh and blood, but against the principalities, against the powers, . . . against the spiritual hosts of wickedness in the heavenly places" (Eph. 6:12). Part of the blindness of our generation is a direct result of man in his arrogance saying, "I reject the whole concept of evil spirits and demons. It is intellectually unacceptable to me." The blindness of that attitude precludes any defense against evil.

The Test

You must remember that you can never recognize this kind of error by simply reading the arguments. I am not saying it is wrong to read the arguments, but you will not see the error in them that way. Taken by themselves, they always sound clear, convincing, and logical. That is the way error makes its approach to us. The only way to discover it is to do as John says—test it. Test these spirits, try them. Lay them alongside a measuring stick, and if they do not match, throw them out. Well, what is the test?

> By this you know the Spirit of God: every spirit which confesses that Jesus Christ has come in the flesh is of God, and every spirit which does not confess Jesus is not of God. This is the spirit of antichrist, of which you heard that it was coming, and now it is in the world already (1 John 4:2,3).

300 / M<small>AINTAINING</small> L<small>OVE</small>

The test consists of two things: first, the acknowledgment of the historical incarnation of the Son of God, his appearance in history as a man in the flesh. I think almost all biblical scholars are agreed that verse 2 should read this way: ". . . every spirit which confesses that Jesus is Christ, come in the flesh, is of God, . . ." Jesus is his human name. He never was called Jesus before the incarnation. It was only when he was born as a babe in Bethlehem and grew up in Nazareth that he bore the human name of Jesus, "Jesus of Nazareth." But the whole teaching of Scripture is that this historical Jesus who prayed and talked and taught men is the Messiah (Christ) of the Old Testament, the predicted One, the Son of God who was to come—they are one and the same. This is the spirit of truth. Jesus *is* the Christ, come in the flesh. Jesus of Nazareth is identical with—and indivisible from—that promised Messiah of the Old Testament.

It is clear that Jesus makes this claim about himself. In John 10 he says of certain ones who have gone before him,

> Truly, truly I say to you, he who does not enter the sheepfold by the door but climbs in by another way, that man is a thief and a robber [that is, if someone comes to you by another process than the predicted way, the way that has been announced, he is a thief and a robber; he is a false prophet, he is a false Christ, he is an antichrist]; but he who enters by the door is the shepherd of the sheep. To him the gatekeeper opens; the sheep hear his voice, and he calls his own sheep by name and leads them out (John 10:1–3).

He is saying, "I am that good shepherd. I came in the predicted way, the way the prophets announced. I was born in the right place, at the right time, in the right way. I came exactly as it was announced. I am the door and I am the shepherd of the sheep." Now any teacher of spiritual matters who confesses this of Jesus, John says, is of the truth, is of God. But any teacher who stands up and professes to teach men about God but who does not confess this is not of God. Do not listen to him; pay no attention to him. Regardless of how beautifully he talks, he is not of God. He is of the spirit of error, the spirit of antichrist that has already gone out into the world.

Plain language, is it not? It is amazing how we have forgotten and neglected it. This is the paramount doctrine which must never be compromised, the divine-human person of the Lord Jesus Christ. It is the one thing that is basic and fundamental to all Christian faith. He appeared in the flesh; he came as a man, humbled himself, and became obedient unto the death of the cross.

More Than Profession

The second thing that John brings out here is that a teacher must not only acknowledge this as a historical fact, but must also *confess* it. There must be a commitment of his life to this truth. This is what confess means here. It is more than a mere acknowledgment or a profession that this is true; it is a commitment. It means actually to trust this great declared fact and this great historic person. If anyone does not actually trust him and live by him, do not listen to him either.

In the gospel accounts there are demons that acknowledged the deity of the Lord Jesus. When he appeared before them they said, "We know who you are, the Holy One of God." They acknowledged what the Jews were too blind to see, the full deity of Jesus Christ, as well as his humanity. But though demons acknowledged this, they never "confessed" it. They never trusted him. They did not commit themselves to him; they did not live by this truth. Through the course of history there have been many religious leaders, popes, priests, and others, Protestant and Catholic alike, who have acknowledged the deity of the Lord Jesus and his humanity, but who have never committed themselves to him.

There you have the fundamental questions that we

must ask every group or any teacher of religion today: Do you acknowledge the entrance into history of the Son of God as Jesus of Nazareth, the man who labored and loved and died and rose again from the dead? Do you acknowledge that he who was with God from the beginning, and is God, became man and lived among us? Do you acknowledge that? That question ought to be asked of every religious teacher, everywhere. Then, it must be asked, do you follow him? Do you live by this? Are you committed to him—is he your Lord, your strength, and everything you need? How many would fail if we gave that test? How many fail, even at the first question? Just test in your mind some of the voices that speak today in the name of Christ.

There are those who style themselves liberals who say that the Jesus of history is not important to us; that his virgin birth, his miracles, his resurrection, and even his crucifixion are but myths, legends gathered about the figure of the man, Jesus—highly exaggerated ideas that the churches added to the facts. They tell us that these things are not important and that it does not make any difference if he rose from the dead, or if he died on the cross, or if he was born in a manger, of a virgin. These do not make any difference; the great thing is the truth he taught, the things that he said—those are the important things. But John says if they do not confess that Jesus is the Christ, come in the flesh, this is the spirit of error, of antichrist.

I once knew a young man who grew up in a godly home and became a Christian through the influence of his family. When he went away to college his faith was undermined by the clever presentations of teachers who challenged him to think for himself. There is nothing wrong with that, but what was omitted was a standard of thinking, a measurement by which human thought could be evaluated. When that is omitted the result is always that the individual himself becomes the final measuring stick, the standard. This young man fell into that trap. He began to measure everything by what he thought, including the gospel and the Bible and all the things that are in it. Little by little he drifted off into liberalism, or modernism. He became a minister of a liberal church, involved in social crusades, declaring nothing of the gospel, the Word of God, the life-changing message that Christ came to give. But there was an increasing emptiness in his heart and life.

Gradually he found his ministry crumbling, and he was unable to accomplish the things he wanted. He was sincere, earnest, dedicated, but increasingly hungry for something real. Finally, a word from his wife, which irritated him immensely when he first heard it, struck a note of fire in his heart, and the Lord used it to wake him up to the great and saving truth that Jesus Christ alone can change the hearts of men. No social revolution is worth the snap of your finger if it does not rest upon that. He began to preach this and soon his church was changed. His congregation began to come back, the pews began to fill up, and his church became a living force in his community.

Today's Voices

Now measure some of these voices today. Here is the Christian Scientist, who says that Jesus was a man upon whom the Spirit of Christ came. The spirit of Christ is the eternal One and he came upon Jesus at his baptism and left him again before he died upon the cross. Jesus, therefore, was born as a mere man and died as a mere man, and the only part of his ministry that is worth anything to us is his public ministry of teaching, when he was influenced by the Spirit of Christ. But that is not what John says. John says that the spirit which confesses that Jesus *is* the Christ—that the two are identical, one and the same, never to be separated—that is the Spirit which is of God. Anything else is the spirit of error and of antichrist.

Take the gospel of the Mormons. They say that Jesus was a man who became God and came to show us how we, too, might become gods some day. Is that *the* Gospel? Of course not. It is the spirit of error, of antichrist.

There are even many who are orthodox in doctrine and who say "Yes, of course we believe Jesus is the Christ come in the flesh. We have that in our creed; we can show it to you. It is written in our hymnbooks. We confess it every Sunday morning when we stand up in church. 'We believe in God the Father Almighty, and in Jesus Christ, His Son, our Lord.'" But do they *confess* him, do they live by him? Have they committed themselves to this One in whom they profess to believe? This is the searching question John asks. If they do not confess him, if they do not live by him, then do not follow them. Their error is as deadly as those who deny that he came in the flesh. Many young people are finding today that dead orthodoxy has no more power to deliver than heresy and apostasy.

If you do not follow him you can never be my theological teacher. I do not want to listen to any voice that professes to talk about the inner things of man's life and his relationship to an eternal God, who does not confess that Jesus is Christ come in the flesh, or who does not demonstrate in his life that he lives by that principle. Test the spirits!

That is where we must begin. The gospel, the good news, stands or falls by faith in Jesus Christ come in the flesh, and by the availability of his life to us now by which to live and move and have our being. God help us to be unbelievers in error as well as believers in truth.

28

God Is Greater

In the section we come to now, John continues to unfold certain factors relative to the whole matter of truth versus error.

> Little children, you are of God, and have overcome them; for he who is in you is greater than he who is in the world. They are of the world, therefore what they say is of the world, and the world listens to them. We are of God. Whoever knows God listens to us, and he who is not of God does not listen to us. By this we know the spirit of truth and the spirit of error (1 John 4:4–6).

You will note that each of these three verses begins with an emphatic pronoun. That is true both in the Greek and the English. There is first "you"—"*you* are of God." Then in verse five, "*they* are of the world" and in verse six, "*we* are of God." There are three distinct groups set forth here.

The first group is addressed as "little children," the readers of this letter, and they are said to be "of God." Obviously these are Christians who, John declares, have overcome the false teachers; that is, they have escaped their blandishments and have not been deluded by their error. They have heard all the arguments of the false teachers and have been enabled to see through them. So he says, "You are of God and have overcome these false teachers."

The important thing in this verse is to note the ground of their victory. How was it that they overcame? If there is any way that we can escape the extreme pressures of theological error today, it will be by this same method. This way is indicated not so much by what he says as by what he does not say. These "little children" who are "of God" overcame the false teachers, but not because they had a superior intelligence. John says nothing about them being smarter than the teachers. Nor was it because they had been subjected to intensive training in the cults. There is no word about that, either. Nor is it that they had been supported and bulwarked by clever arguments with which they were able to answer the errors of the teachers. Nor was it their broad theological knowledge. What John says is, "You overcame them *because he who is in you is greater than he who is in the world.*" In other words, it was not anything these Christians had in themselves that delivered them; it was the One who dwelt within them. It was the greatness of God that kept them straight. It was the fact that God was greater than the spirit that was at work behind the teachers of error. This is what will keep us straight today.

Despite all the appearances, God is greater than the power of the enemy. In fact, it is almost ludicrous to put it that way. God is so much greater that there is simply no contest. This is where the eye of faith must always turn in hours of darkness, discomfort, or despair; turn to what the Scriptures reveal as the truth about God and how incomparably great he is. Read of God's greatness in Isaiah 40, where the prophet cries out at the unbelief of the people of God in verse 21:

Have you not known? Have you not heard? Has it not been told you from the beginning?

"What is the matter with you people?" he is saying. "Why all this gloom and despair? Why this mood of pessimism? Why this wringing of the hands and rending of your clothes? Haven't you been told what God is like?" He goes on:

Have you not understood from the foundations of the earth?

It is he who sits above the circle of the earth, and its inhabitants are like grasshoppers; who stretches out the heavens like a curtain, and spreads them like a tent to dwell in; who brings princes to nought, and makes the rulers of the earth as nothing. . . .

To whom then will you compare me, that I should be like him? says the Holy One. Lift up your eyes on high . . . (Isa. 40:21–23,25,26).

That is what people need to do in these days of darkness.

Lift up your eyes on high and see: who created these? He who brings out their host by number, calling them all by name; by the greatness of his might, and because he is strong in power not one is missing.

Why do you say, O Jacob, and speak, O Israel, "My way is hid from the Lord . . ." (Isa. 40:26,27).

He is saying, Do you think that God is unaware of what is happening in your life and the problems that you are going through? Why do you talk like this? "'. . . and my right is disregarded by my God'?" (Isa. 40:27). Would that we could get men to hear that today when so many are insisting upon their rights and saying that no one is standing up for them. The prophet says, "Imagine thinking that your right has been disregarded by God."

Have you not known? Have you not heard?

The Lord is the everlasting God, the Creator of the ends of the earth.

> He does not faint or grow weary. . . . He gives power to the faint, and to him who has no might he increases strength (Isa. 40:28,29).

Do you remember what Paul says in his first letter to the Corinthians? As he came into Corinth, that beautiful city of the golden age of Greece, with its great love of wisdom, he foreswore every approach on the basis of human wisdom and said, "I decided to know nothing among you except Jesus Christ and him crucified" (1 Cor. 2:2). The reason he gave was that the weakness of God is stronger than men and the foolishness of God is wiser than men. That is, even when God acts in some way that seems to be utterly weak, it is still stronger than anything that man can do. When God says things that appear to be utter folly, if followed they will prove to be wiser than anything man has ever said. That is the greatness of God. God is greater than all else. "He who is in you is greater than he who is in the world."

I love that wonderful cry of triumph from the apostle Paul in Romans 11, after he concludes his great treatise on the providence of God and the free will of man:

> O the depth of the riches and wisdom and knowledge of God! How unsearchable are his judgments and how inscrutable his ways! For who has known the mind of the Lord, or who has been his counselor? Or who has given a gift to him that he might be repaid? For from him and through him and to him are all things. To him be glory for ever. Amen (Rom. 11:33–36).

Now the point of all this, as John brings out, is that all this incomparable wisdom is available to the humblest Christian believer. Therefore, there isn't a chance that he will be swept away by the silken errors of the day, attractive and alluring as they may be, *if* he combines the two things that John mentions here. These two factors guarantee deliverance: They are to be "of God" and to be "little children."

It is not by accident that John uses this title, "little children," for that name indicates the childlike trust of one who believes the Word of God. You don't have to fully understand it; simply accept it, trust it, and act on it. You will discover that all the wisdom and greatness and superior intelligence of God is imparted through that simple word, and though it may appear foolish to others it is wiser than men. He who in childlike faith trusts the Word to guide him through life will find that he will be safely kept through all entrapping errors. He can sing,

> Thro' many dangers, toils and snares,
> I have already come;
> 'Tis grace hath bro't me safe thus far
> And grace will lead me home.

God is greater, and it is this simple trust in his wisdom that makes it possible for us to lay hold of the greatness of God.

Now it is right here that the subtle attack of the enemy occurs, as I mentioned briefly in the last chapter. The world, in its general outlook, is hostile to the faith of Christians. But often in colleges and universities there is a clever and subtle approach to unbelief. It always begins the same way, with the suggestion that it is necessary for each to think for himself, to judge everything by the light of whether it appears reasonable to him. Thus the mind of man becomes the ultimate test, the ultimate authority of all life. It *is* necessary for man to reason and it *is* necessary for him to think for himself and to examine things. But we are creatures under God, and we can never examine accurately or rightly until we begin with the basic recognition that all of man's thinking, blinded and shadowed as it is with the confusion of sin, must be measured by the Word of God which is the ultimate authority.

That is what can help us to know whether we are right or wrong, whether we are living according to reality or drifting off into a never-never land of relativity and fantasy. The drift into error begins by forgetting that the authority being challenged is that of Jesus Christ. The authority of the Scriptures is the authority of Christ. He himself said the Scriptures are the Word of God. He is the one who solved the most unsolvable problem of human life; he rose from the dead! Who else has done that in human history? Who else has ever presented that kind of credentials to be believed? So it all comes back to the authority of Jesus Christ.

But in arguing with unbelievers you don't begin with the authority of the Scriptures. It is wrong for Christians to think that the first thing we have to do in presenting the Christian faith is to convince people to accept the Bible as true. What they should be asked to accept is the living Christ, the Lord Jesus; to come into a personal relationship with him. Then, having come to know him, and having discovered in their own life that he is real, that he lives, that he delivers, that he changes, that he transforms, on *that* basis, they are to accept the authority of the Word of God. That is a quite different approach, isn't it? When they once come to Christ, then they are to accept the Word, and if they trust it in simple, childlike faith, they will discover that it has a way of taking them safely past all the devious errors of men and all the clever stratagems of the enemy, into life as God intended it to be lived. One of the most helpful passages to me, as a young Christian, was Proverbs 3:5,6:

> Trust in the Lord with all your heart, and do not rely on your own insight. In all your ways acknowledge him, and he will make straight your paths.

What a safe guide through life that is! God is greater than the spirit of the world.

Now look back to 1 John 4:5:

> They are of the world, therefore what they say is of the world, and the world listens to them.

"They" here are the false teachers of all varieties, including both those who rant and rave and those who speak in cultured tones and with apparent logic. They are "of the world." The one revealing thing about them is that they say what the world wants to hear; therefore, they are almost invariably popular. Let some theologian come out with a startling statement that denies some fundamental Christian truth and it is spread across the papers immediately. Soon a "school of thought" is formed and begins to spread as others jump on the bandwagon.

The world listens to them. Why? Because they are saying what the world wants to hear. And what is that? Well, if you analyze what they are saying, you will find, running as an undercurrent through everything they say, a basic assumption of the greatness and glory of man. The world loves to hear man exalted. "How smart we are. How mature we are. We have 'come of age' at last. We are right on the verge of being able to manipulate every earthly force to our advantage. How clever we are at solving the problems of man." That is said in the face of the most astounding and appalling chaos existing on every side and growing every moment. Isn't it amazing that man can have such intellectual pride in the face of such momentous failure? Yet that is what the world wants to hear, and so the popularity of these false teachers is assured.

Now John concludes in verse 6: "We are of God." Who does he mean? Here he is speaking of the apostles, of which he was one. "We apostles," he says, in union with you who are Christians, are "of God." We form a special band of authoritative apostles who were with the Lord Jesus and have been commissioned to the task of declaring authoritatively the full message of Christianity.

> We are of God. Whoever knows God listens to us, and he who is not of God does not listen to us.

John could say that the apostles were of God because

he, with the other twelve, was one with Jesus Christ. They had entered into a union and a relationship with him that grew out of hearing his teachings. John, in his Gospel, says this awareness came to them all rather gradually. They watched him. They listened to him. They followed him. They saw the things that he did, and gradually an increasing awareness dawned on them, which John records in these words—

And the Word became flesh and dwelt among us, full of grace and truth; we have beheld his glory, glory as of the only Son from the Father (John 1:14).

Their growing faith was weakened and shattered by the crucifixion, but on the morning of the resurrection they were convinced again, almost against their will. They could hardly believe this incredible thing, that he who was dead was alive again. But they had to acknowledge it by the evidence of their own senses. Here was one who had broken through the bonds of death. They saw him, they handled him, they felt him, they touched him, they lived with him again for forty days and forty nights, and they were convinced.

Then finally, on the day of Pentecost, all doubt was taken away forever when, in the courts of the temple, as the Lord Jesus had promised, the Holy Spirit was poured out upon them and they were commissioned to begin the task of heralding this great message unto the far corners of the earth. That is why he says "we are of God"; therefore, those "who are of God listen to us."

Here is another test of truth and error. He says,

By this we know the spirit of truth and the spirit of error.

Do men receive the apostolic witness, or do they think that to sit behind a desk in some American city, removed by some five thousand miles from the scene of these amazing events and by twenty centuries of history, somehow makes them know more than the apostles of the Lord Jesus? "No," John says, "we are of God and those who are of God listen to us."

That was one of the things which encouraged the apostle Paul when he came into the Greek city of Corinth. He had encountered much opposition there. A rising tide of resistance was mounting against him. One night the Lord appeared to him when he was sorely tempted by discouragement and said to him, "Do not be afraid, but speak and do not be silent; for I am with you, and no man shall attack you to harm you; for I have many people in this city" (Acts 18:9,10).

Now what did he mean? These "many people" were not Christians yet. They were pagans. But they were "of God" in the sense that they were willing to listen. They were open to the Word of God. They were ready to hear what God had to say. So Jesus said, "Paul, while you go about the city preaching the Word of God, don't worry. Out in that crowd, though you won't be able to tell them from any others, are some in whom my Spirit is working, and they will hear what you have to say. Others will not hear, but those who hear will come to you." This is what Jesus meant when he said, "All that my Father has given me shall come unto me." This is the sign then of truly open hearts. Do they hear the apostolic witness? Do they believe what the apostles have said?

29

Love Made Visible

The Christian faith has always emphasized two very important things: truth and love. Jesus Christ himself was the preeminent expression of both of these, truth and love, held in perfect balance. He was fully the expression of truth, and fully the expression of love. Therefore Christianity, which is but the expression of his life in the world, is to be an experience of "truthing in love." That is the literal rendering of the phrase which Paul uses in Ephesians, "speaking the truth in love" (Eph. 4:15). Christianity is to be "truthing in love," living the truth in love.

Among the tactics of the devil, by which he seeks to overthrow and disrupt Christian faith, one of the most common is simply to overemphasize a truth. This is what he does in this matter of truth and love. All he needs to do, to distort Christianity, is to produce the one without the other.

To emphasize love at the expense of truth is to produce what is usually called liberalism, with its blindness to the hard realities of sin and evil in human life, and its glowing proclamations of sweetness and light. On the other hand, to emphasize truth at the expense of love produces a cold, legalistic fundamentalism which, though it holds to the right creed, is as empty of genuine Christian life as is

314

the former. Increasingly I meet individuals whose Christian faith has been sorely shaken, if not completely disrupted, by exposure to vicious attack and railing abuse from certain Christians who are self-appointed defenders of the faith and accusers of the brethren. In the light of what the apostle John has to say to us now, beginning with verse 7 of chapter 4, this kind of conduct on the part of professed Christians raises serious questions about the genuineness of their faith.

> Beloved, let us love one another; for love is of God, and he who loves is born of God and knows God. He who does not love does not know God; for God is love (1 John 4:7,8).

Three times in the immediate context of this passage the phrase "love one another" occurs. It is here in verse 7, also in verse 11, "Beloved, if God so loved us, we also ought to love one another," and in verse 12, "No man has ever seen God; if we love one another, God abides in us. . . ." Obviously, the primary exhortation here is this threefold repetition, "love one another."

Each Is Another

The nature of this love is inherent in the very statement John makes. "Love one *another,*" he says. Thereby it is indicated that love is not to be only for those who are pleasant to us, or who are nice, congenial, clever people. We are not to love because people are lovable, but because each is *another.* Every one is a person, capable of a unique relationship to God, and therefore not a "thing" to be dealt with impersonally, or to be opposed or accepted as it suits our purpose, but a living, breathing, searching creation of God, just like us. That is why we are to love one another, without regard to what that person is like.

This is the sort of love the Bible talks about. True love is an interest in, and a concern for, another person just because he is a person, and for no other reason. It does not matter whether he is rich or poor, black or white, old or young, male or female, Republican or Democrat; it makes absolutely no difference. He or she is a person. Love takes no notice of what a person is like, or what he does, or how he dresses, or anything about his background. It sees one thing only and that is, "Here is another person, another one like me with all the longings, the heartaches, the hopes, dreams, and frustrations of life like me. Here is another one, struggling as I am to face the problems of life. What can I do to help?" That is love.

As John marvelously declares, that kind of love can only originate with God. This kind of love is "of God." In fact, God *is* this kind of love, God *is* love. Therefore, wherever the life of God is present that love is found. And if that love is not found, the life of God is not present. The argument is clear, is it not? It is no good claiming that you know God if the love of God is not found in your life. If you cannot treat people objectively and see through the irritating qualities that may offend you and be nice to them because they are in need of love; if your reaction to those who offend you is one of opposition, rejection, and instant antagonism, then it is no good saying you belong to God. That is not God's life; that is not God's love. John's argument is that if the life of God is present in us then the love of God will be there, too.

The Fountain of God's Activity

Here we come face to face with that tremendous declaration of the Scriptures, "God is love." As John Stott says, "This is the most comprehensive and sublime of all the biblical affirmations of God's being." It means that at the root of all God does is love. No matter how difficult it may appear to us, the fountain from which all God's activity stems is this kind of self-giving love. Even his judgments and his condemnations arise from love. We need to understand this. Judgment is not something separate from love. If you convince me that a holy, loving God cannot judge an evil being, then you will also convince me that he cannot love him. It is inherent in the quality of love to be antagonistic to that which opposes the thing loved.

You see that in every mother. Attack a child with the mother present and see how that mother-love flames out in immediate antagonism to all that threatens her loved one. God's love is the same. Inherent in it is the quality of judgment. God is a purifying fire, consuming and burning away the dross in order that he might preserve the gold. That is exactly how the Book of Hebrews describes him: "Our God is a consuming fire" (Heb. 12:29). Love is not always easy to live with because of that very quality. Yet it is the most attractive and wonderful thing in the world because of its all-embracing inclusiveness.

Dr. H. A. Ironside used to tell of a woman who came to him and said, "I don't have any use for the Bible and for all this Christian superstition. It's enough for me to know that God is love." He said to her, "Well, do you know that?" She said, "Of course I know that; I've known it all my life." "Well," he said, "do you think that everyone knows that?" "Oh, yes," she said. "Everyone knows God is love."

"Well," he said, "do you think that the woman over in India, who is persuaded by her religion to take her little child and throw it into the river as an offering to the crocodile god has any concept or idea that God is love?" She said, "Well, no, but that's mere superstition." "Do you think that the savage in Africa, bowing down to his idols of wood and stone, trembling with fear lest they should strike back at him and destroy his crops and take away his children and even injure his own person, has any idea that God is love?" he asked. She said, "No, but in every civilized country we know that God is love."

"How do we know that?" he asked. "How do we know that God is love? Do the ancients teach this? Do the other religions of earth teach that God is love, and show that God is love? Let me tell you something: The only reason we know that God is love is because he sent his Son and manifested himself as love. The book that tells about the Lord Jesus Christ is the only book in the world that contains the idea that the God behind all created matter is a God of love. Creation reveals his power, his greatness, and his might, but there is nothing in nature that says 'God is love.' The only way we know it is that God manifested his love in the giving of his Son."

John moves on to declare this, in verses 9 and 10:

> In this the love of God was made manifest among us, that God sent his only Son into the world, so that we might live through him. In this is love, not that we loved God but that he loved us and sent his Son to be the expiation for our sins.

Note again the character of love; it is love for the unlovely. "God so loved the world. . . ." What world? Why, the world made up of men and women like you, like me. The world that consists of the people who fill the pages of our newspapers with the ugly reports that are so abounding these days. Some time ago a mother said to me, "I've come to the place where I almost hate my son." Why? The evil in her son had turned her against him. The evil in him had so offended her, that which was ugly and wrong in him had loomed as such a frightful thing, that she had found her love almost turned to hate.

Some time ago a husband and wife who were in my study for counseling became so angry that the husband stood up, right in my presence, and spat in his wife's face. Yet he had promised to love, honor, and cherish her until death should part them. Why would he do such a thing? Because the evil and ugliness of sin in his wife (though he was not seeing the same in his own life), so enraged him that he struck out against it. It offended him; it was repulsive, revolting to him.

God's Response

How angry we get sometimes at the stubbornness and insolence of others, the rudeness and hate that is manifested toward us. It makes our blood boil and our tempers rise; we burn and writhe within. Yet that evil is in the heart of all those born of Adam. It is constantly revealing itself to the eyes of God. It may be hidden away from others, and even from our own eyes, but God, who sees all things, sees the world of men in all their blatant ugliness and evil. And what is his response? Is it anger? Is it rejection? Is it judgment? Did he pour out the fires of wrath upon a world so repulsively ugly as that? Oh, no, he responded with the most costly of all loves: he gave himself; he sent his Son. In the Person of his Son, God himself came and lived among us and died upon a cross of shame in the very world his hands had made. Why? As John says: "that we might live through him." Is that not love? Does that not grip you? He did it so that all the chains of fear, hate, and evil which bind us and shackle us might be broken, and quarreling and abuse might cease between human beings. He came so that it all might be replaced, not by negative nothingness, but by patience, acceptance, and the power to remain calm—"in order that we might live."

John says if you want to measure love, use that as your standard. Do not measure love by the warm affection of your heart toward God, the gratitude you feel toward God. Naturally, if God has blessed, helped, and strengthened you, you will feel a warm affection toward him arising within you, but that is not the measure of love. God is altogether lovable, but do not define love as that quality of warmth and gratitude which rises up when you meet a lovable and lovely person. That is not love. "In *this* is love, not that we loved God but that he loved us and sent his Son to be the expiation for our sins." That is the sign of love. Stamped forever in human history, the greatest sign of love is a bloody cross. If you have ever been to that cross and seen the love of God manifested there, you never can go back to a life of selfish indulgence and quarreling behavior.

Will you notice, in verse 10, the linking of love and expiation? There are those who tell us that God's love is comparable to that of an indulgent grandfather, that he loves us so much that he will let us get away with anything. He will forgive solely on the basis of his kindness to us. He will not demand an accounting, nor will his love ever insist on any punishment. But no; "in *this* is love, not that we loved God but that he loved us," and—what? "sent his Son to be the expiation [a propitiation] for our sins." He came to satisfy justice, to meet the demands of a broken law, to pay the full debt, to satisfy the penalty. It all must be met; it cannot be ignored. God's law is also involved. God's love is just—love must be just—and therefore the only love that is worth talking about is a love that satisfies justice. Love that satisfies justice is righteousness.

Our Debt to Others

Now in this last pair of verses, we will see a declaration of the possibility of this kind of love among us, as well as its perfectibility.

> Beloved, if God so loved us, we also ought to love one another. No man has ever seen God; if we love one another, God abides in us and his love is perfected in us (1 John 4:11,12).

Verse 11 is the answer to every lame excuse on our part which says, "Oh, I just can't love that person. You don't know what she's like. If you had to live with her (or him) as I have to, you wouldn't be able to love her either." But

John says, "Beloved, if God so loved us. . . ." If you have experienced this kind of love, if you have been to the cross and have felt the overwhelming cleansing of God's love for you, despite the antagonism and hatefulness you have shown him, then, John says, you not only *can* love someone else but you "ought" to—you owe it to them. This is why Paul cries in Romans, "Owe no man anything, except to love one another" (Rom. 13:8). We owe it, because we have within us the fountain of love in the life of God.

Of course, if you do not have the life of God, you cannot love one another like this. Do not try—admit that you cannot. Above all, do not come up with a shabby, sleazy imitation of love, that is nice to another's face but cuts him to death behind his back. That is not love, nor is love merely to tolerate another for a time. Unless you have the life of God you cannot love. But if you *have* the life of God—that is the whole point—you can love like this, and you ought to do it. God, in you, can love through you and will love through you. All he is waiting for is the acquiescence of your will, your willingness to love; then he will do the loving.

Verse 12 declares a great and daring concept. It recognizes that God is invisible and that no man has ever seen God. How true this is. Even in the Old Testament days, though manifestations of God appeared in human form, these were but God in human disguise. It was not God made visible. There is a sense in which it is possible to say, "I have never seen you, and you have never seen me." You see this tabernacle, this shabby, rather tattered tent in which I live. But you have not seen me, and I have not seen you. Men, like God, are spirits and invisible. I can feel the force of your personality, and I can certainly see that there is a spirit living in that tent of yours, but I have not seen you, and you have not seen me. So also no man has ever seen God at any time. God is a Spirit, and therefore invisible. This is why the love of God cannot be demonstrated in nature, cannot be made visible in God's creation. Well, where is it made visible? John says, "If we love one another, God abides in us and his love is perfected [reaches its final end] in us" (v. 12). That is where men see God's love, and it is the only place it can be seen.

The fact of an indwelling God becomes visible only when we manifest love one to another, the kind of love that we have been talking about. As long as we are nice only to our friends or to those who are nice to us, no one has any idea that God is around. But when we start being nice to those who are nasty to us, when we start returning good for evil, when we start being patient, tender, thoughtful, and considerate of those who are stubborn, obstinate, and selfish and say difficult things to us, then people get the sense that God is somewhere around, close at hand, that he is in the situation. Then God's dwelling in us becomes visible to them.

The Gospel According to You

Men today are unacquainted with the Gospel according to Matthew or Luke or John, but every man is somewhere reading the Gospel according to You. If they cannot read it clearly it is because there is not much manifestation of the love of God in your life, as a Christian. But it is there if God's life is there. So the appeal of the apostle John is, "let us" do this. This is not an automatic thing; it demands also the agreement of our will. Let us deliberately love one another. Let us make channels for this life to be manifested. Let us allow it to be expressed in deliberate activities of kindness, thoughtfulness, and consideration, one to another, and of understanding, patience, and tolerance of each other's views.

The result is staggering: What John says is that God's love, this love pouring out from this amazing Being whose concern for the vast millions of earth is individual, each one wrapped in his amazing love, *this* love is perfected only when it becomes visible in us. Is that not amazing? God's love reaches its ultimate and final conclusion *only* when it becomes visible in us. It is an abortive thing, incomplete, and therefore untouchable, incomprehensible, until it finds its manifestation in a living human being, in flesh and blood, incarnate again in you and me.

30

Love's Accomplishments

God loves the world. As John says, he manifested his love in the sending of his Son. He came into the world, the very world his hands had made, and died here upon a cross of shame. In the mystery of those hours when darkness fell across the face of the land, some strange and remarkable thing happened to the lonely Sufferer upon the cross. The sins of the world were laid on him and he became the propitiation for our sins. His total willingness to do that marked the full extent of his love for us.

Now where God's life is, God's love will be. This is the whole argument of the central part of John's letter. As we saw last, he says in verse 12, "No man has ever seen God; [but] if we love one another, God abides in us and his love is perfected in us." These two themes—God's abiding in us and the perfecting of his love—form the subject of John's conclusion to this section.

First, there is the relationship of belief to love:

By this we know that we abide in him and he in us, because he has given us of his own Spirit. And we have seen and testify that the Father has sent his Son as the Savior of the world. Whoever confesses that Jesus is the Son of God, God abides in him, and he in God. So we know and believe the love God has for us. God is love, and he who abides in love abides in God, and God abides in him (1 John 4:13–16).

If you will recall, this chapter began with a warning against wrong belief. "Test the spirits," says John; "don't believe every voice that speaks in the name of Jesus these days, but test the spirits, whether they be of God." There is one supreme test, doctrinally. There must be an acknowledgment that Jesus is the Christ, that he has come in the flesh. By this you can tell the difference between the spirit of truth and the spirit of error. That is John's emphasis on belief. Then, in verse 7, he moves right on to talk about love, with an exhortation to love one another.

Product of Faith

In this present section, he brings these two together, belief and love, and shows us the relationship between them. It is belief that produces love! Perhaps you have never thought of it that way, for most of us think love is produced by happy circumstances, or by nice people, or by spending time together. But John tells us where love really originates. "Faith," he says, "produces love," and he proves his point here. In verses 13 and 14 he is referring to himself and the rest of the apostles: "By this," he says, *"we* know that *we* abide in him." That is, we apostles understand that we are of God and have a continuous relationship to God. How? "Because he has given us of his Spirit." It is not "because he has given us his Spirit." It is true that on the day of Pentecost when the Spirit of God was poured out upon these apostles and the other believers, all their doubts about Jesus Christ were forever settled. When the Spirit of God came to perform his function of taking the things of Christ and making him real to them, they realized that they knew Jesus better on the day of Pentecost than they had ever known him when he was here in the flesh. They understood his purposes and his program far more clearly then than they ever did when he walked, lived, and talked among them. The Spirit could make Christ more real than he ever was when they knew him in the flesh, and that convinced them that they were "of God."

But what he really says here is, "he has given us *out of* his Spirit," he has poured out from his Spirit, by means of his Spirit, something. The context helps us to know what that is: it is love. Remember that Paul says, "God's love has been poured into our hearts through the Holy Spirit which has been given to us" (Rom. 5:5). Love, God's love, the kind that accepts people for what they are regardless of what they are like, is a product only of the Spirit of God. He has given us *out of* his own Spirit, and John says, that is why we know that we are of God, because the kind of love that only God can produce is in our lives and in our hearts. Now he goes on:

And we have seen and testify that the Father has sent his Son as the Savior of the world (v. 14).

Here you can see clearly that he must mean only the apostles. "We have seen him," he says; "we beheld him, we touched him, we felt him, we knew that he was alive from the dead, and we now testify that he was sent as the Savior of the world." This kind of witnessing, of course, followed the coming of the Spirit on the day of Pentecost, as Jesus had said it would. "You shall receive power when the Holy Spirit has come upon you; and you shall be my witness . . . to the end of the earth" (Acts 1:8). They began to testify *after* they received the Holy Spirit. John reminds us that they had the evidence of his love by the Spirit, and they began to pour out in power the testimony that the Father had sent his Son to be the Savior of the world.

Always the Son

Notice something important about that witness: he says that "the Father sent the Son." Many people are confused about this and think that Jesus became the Son of God when he was born in Bethlehem. But he was the Son *before* he came. The Father sent the Son. Christ Jesus was the *eternal* Son of God, and always the Son. This relationship of Father and Son is an eternal relationship. It was as the Son that he came to become the Savior of the world.

Again, notice that it does not say that he came to save the world. He does not save the world. He came *as* the Savior of the world; that is, all the world could be saved if they would be. But as the Scriptures make abundantly clear, it is only those who believe who are saved. Jesus said to certain Jews of his own day, "You will die in your sins unless you believe that I am he" (John 8:24). So, though he came to be the Savior of the world, in the sense of providing a redemption adequate for everyone everywhere, it is only effective to those who lay hold of it by faith in his word, and make it personal in their lives.

Now John says that what happened to the apostles will happen to you, if you believe:

Whoever confesses that Jesus is the Son of God, God abides in him, and he in God. So we know and believe the love God has for us. God is love, and he who abides in love abides in God, and God abides in him (1 John 4:15,16).

When you believe and confess that Jesus is the Son of God (that is, you take him as *your* Lord), it means that God's life is in you. Where his life is, his love will be, because love always follows the life of God. Therefore, you will begin to love. Faith produces love. Your faith produces the love that accepts persons without distinction. Put in another way, the theology which robs Christ of his deity also robs man of the one belief that can generate love within him. Thus, to weaken faith is to deaden love.

John goes on now to show us the tremendous practical effects of this kind of love. First, there is confidence in the day of judgment:

> In this is love perfected with us, that we may have confidence for the day of judgment, because as he is so are we in this world (1 John 4:17).

Confidence in the day of judgment! I doubt if there is a single person who does not realize, deep in his heart, that at the end of life there is an accounting. We must stand before the Lord our Maker. It does not make any difference whether we are Christians or non-Christians. Our relationship with him may be different but we must all come face-to-face with the Lord himself. He stands at the end of every path anyone may take. This is what Paul declared to the Athenian intellectuals on Mars Hill, God "has fixed a day on which he will judge the world in righteousness by a man whom he has appointed, and of this he has given assurance to all men by raising him from the dead" (Acts 17:31). That day lies ahead for us all.

The Crucial Test

But when we stop to think about it we cannot help but ask ourselves: how am I going to do in that day? Can I pass the test that Jesus speaks of in Matthew 25, when he stands to judge the nations and places the sheep on his right hand, the goats on his left? He will say to the people on his right, "Blessed are you of my Father; enter into the inheritance which the Father has prepared for you from the foundation of the earth." Why? "Because when I was naked and hungry and in prison and sick, you visited me, you helped me, you did something for me, you ministered to my need." Do you remember their reaction? "Lord, *when* did this happen? We weren't aware of it. We don't remember seeing you, we don't remember doing these things."

Again, he says to those on his left, "Depart into everlasting judgment." Why? "Because when you saw me weak and sick and in prison, you did nothing about it. You passed on your way, you showed no concern, you displayed no compassion, you did nothing." Again, remember that they said, with surprise, "Why Lord, *when* did this happen? We don't have any memory of it. We don't recall it. If we had seen you we'd have done something, but we don't even remember seeing you." Of course the searching revelation of that passage is that this is now happening all about us. Christ is in all these situations of need, and when we are confronted with someone who has a need it is Jesus who is asking our help. Our reaction to that person is our reaction to him.

Notice that John says it is love "perfected" which gives us confidence in the day of judgment. Love which is perfected is love made visible in deeds. We saw that in verse 12: "If we love one another," he says, "his love is perfected in us." Love perfected expresses itself in deeds, as he said in chapter 3: "Little children, let us not love in word or speech but in deed and in truth" (v. 18). Love, even God's love, can never find its end, its perfection, until it is expressed in a deed or word or compassionate act. Therefore, note what John is saying. If you want to have boldness and confidence in the day of judgment, let love express itself, because it is when love is perfected that we have confidence for the day of judgment.

Will you pass that test? You will if you understand what John means by this wonderful little phrase at the end of the verse: "because as he is so are we in this world." That is one of the most profound statements in the Word of God—yet it is couched in the simplest of language—every word is a monosyllable. "As he is so are we in this world." That simply means that as Christ is now, invisibly, we are, in this world, visibly. That is to say, the secret of Christian living is not in our feeble efforts to do something in imitation of him or in response to his command; it is to recognize his willingness to do all that he demands in us, to live in us. Paul says, "It is no longer I who live"—no longer I, trying my best to imitate and obey the commands of Jesus Christ—"but Christ who lives in me; and the life I now live in the flesh I live by faith in the Son of God" (Gal. 2:20). All that he is, is continuously available to me; therefore whatever I do by faith, it is he who is doing it.

You can see what confidence this gives in the day of judgment. If he is going to look at my life and see the activity of himself in me, he will certainly not deny himself at the day of judgment. I know that what I am doing, if it stems from this source, is wholly acceptable to him, and therefore I can have confidence in his presence.

Some years ago a group of us were in Newport Beach, California, having a prayer breakfast together. It was one of those times when it was very evident that the Spirit of God was working in unusual ways. Afterward, I overheard two men speaking together. One of them said, "Oh, wasn't this wonderful! You know, I think God was really pleased at what happened this morning." And the other one said, "Well, he ought to be; he did it." That says it exactly, does it not? It is God's activity in us that is the basis of his approval on the day of judgement.

Fear's Restraint

The second thing that love accomplishes is in verse 18:

> There is no fear in love, but perfect love casts out fear. For fear has to do with punishment, and he who fears is not perfected in love.

Love accomplishes something, not only for the future, but for now. It casts out fear now. It gives us complete freedom from fear. Before we look further at this I want to adjust the translation a bit. Where it says that "fear has to do with punishment" it should read, "fear *has* punishment." Even more literally, perhaps, since this word for punishment comes from a root word which means to limit or to restrain, John is saying that fear has limitation, fear imprisons us. Anxieties, tensions, worries, apathy—all these forms of fear literally imprison us, they limit us. I have known people who were unable to go outside the door of their house because of fear. I have seen Christian people who were unable to drive their cars, or who were afraid to meet people. Fear limits our life, pushes us into corners and keeps us there, and we cannot live as God intended us to live.

John puts his finger on what is wrong when such fears arise. He who fears is not perfected in love. That is the trouble; that is the diagnosis. Love may be in him, if the life of God is there, but it is not perfected; it is not taking the form of deeds and words, but is all inside. That is the trouble. Love, perfected, casts out fear. Do you dare try that? What a dramatic solution to the problems of fear and anxiety, and yet, how wonderfully effective it is.

There are those who have the life of God and yet never let it out. Their pride and self-pity bind them up, and they do not want to show love; they are afraid to. They are afraid it will open them up to be hurt, or that it will give someone an advantage over them, and so they bottle it up, keep it in, and then they wonder why they are oppressed by anxieties, tensions, and problems of nervousness. They are limited, unable to move and do as they ought to.

But love, perfected, casts out fear. John is not talking about a perfect kind of love; but love that accomplishes its purpose. I have often seen people begin to show love to someone else, feebly at first, tentatively, perhaps just saying a kind word, but beginning to minister to another's need. As they continued to do so they found their own hearts flooded with release and deliverance. Gradually they were set free and able to be what they were intended to be.

Trapped in Self-Pity

I remember a woman who told me how empty her life had become. She had a husband whom she loved, and a child, and she wanted to show love toward them, but she said, "Every morning when I get up I feel so dead and dull, so lifeless. I lack motivation to do my housework. I just sit around. I don't want to talk to people." What is this but a description of imprisonment? As we talked together I explained to her that her problem was self-pity. She was feeling sorry for herself and blaming it on others, blaming everything that was wrong on something else.

She went back home and time went by. I did not know how things were going until one day a letter came. She wrote, "I just want to tell you what God has done in my life. When I went home after our talk, I heard what you said, but I didn't agree with you. I spent weeks trying to fight what was wrong, and I kept trying to blame everyone else—my husband, my in-laws—everyone else was wrong. I was feeling sorry for myself, but I kept hearing that little voice within saying, 'The trouble is you. It is you. You're not showing love; you're not laying hold of the possibilities God has given you.' One day I became so sick and tired of being miserable that I decided I'd try it. I decided to forget about myself and show some love and concern to others and to rejoice in what God was to me, refusing to blame others. I still have problem periods, but oh, what a difference! Now I love to get up in the morning. The day looks exciting and adventurous to me, and I find myself filled with joy and love once again." What had happened? Why, love perfected had done what God says it will do; it had cast out fear.

Finally, in these last verses, look at love's possibility:

We love, because he first loved us. If any one says, "I love God," and hates his brother, he is a liar; for he who does not love his brother whom he has seen, cannot love God whom he has not seen. And this commandment we have from him, that he who loves God should love his brother also (1 John 4:19–21).

I like the bluntness of this apostle. He lays it right on the line. Look, he says, where does love come from? Don't forget, we love because he first loved us. If you know the love of God, if you know how fully he accepts you, even as stinky, nasty, and miserable as you are, then you know what love is. You can love, because you have been loved. "We love, because he first loved us." It does not say, "We love *him*"; it says, "We love—anyone—because he first loved us."

Then John really takes the gloves off. He says, "Look, don't be self-deceived about this. It is very easy to kid yourself. But if you can say, 'I love God,' and yet you hate your brother, you're kidding yourself. You're a liar. How can you love God, whom you can't see at all, and not love your brother, when you can see his needs, and what love can do in his life? God doesn't need your love, but your brother does." Also, the commandment of God, always based upon his availability to make it possible, is, "that he who loves God should love his brother also." If we have the life of God, we can show the love of God.

People will scratch and fight like wildcats to say they cannot love someone, when God says that they can. We want to find an excuse for lovelessness. But it is not that we cannot love; it is that we will not. Is that not true? Then let us face it. John deals bluntly and honestly with us. If you *really* cannot, then you are not a Christian, he says. You are a liar when you say you love God. But if you love him, and you know you do, then you can love your brother—and you must!

Book Five

Maintaining Assurance

31

We Shall Overcome

In this last chapter the apostle John discusses the fifth of the series of themes that he has taken up in this Epistle. The first was the theme of maintaining fellowship, then followed maintaining truth, maintaining righteousness, maintaining love, and now he concludes with the theme of maintaining assurance, or confidence.

The relationship between these five themes is extremely important. The first of these links with the last; that is, fellowship with Christ ends in assurance or confidence. Who of us does not desire to be an adequate person, confident, self-assured, poised, able to cope with life? This is the image of humanity that is idealistically present in every human heart—we each want to be this kind of a person. And this is exactly what Christianity is designed to produce! To me, the glory of our Christian faith is never that it is religious, but that it is so gloriously secular. It is designed to produce life, to fit us for living, so we can be the kind of person God intended us to be—confident, able, adequate.

The secret of that confidence is fellowship, the sharing of the life of Jesus Christ, which also explains the three intermediate themes that John discusses. This confident life will be manifest in a threefold way: as truth, as righteousness, and as love.

These three form the test of authentic Christianity: truth, righteousness, and love. John says, first, that if you claim to know God but yet walk in the darkness of disobedience, you are a liar (1 John 1:6). He does not hesitate to use this extremely direct term. If you claim to know God and yet you walk in disobedience, you lie and do not live according to the truth. The absence of righteousness in your life makes a lie of all your claims to be Christian.

In chapter 2 he says that to claim to possess the Father and yet deny the deity and incarnation of the Son is also to be a liar (2:22). There is an absence of truth in the life; therefore it is not genuinely Christian.

Third, to claim to love God while you ignore or mistreat your brethren is to lie. You are a liar if you say you love God and yet you do not love your brethren (4:20). This is the absence of love. The presence of habitual sin, of a doctrinal denial of Christ, or of selfish hatred despite a professed Christian experience will expose all claims to Christianity as phony. These three must all be present. This is the whole argument of the Epistle of John. They must all be present and in an ever-increasing degree. Truth, love, and righteousness are the marks of authentic Christianity.

Coherent Fabric of Life

In this last section, which deals with assurance, the apostle brings all three of these together. In the passage we look at now we shall find these intertwined together, one coherent fabric of life from God which produces assurance and confidence and victory, manifest as righteousness, truth, and love.

> Every one who believes that Jesus is the Christ is a child of God, and every one who loves the parent loves the child. By this we know that we love the children of God, when we love God and obey his commandments. For this is the

love of God, that we keep his commandments. And his commandments are not burdensome. For whatever is born of God overcomes the world; and this is the victory that overcomes the world, our faith. Who is it that overcomes the world but he who believes that Jesus is the Son of God? (1 John 5:1–5).

Notice in verse 1 that truth and love belong together. One produces the other. "Every one who believes that Jesus is the Christ is a child of God," or literally, "Every one who believes that Jesus is the Christ has been begotten of God, and every one who loves the Father loves the child." In verse 21 of chapter 4 he has just been talking about loving our brother. This is a command from God, he says. "He who loves God should love his brother also." Now he answers a question that is continually being asked though not always expressed vocally. What does it mean to love my *brother?* Who is my brother, anyway? The answer is, "Every one who believes that Jesus is the Christ has been begotten of God." There is your brother. Such a one is part of the family. Thus if you love the Father you will inevitably love the other children of the Father anywhere you meet them.

What a condemnation this is of all denominational and sectarian spirit! Christians often feel they are responsible to love only those who belong to their particular group, whatever it may be. If we are Presbyterians, we love Presbyterians, but we do not like the Baptists or Methodists. All this is a denial of what John is saying here. We are to love the members of the family, wherever they are. Our brother is he who shares the life of Jesus Christ, who is born of God, who believes that Jesus is the Christ. Every one who believes that Jesus is *his* Lord, his supreme concern and authority in life, the One around whom his life is built, that one is in the family. It does not make any difference whether he differs with you about the pre-tribulation rapture, or the method of baptism, or anything else; if he has the life of the Father and believes that Jesus is Lord, then he is a brother.

Perhaps you may ask whether Christians are to love only other Christians, and no one else. No, but that is where love is to begin. Love begins within a family circle, does it not? We first love the members of our own family before we find it possible to love those outside. If love begins there it will reach out finally to encompass the world as well. The love of a Christian is never limited to "brothers," those who share the life of the Lord Jesus, but it must at least begin there.

Love Expressed by Righteousness

Verses 2 and 3 link together love and righteousness. These are the three tests: truth, love, and righteousness, and in the center is love.

> By this we know that we love the children of God, when we love God and obey his commandments. For this is the love of God, that we keep his commandments. And his commandments are not burdensome.

Here another sticky question that is often raised is answered for us. Someone says, "How can I know that I truly love my brother? Sometimes there are differences of opinion between us; sometimes we do not agree. There are times when I must do things that seem to offend my brother, and I don't always please him. Does this mean that I don't love him?" The answer is found in verse 2:

> By this we know that we love the children of God, when we love God and obey his commandments.

When our actions toward our brother arise, not out of our personal feelings toward him, but out of our love for God and our desire to obey his Word—in other words, when love is expressed by righteousness—then we can be confident that it is really love. Not long ago a Christian girl said to me, "My boyfriend is a Christian, but he wants me to tell a lie for him. He says that if I really love him, I'll tell the lie to protect him. Now should I do this? If I don't do it, he'll be angry with me, and he'll say that I don't love him." I said to her, "Well, tell him this. Tell him you love him enough to refuse to lie for him, because it is wrong and harmful, destructive to his life. Tell him you love him enough to tell him the truth about his lying."

Sometimes love must do the unpleasant thing. If it is prompted by love to God and obedience to his commandments, it is love, even though it makes someone angry, or upsets that person temporarily. Do not be disturbed by that reaction. Love must sometimes be cruel to be kind.

A Way of Pleasing Yourself

Here is the wretchedness of what we ordinarily call "white lies." I have come to regard white lies as the blackest of all. They are the most dangerous; they are the most deadly. They often do more harm than the outright lie. What is a white lie? It is a way of pleasing yourself by avoiding displeasing other people. You tell them a little fib about how they look, or don't look; you say something nice that you think they want to hear, because you don't want them to react toward you with unpleasantness. Thus we avoid making others angry with us by using white lies. But what we are really doing is loving ourselves more than we love them. We do not want to be hurt by their reactions, so we avoid telling them the truth.

What it really amounts to is that we do not love them enough to help them face the truth. Consequently some of them may go on for days, weeks, even years, doing things that offend others and never understanding what their problem is, and we call that love! It is not love; it is a form of hate. It is a refusal to face, and to help them face, the truth. Only the truth delivers; only the truth sets free. If you can gently and graciously help another to see a fault, without yourself becoming self-righteous, priggish, and condescending, then you know that you love that person with God's love. "By this we know that we love the children of God," if we are acting out of love for God and a concern for his commandments.

The wonderful thing is that when you do that you discover the truth of verse 3: "For this is the love of God, that we keep his commandments. And his commandments are not burdensome [or grievous]." They are not difficult, though they seem to be at first. Who of us has not recoiled at having to talk to someone about an unpleasant subject? Who has not wished that someone else would do it? Yet, if we will really love another to the point of helping him face unpleasant truth, we will discover that the results are delightful. If done in the right way we find it easy, producing riches of friendship and blessing.

Some of my dearest friends now are those whom once I didn't like—until they told me the truth. When I faced up to it I discovered that my enmity to them arose, not out of anything in them, but something in me. They became my friends because they dared to tell me the truth. Also, some of my closest friends are those to whom I have gone in love and, painfully perhaps, with great difficulty at first, laid open some wound that was festering and needed to be cleansed. It was not easy to do, but when it was all over and the pain had subsided and the inflammation was gone, there was born a warm and wonderful friendship that has deepened ever since.

His Life at Work

There you have the blending of the three marks of authentic Christianity: belief in the truth, an obedience to God's Word, and a manifestation of love. Those are the signs. These prove that anyone who possesses them has been born of God. Verses 4 and 5 then give us the results that will naturally follow:

For whatever is born of God overcomes the world; and
this is the victory that overcomes the world, our faith.
Who is it that overcomes the world but he who believes
that Jesus is the Son of God?

Here is the whole picture set in focus. When we seek to
show love to others, to obey the Word and to proclaim
these doctrinal truths of the Scriptures, there is sometimes a tendency for us to feel that our success as
Christians is a result of our faithful efforts. We get an
Elijah complex: "We're the only ones left who are true to
God." We tend to regard others as being unfaithful in
varying degrees. But John now declares that though these
activities do overcome the world, it never is a result of
our efforts. Effort is involved, but the results do not
come from them. Victory is a sign that we have the Lord
himself within us. Our efforts are but a sign of the
presence of the life of God, the Lord Jesus himself.
Without that, everything else would be futile. It is not we
who overcome the world, but it is he in us. All that we
contribute is simply the fact that we believe in his life at
work in us. Thus our faith in him overcomes the world.

Now when you consider what is involved in this term,
the world, what it is we are up against, you can see what
John means. This speaks of the moral pressures that we
face in the world today, the outlook and standards of the
godless society that surrounds us.

Think of the temptation to cheat and lie, to get ahead
at all costs, to be dishonest, to overreach, not only in
filling out our income tax but in every aspect of business.
It takes power to be honest in business. To be surrounded by the low moral standards which exist in many
businesses today, to be under constant temptation to take
advantage of people by maneuvering or manipulating or
riding roughshod over other people's rights, and yet to
resist that temptation and do right; that takes power!

These are the pressures that come upon us from the
world; the pressure to sexual looseness which is especially
evident among the young and the unmarried. Pressure to

feed the fire, to satisfy the urge, to give in, to give up, to go the whole way, though it may be wrong and deadly. The pressures around us are tremendous these days, seemingly overpowering at times. There is the pressure to harbor wrong ideas, to react against others the way the world reacts, to strike back, to fight back, and give as good as you get, to be resentful and jealous, to be ambitious and cruel. There are pressures to follow some of the attractive heresies that are about us in these theologically loose days, which offer popularity and social acceptance. Do you not feel all this? The lust of the flesh, the lust of the eyes, and the pride of life—all this is of the world.

How do you overcome it? How can you manifest the life of Jesus Christ in the midst of that kind of pressure? How can you go on, moment by moment, day after day, year after year, living a life that is absolutely contrary to that, enduring not only for ten years, but twenty, forty, sixty years, against this kind of moral pressure? How do you keep steady; how do you keep unmoved in the midst of this—not only unmoved but actually moving out to win others onto your side? John says it is "by faith," that is all. Not by the faith that you once exercised twenty years ago when you first became a Christian, but by faith in the life of Jesus present in you now. By faith in him at work in you, moment by moment, in the midst of the pressure, countering it with the pressure of his own life.

Rod of Dependence

In Exodus 17 there is the story of the Amalekites' attack upon Israel in the desert. That battle at Rephidim waged hot. All the forces of Israel were engaged in combat with this ruthless enemy which was forever standing athwart their pathway, trying to keep them from reaching the goal—the land of promise. We read that the battle went against Israel until Moses went up on the mountainside and raised his rod (which was always the symbol of dependence upon the power of God, the supernatural might of God). Lifting it toward the heavens he found that Israel began to prevail against the Amalekites. Their fighting was then of value, it accomplished something. As long as Moses could hold the rod up, Israel prevailed against Amalek. But Moses' arm grew tired and as the rod fell, the tide of battle turned. Amalek began to conquer, despite all the fighting of Israel. It became very apparent that the issue of the battle did not lie with the armies of Israel but in the symbol of dependence on the power of an invisible God. It was this that turned the tide. When Aaron and Hur came and stood on each side of Moses and held his arms up, the battle was won.

That is a picture of the battle in which we are engaged. How do you win? The issue does not lie in your fighting, although you do need to fight. You do need to pray and read the Scriptures and study and know God's Word—to apply it in every situation. You need to put on the whole armor of God when the enemy comes against you like a roaring lion, sweeping all before him. And you do need to stand. But none of this is of any avail unless you are recognizing that it is the life of God within you that makes the difference. It is he who wins. It is he who overcomes. Your dependence is on his activity in you.

That is the way we overcome the world. If we give in, if we reflect the same attitudes as the world, if our actions are the same as those of worldlings, we have succumbed to the world and are victims of it. We have succumbed to the wiles of the devil. We have lost our testimony and all possible power to witness. But if our dependence is on the life of the Son of God, moment by moment, and his life is in us, then "this is the victory that overcomes the world, even our faith." Who is it that overcomes the world but he who continues to believe that Jesus is the Son of God? The Son of God, the Strong One, the One who could say to his disciples, "Be of good cheer. I have overcome the world." God grant that our faith may be strong in him.

32

Why Do We Believe?

John brings this letter to a close with certain final notes of positive conviction. The last few verses repeat again and again the little phrase, "we know." It is that note of positive assurance that is always a key mark of true Christianity, quite in contrast to the spirit of the age in which we live. Christians are to be dogmatic about certain fundamental things because they have found him who is the truth. We know certain things and we are to say them forthrightly, unabashedly, without any sense of shame and hesitation.

Now we do not know everything, and if we give the impression that we do we are distorting the faith. But there are things we know—certain essential facts of faith. In the early days of Mt. Hermon Christian Conference Center, a Bible teacher named Dr. Joseph Conrad came out from the East. He rather startled the audience at Mt. Hermon in one of the summer conferences by saying something like this: "Dear friends, I want you to know at the very beginning of my ministry with you that I am not dogmatic about the virgin birth of Jesus Christ. I am not dogmatic about the bodily resurrection of Christ, nor am I at all dogmatic about the substitutionary atonement of the Lord Jesus Christ." At this point an unbelieving gasp

346

went up from that conservative audience. But then, marshalling all his force, with great intensity, he said, "No, I am not dogmatic; I am bulldogmatic!"

There is something of that note of intensity conveyed to us by the closing notes of John's letter. "I am bulldogmatic," he seems to be saying, "about certain fundamental issues." The spirit of our age is that nothing is certain, everything is tentative. We are told we cannot know anything for sure. Unfortunately that spirit has permeated the Christian church and we find men standing in pulpits and declaring such nonsense all over our land and the world, in the name of Jesus Christ. According to Philip Wylie, we Americans are rapidly becoming a "nothing" people, "a generation of zeros," because we do not believe anything. We do not think anything can be believed. This is the fundamental philosophy of the age in which we live.

Yet, strangely enough, with the most unreasoning inconsistency, the very same people who hold this philosophy often turn around and accuse Christians of exercising what they call "blind faith," that is, faith without any basis in fact. They charge us with accepting the Scriptures by an act of will, saying that we simply choose to believe them without any reasonable evidence. They say to us, rather condescendingly at times, "I would love to believe as you do, but I simply cannot." By that they imply that they cannot so divorce their will from their reason as to believe a thing without any basis in fact. But the whole genius of the Christian faith is that it rests upon facts. These facts are the acts of God in history, the incontrovertible movements of God which cannot be explained away or dismissed by a mere wave of the hand. They are imbedded in the record of the human race. A careful survey of these acts of God in history actually serves to compel belief, showing that it is not belief that is unreasonable, but unbelief. One must struggle and exert painful effort to convince oneself that these facts are not true.

Surveying the Evidence

Thus John, as he comes now to the close of this letter, quickly surveys for us the evidence for our faith. He declares why it is that we believe what we believe, using, for the sake of brevity, certain very eloquent symbols:

> This is he who came by water and blood, Jesus Christ, not with the water only but with the water and the blood. And the Spirit is the witness, because the Spirit is the truth. There are three witnesses, the Spirit, the water, and the blood; and these three agree (1 John 5:6–8).

Those who use the King James Version will note that a verse is apparently omitted from the Revised Standard Version text, verse 7. This verse is properly omitted because it has no manuscript support earlier than the fifteenth century, A.D. The King James translators did not have access to the number of manuscripts that are available today and therefore did not recognize this. But it is universally agreed today among Bible scholars that the statement concerning three witnesses in heaven—the Father, the Word, and the Spirit—is not a genuine part of the Scriptures and so is omitted from the RSV text. The RSV takes part of verse 6 and makes it verse 7 so that the numbering carries right through.

Now as John declares in this text, there are three witnesses. Two of them are external and historical, and one of them is internal and personal; but all three are intricately related, forming a marvelous fabric of testimony that is powerful in the extreme. Ecclesiastes says "a threefold cord is not quickly broken," and here are three mighty testimonies to the fundamental facts upon which Christian faith rests. Faith is not merely believing a set of facts, but acting upon the facts which you believe. It is necessary to interject that element of activity before belief becomes faith. Faith, however, rests upon facts, and here are the three facts.

There are those, first of all, symbolized by the water and the blood. These mark events which lay at the beginning and end of our Lord's public ministry on earth: the water of baptism at the beginning; the blood of the cross at the end. Christ, himself, is the centering ground of Christian faith. This is always true. It is Jesus Christ himself who is the supreme fact upon which Christian faith rests. But two unique qualities mark his life, symbolized here by the water and the blood.

A Sinless Life

The water, of course, refers to that event at the Jordan River when our Lord went down to be baptized by John the Baptist. After he came up out of the water, the Holy Spirit came upon him in the form of a dove and a voice from heaven declared. "This is my beloved Son in whom I am well pleased." That event thus declared the sinlessness of his life. The water of baptism was the water of cleansing. For the sin-defiled members of the human race it was necessary as a symbolic representation of what God did when a sinner returned to his Lord. There must be a cleansing, a forgiveness of sin.

But the Lord Jesus did not personally require such a cleansing, and it was this that gave pause to John the Baptist when he saw the Lord coming toward him. He said, "Are you coming to be baptized of me? Why, I ought to be baptized of you." And you remember Jesus said to him, "Allow it to be so, for thus it behooves us to fulfill all righteousness," that is, "Go ahead anyway, because I am taking the place of man, as representative man, and as representative man I am assuming the burden of guilt and sin for the whole race. Therefore I need to be baptized." Yet the Father's voice made very clear that there was not one stain, one spot in the Son to mar the record.

Water, therefore, was the sign of a perfect humanity. Here was one who all his life had done that which pleased the Father and who had never once stepped outside the bounds of the Father's will. Again and again during his public ministry he held up his stainless record before his enemies, challenging them to find any fault in it. "Which of you," he says, "convinces me of sin?" It is this unblemished, spotless record that is testimony of a life that came from God. How else can you explain the person of the Lord Jesus Christ if he is not from God, God manifest in the flesh? This is part of the proof of our faith, this sinless life.

No Right to Live

Ah yes, says the liberal, I am willing to accept that. I believe that he came as the perfect example for us to imitate. If we simply follow the life of Jesus and imitate his example, we too will live the kind of life that is pleasing to God. But notice that John, in symbol, denies that. He says, "He came not with water only, but with water *and* blood." A sinless life is insufficient for faith. It does not really help us. To look at the spotless, stainless life of the Son of God is the most condemning thing I know. It shames me; it discourages me. I could never approach that kind of living, and I do not know anyone else who can. No, faith requires something else. It requires an atoning death; it requires blood. To the Hebrew mind this is most eloquent, speaking of life poured out, forfeited life. It is life that no longer has the right to live, blood poured out as a sacrifice.

Yet again, it was not for himself. He was put to death, not for his own sins, but for the sins of the world. The death of Jesus only makes sense as we see that it was for others. As the prophet Isaiah predicted,

> He was wounded for our transgressions,
> he was bruised for our iniquities;
> upon him was the chastisement that made us whole,
> and with his stripes we are healed (Isa. 53:5).

It was what those passersby threw in his face as he hung upon the cross: In unconscious irony they cried out, "He saved others; himself he could not save." How true it was. His life was for others, he laid down his life on our behalf.

It is this, John says, that is the ground of faith. How else can you explain the fact that the Gospels give the greatest part of their account to the record of the death of Jesus? Though his words captured the attention of men, for crowds followed him everywhere to hear him, and though those words still startle and amaze men as they read them today, yet the focus of the Gospel is not upon the teachings of Jesus but upon the death of Jesus. That last memorable week, with all its significant events, occupies the greatest part of each of the Gospels. The attention of heaven and earth seems to be focused upon the mighty event when the Son of God hung upon a bloody cross on a hill outside Jerusalem, when the sun became dark for three hours.

This becomes an essential ingredient of the Good News that Christians declare. Paul said, "Christ died *for our sins*" (1 Cor. 15:3). That is the point of it, *for our sins.* If we do not add that, the death of Christ is a pointless experience. There is no adequate explanation for the cross apart from this. Thus the sinless life of Jesus and his death on behalf of others can only be explained in terms of God entering human history to do a most remarkable thing on behalf of men. They are sturdy facts upon which faith can rest.

Themselves Involved

But beyond these two historical evidences, John says, lies yet a third: that mysterious, subjective, yet powerfully compelling evidence of the witness of the Spirit within. By this he means that when the story of the sinless life and the cross is told, whether it be told simply or with eloquence, the Spirit of God works in the hearts of many to make it extremely personal. Such listeners suddenly see themselves as involved in the incidents, as caught up in the mighty sweep of these events and becoming part and parcel of them. The whole meaning of it becomes personalized for them so it is no longer, "Christ died for the world," but "Christ died for me." That is the witness of the Holy Spirit.

John Newton, who wrote so many of our hymns, was for many years of his life a reckless, dissolute reprobate, living the wildest sort of life, until he became, at last, a slave even to slaves. With his health ruined, he was on a voyage back to England from Africa when, in the midst of a storm, God spoke to his heart and he found the Christ he had long rejected. He became one of the outstanding spokesmen of the gospel of his day, and he put his own testimony in these simple words.

> In evil long I took delight
> Unawed by shame or fear
> Until a new object met my sight
> And stopped my wild career.
>
> I saw One hanging on a tree
> In agony and blood
> Who fixed his languid eyes on me
> As near His cross I stood.
>
> Sure, never till my latest breath
> Will I forget that look
> It seemed to charge me with His death
> Though not a word He spoke.
>
> My conscience owned and felt my guilt
> And plunged me in despair
> I saw my sins His blood had spilt
> And served to nail Him there.
>
> A second look He gave
> Which said, "I freely all forgive.
> My blood was for thy ransom paid
> I died that thou may'st live."

That is the witness of the Spirit, that personalizes the work of the cross, bringing it home to the individual in power. When the word of pardon is believed, the Spirit also gives a wonderful sense of forgiveness, a lifting of the burden of guilt, the sense of washing away of sins, and the peace of God is spoken to a guilty heart.

This is perhaps the greatest need of humanity in our day. Billy Graham reported that when he was in London one of the heads of a mental hospital said to him, "Half of our patients could be immediately dismissed if they could obtain somehow the assurance of forgiveness." Forgiveness is the work of the Spirit. "His Spirit," Paul writes to the Romans, "bears witness with our spirit that we are the children of God." That is an internal, personal, present confirmation of the one great fact declared by the sinless life (the water), and the atoning death (the blood), of the Lord Jesus Christ. These three mighty witnesses agree. What do they agree to? That, "he who knew no sin [that is his sinless life] was made sin for us [that is his blood], in order that we might be made the righteousness of God in him [that is the testimony of the Spirit]," (2 Cor. 5:21). There you have the gospel, resting upon these three inescapable facts.

Risky Undertakings

For this reason it is actually unbelief that is unreasonable, as John goes on now to argue:

> If we receive the testimony of men, the testimony of God is greater; for this is the testimony of God that he has borne witness to his Son. He who believes in the Son of God has the testimony in himself. He who does not believe God has made him a liar, because he has not believed in the testimony that God has borne to his Son (vv. 9,10).

One of the most common experiences of life is to act upon the word or testimony of another person, often even that of a stranger. We will sometimes do the most amazing things in response to the simple declaration of a person we have never met before. Years ago I had the privilege of leading a group of pilgrims to the Holy Land. We were innocents abroad, indeed. Most of us had never been there before, including the leader. But we had been given assurance by means of a letter from a person in New York whom I had not met, that someone would meet us at every place we landed, help us get through customs, and take us through all the intricacies of entering a foreign land. On the strength of that letter some twenty-five of us committed ourselves to the tender mercies of a stranger, and discovered that it all proved true. Everywhere we went someone showed up to help us.

Now, is not God more dependable than man? That is John's argument. If you will take the word of a stranger and act on it, can you not believe the Word of God, especially when he has caused the testimony to be written down by the eyewitnesses of these events? In addition, when faith is exercised on the basis of that objective testimony, a confirmation of the Spirit within makes it wholly believable. Can you not exercise faith on that basis? Well, John says, if you refuse to do that then you are treating God as though he were a liar. You insult God if you do not believe the record he has given.

Suppose you were to state something to someone, and they said to you, "Well, you know, I'm trying to believe you." Would you not take that as an insult? Would you not feel that they were definitely questioning your integrity, your character? Would you not say, "Why can't you believe what I say? Do you think I'm a liar?" How much greater cause has God to say that to us when he has given us the record, indelibly engraved in history and confirmed by the witness of the Spirit within.

John moves at last to the heart of the whole matter:

And this is the testimony, that God gave us eternal life, and this life is in his Son. He who has the Son has life; he who has not the Son of God has not life. I write this to you who believe in the name of the Son of God, that you may know that you have eternal life (1 John 5:11–13).

Here is the testimony, he says. The whole point of the matter is that God has given to man the thing he lacks, eternal life. Not life in quantity, although it does include that—it is endless life—but primarily life in quality. Life abundant, life exciting. Life that is adventurous, full, meaningful, relevant, all these much-abused terms that are so widely used today. Life that is lived to the fullest, that is God's gift to man. He who has the Son has life, because the Son is life. That is the whole point of this letter.

Under the Thumb

Dr. H. A. Ironside used to tell of a man who had great doubts about whether or not he was a Christian. He had been troubled by certain theorists who said that God only elected certain individuals to be saved; if you were not of the elect there was no chance for you. The perfectly proper biblical truth of election had been distorted to extreme proportions, and he felt that there was no way he could know whether or not he was among the elect.

One day he went home after hearing a sermon on the verse. "As many as received him, to them gave he power to become the sons of God" (John 1:12, KJV). "He that believes on the Son has eternal life" (paraphrase of John 3:15). He got down on his knees and said, "Now, Father, I want to settle this question. Show me whether I have eternal life or not." And opening his Bible, his eyes fell on these verses, "He who does not believe God has made him a liar, because he has not believed in the testimony that God has born to his Son" (1 John 5:10).

He said in his prayer, "Father, I don't want to make you a liar and it says here that if I don't believe the testimony that you give about the Son, I'm making you a liar. Now I don't want to do that. What is the testimony?" And he read the next part. "This is the testimony," and he stopped right there. He was so overwrought that he put his thumb over the rest of the verse and said, "Lord, it says here that if I don't believe the testimony that you gave concerning your Son, I'm making you a liar, and I don't want to make you a liar. I believe that I have what that testimony is right under my thumb here, and I'm going to take my thumb off and read it, and Lord, help me to believe it, because I don't want to make you a liar." With great trepidation he raised his thumb and read, ". . . that God gave us eternal life, and this life is in his Son" (v. 11). Suddenly it came home to him. John makes it so clear, "He who has received the Son has the life; and he who has not received the Son has not the life." No matter what else he may have, no matter how religious he may be, if he has not received the Son he does not have life.

This is the testimony. God has given us something, and it is wrapped up in a person, the Son of God. If you have received the Son, you have his life—manifested, of course, by the things John has been talking about in this letter: righteousness, truth, and love. If you have not received the Son of God, no matter how earnest you are, no matter how devoted you have been, no matter how religiously intent you have been, seeking to do everything you could think of to please God, if you do not have the Son, you do not have life. That is the issue, is it not? Either you have him, or you do not have him; either you know Jesus Christ, or you do not know him. There is no middle ground; it is one or the other.

So, John concludes,

> I write this to you who believe in the name of the Son of God [in order] that you may know that you have eternal life (v. 13).

The purpose of this letter is to move us from doubt to certainty: "that we may know that we have eternal life." What about you?

He who has the Son has life; he who has not the Son of God has not life (v. 12).

33

Praying Boldly

It certainly is not an accident that John closes his letter with an emphasis upon the subject of prayer. He has been writing about the life of Christ—the only life that can truly be called a Christian life—which is characterized by truth, love, and righteousness. Prayer is the perfect expression of all three of these: love is prayer's motive, truth is its expression, and righteousness is its goal.

A deep-seated instinct for prayer lies buried within each human being. Given enough stress, given the right circumstances, it will come out; as it is said, "There are no atheists in fox-holes." I remember hearing of a sea captain who described the violence of a storm by saying, "God heard from plenty of strangers that night."

Perhaps no aspect of Christian faith is so puzzling to so many as that of unanswered prayer. Almost all the problems in prayer are a result of ignorance as to its nature. Many have lost faith in prayer because, not having a proper understanding of its nature and purpose, their prayers have gone unanswered. They conclude that prayer—and even God himself—is a failure.

A Sure Thing

Prayer does not appear to be very difficult or complex, and it is available to the simplest of people. Even children can pray successfully and effectively. Yet the nature of prayer is infinitely complex and requires considerable knowledge before prayers are answered regularly. In this closing section of his letter John gives us certain general principles about prayer. Then he follows them with a specific illustration. We have first the general principles:

> And this is the confidence which we have in him, that if we ask anything according to his will he hears us. And if we know that he hears us in whatever we ask, we know that we have obtained the requests made of him (1 John 5:14,15).

For many Christians prayer is a venture, an experiment. There is nothing very certain about it. We often pray because we do not know what else to do. But you do not see that attitude in the apostle John. What is his reaction to this matter of prayer? "This is the confidence which we have in him," he says, "that if we ask anything according to his will, we know he hears us." There is a ringing note of certainty there. Prayer is not an experiment; prayer is a certainty with John, a sure thing. He knows it works, and he knows how it works. That confidence is expressed by the word he chooses, "confidence," or "boldness." "This is the boldness which we have in him, that if we ask anything according to his will he hears us."

You cannot read the New Testament without realizing that God delights in bold praying, and in bold people. Read the Epistle to the Hebrews and see how many times that word appears. "Let us then with *confidence* draw near to the throne of grace, that we may receive mercy and find grace to help in time of need" (Heb. 4:16). And again, "We have *confidence* to enter the sanctuary by the blood of Jesus, by the new and living way which he opened for us . . ." (Heb. 10:19,20). This is what ought to characterize prayer. It should be bold, confident, certain.

This kind of certainty arises from the knowledge of two fundamental principles of prayer which John gives us here: the certainty of hearing and the certainty of having. First, "If we ask anything according to his will *he hears us.*" Perhaps the major reason for most of the unanswered prayers of the world is that they are not according to God's will and therefore they are not heard. John makes it explicitly clear that a prayer that is according to God's will is always heard. Thus at one stroke he demolishes all those concepts of prayer which imply that prayer is a means of getting God to do our will.

Heavenly Bellboy

Many people regard prayer as some kind of mysterious device by which human beings can get God to do what we want him to do, a kind of Aladdin's lamp to cause the great Genie of heaven to appear and give us our requests. God becomes a kind of heavenly Bellboy, rushing to our aid when we push the button of prayer. It is this concept which has resulted in some of the frightful perversions of prayer. For instance, there are faith healers who make arrogant, blasphemous demands upon a patient and long-suffering God, commanding him to do things which they insist are their right to ask, though it is very evident that God is regarded as a junior partner in their business relationship. But that is not prayer. Prayer is a means of obtaining the will of God and is limited always by the will and purpose of God. If we pray outside his purpose there is no assurance at all that our prayers are heard, and certainly not that they will be granted.

Sometimes our prayers are not according to the will of

God because our motives are wrong. Sometimes we pray "wrongly" as James says, "to spend it on your passions" (James 4:3). We want what *we* want, not what God wants. Some time ago I ran across a wedding prayer that illustrates how subtly this can be done. This is a girl praying on her wedding day:

> Dear God. I can hardly believe that this is my wedding day. I know I haven't been able to spend much time with You lately, with all the rush of getting ready for today, and I'm sorry. I guess, too, that I feel a little guilty when I try to pray about all this, since Larry still isn't a Christian. But oh, Father, I love him so much, what else can I do? I just couldn't give him up. Oh, You must save him, some way, somehow.

> You know how much I've prayed for him, and the way we've discussed the gospel together. I've tried not to appear too religious, I know, but that's because I didn't want to scare him off. Yet he isn't antagonistic and I can't understand why he hasn't responded. Oh, if he only were a Christian.

> Dear Father, please bless our marriage. I don't want to disobey You, but I do love him and I want to be his wife, so please be with us and please don't spoil my wedding day.

That sounds like a sincere, earnest prayer, does it not? But if it is stripped of its fine, pious language, it is really saying something like this:

> Dear Father, I don't want to disobey You, but I must have my own way at all costs. For I love what You do not love, and I want what You do not want. So please be a good God and deny Yourself, and move off Your throne, and let me take over. If You don't like this, then all I ask is that You bite Your tongue and say or do nothing that will spoil my plans, but let me enjoy myself.

Prayer that lies outside the will of God is an insult to God. As the psalmist has said, "If I regard iniquity in my heart, the Lord will not hear me" (Ps. 66:18, KJV). Prayer must be according to God's will, John says, in the direction God is going, with a view to obtaining the purposes he intends. As Romans tells us, the Spirit of God helps us in our infirmities by prompting our desires, by creating deep urges within us, unutterable yearnings, hungerings after more of the real life that satisfies, not only for ourselves, but for others. Thus the Spirit is our Helper that we might pray according to his will.

Everything in the Catalog

Now "according to his will" includes a tremendous amount, for much of the will of God is already revealed to us. I grew up as a boy in Montana. About the only reading matter we had during the long winter months was a Sears and Roebuck catalog. It was limited reading, but what a great number of things were included! It took us weeks to go through only one section of it. We could order anything we had the money to pay for, but it would have been utterly futile to send in an order for something that was not in the catalog. So it is with prayer. Within the will of God there are vast numbers of gifts he has provided for his own. The will of God includes all that we need. All that we really want is available to us and to our loved ones and friends within the will of God. There is nothing we need to pray for outside of it. Outside are only things that harm, injure, and destroy us.

Perhaps we do not know exactly whether or not a request is the will of God for us, and the examples of Scripture make clear that it is not wrong to ask even for these things. But we must then always add, as Jesus himself added in the garden of Gethsemane, "nevertheless, not my will, but thine be done," for prayer is designed only to obtain that which is within the will of God.

Thus John says that if you know that what you are asking for is within the will of God, if you have found a promise of God in Scripture or, in seeking the mind of God there has come a deep and settled conviction in your heart from the Spirit of God that something is the will of God, then you know that he hears you when you ask for it. God *always* hears every prayer voiced within the boundaries of his will. This is the first certainty that forms the basis of prayer—we know we are heard. Jesus could say, "I thank you, Father, that you always hear me," because everything he did lay within the boundaries of the will of God.

That brings us then to the second certainty of prayer, the certainty of having. "If we know that he hears us," John says, "then we know that we have obtained the requests made of him." Think of that! If we know it is heard, we know that we have it. God has already granted the request. In other words, God never says no except to that which lies outside his will. As Paul says to the Corinthians, "All the promises of God find their Yes in him [Christ]" (2 Cor. 1:20). There are no negatives; everything we ask within this vast area of the will of God, God grants without exception. Is that not a wonderful thing? Do you dare to believe that?

The Secret Is to Take

God plays no favorites and has no special pets. He has intimates, but anyone can be his intimate who desires to be and moves within the program he has outlined. He has intimates to whom he gives much more than others, but he has no favorites, and no limitations as to who can enter into these things. Anyone can who will. But the secret of prayer, as John suggests here, is to take, to believe that God has granted everything we ask within his will. "You have it," John says. "We know that we have obtained the request made of him."

Now John is not trying to kid himself. He is not

pretending that God has given him something that is right there, if he will just open his eyes to see. There is no psychological gimmick here. What he is saying is that when we pray within the will of God the answer is absolutely sure, and it is only a question of God's timing as to when it appears. It is up to God when that answer will come but the request has been granted and therefore we can give thanks. We can take from him and thank him for that which has been given, expecting it to appear in God's time. Remember that Jesus warned, "The times and the seasons are not for you to know." Time is the only uncertain aspect about prayer. There are often delays in God's fulfillment of answers. This matter he reserves to himself. But as to the ultimate giving of the things requested, there is no uncertainty whatsoever.

Jesus made clear that God is not like a reluctant neighbor who needs to be wheedled, cajoled, and enticed to give something. He gives eagerly, gladly, willingly. As Jesus said, "Ask, and it will be given you; seek, and you will find; knock, and it will be opened to you" (Matt. 7:7). Many church prayer meetings are often pools of unbelief. Prayers are uttered in a wheedling, begging tone of voice, as though the petitioner felt he had to twist God's arm a bit to persuade him to come through. But God is never like that, says Jesus. "What father of you, if your son comes and asks for a fish, will give him a serpent; or for bread, will give him a stone?" You would not do that, and God is much better than you. "If you who are evil know how to give good gifts to your children, how much more will your heavenly Father respond to your needs in prayer?" (Matt. 7:9–11).

Now John comes to the specific illustration of this principle in a passage that troubles many:

> If any one sees his brother committing what is not a mortal sin, he will ask, and God will give him life for those whose sin is not mortal. There is sin which is mortal; I do not say that one is to pray for that. All wrongdoing is sin, but there is sin which is not mortal (vv. 16,17).

These two verses are an illustration of a request that is in the will of God, as contrasted with one that is not in the will of God. He has just been urging us to pray only concerning that which is in the will of God, so he gives us these two illustrations, one of which is in the will of God, one of which is not. The "sin which is not unto death" is the kind which permits a concerned brother to ask God for deliverance from that sin for an erring brother, and the will of God is to grant that request. The "sin which is unto death" is the kind to which God has already determined upon a certain response, and no prayer is going to change his mind. Therefore, it is useless to pray. That is why John gives us this illustration.

Nothing to Do with Salvation

Now let us come to the moot question, what is this sin unto death? There are three major explanations of this passage and particularly of this phrase, "the sin unto death." The first view regards it as some specific sin which is so terrible as to be unforgivable, such as suicide, murder, idolatry, or even adultery. This view (which has been held by many through the Christian centuries) gave rise to the Catholic distinctions between mortal and venial sins. This is, perhaps, why the RSV translates this "sin which is mortal" and "sin which is not mortal." But that translation is unquestionably wrong. It should never be translated "mortal sin" for it has nothing to do with the question of salvation. There is no warrant whatsoever in Scripture for distinguishing between mortal and venial sins—sins which can be forgiven (venial), and those which can never be forgiven (mortal). Scripture makes no such distinctions. As a matter of fact, this sin is not any one specific sin. The Greek makes very clear here that this is simply sin in general. It is not a particular sin which is unto death; any sin can become sin unto death.

There is a second view which links this with the words of Jesus concerning the blasphemy against the Holy

Spirit. Remember that on one occasion he warned that the blasphemy against the Holy Spirit can never be forgiven, either in this age or in the age to come. The death which is mentioned in this passage in 1 John is thus taken to mean spiritual death. This is a description of what we generally call apostasy. An apostate is someone who has made a profession of faith in Christ but begins to drift away and ultimately comes to the place where he actually blasphemes the name of the Lord Jesus and the things of Christian faith, denying them and turning his back upon them. Hebrews 6 and 10 and other passages made clear that such an apostate is in a terrible situation. He has committed blasphemy against the Holy Spirit, the flagrant rejection of the testimony of the Holy Spirit to Jesus Christ, and that is unpardonable.

But it is equally clear that this sin can never be committed by a genuine born-again Christian. It is only committed by those who have made a profession of faith but have never entered into new birth in Jesus Christ. But the word here is, "if any one sees his *brother* committing what is not a sin unto death," and the term *brother* is reserved for other Christians. John says that every one who believes that Jesus is the Christ is a child of God, and every one who loves the Father loves the child (1 John 5:1). That is, such a one is my brother. He, like me, is a member of the family of God through faith in Jesus Christ. Therefore it seems likely that the sin unto death mentioned here is limited to Christians, and cannot refer to apostates.

That brings us to the third view, which I believe is the correct one, which views death here as physical death. Let us take another look at these verses:

> If any one sees his brother committing what is not a sin unto [physical] death, he will ask, and God will give him life for those whose sin is not unto [physical] death. There is sin which is unto [physical] death.

There is sin which a Christian can commit which will result in God taking him home in physical death. John goes on to say,

> I do not say that one is to pray for that. All wrongdoing is sin, but there is sin which is not unto [physical] death.

Certain examples of this sin unto death are given in Scripture which, if one studies them through carefully, will reveal the element that turns ordinary sin into sin which is unto death. "All wrongdoing is sin," says John. All unrighteousness is sin, let us not misunderstand that, but there is sin which has a certain element about it, a certain characteristic which will result in physical death, physical judgment. Let us look at some of the instances of this in Scripture.

Premature Death

Moses, for instance, committed a sin unto death when God commanded him to speak to the rock in the wilderness so that water would come forth to meet the needs of the children of Israel. Previously he had been commanded to strike the rock for the water to come out, but on a second occasion he was told to speak to the rock. This change was important because the rock was a type of Christ and to strike it was a picture of the judgment of the cross.

The cross is the way by which the refreshing water of grace first comes into our life as Christians, but after we have become Christians we are not to strike the rock (crucify Christ again) but to speak to it. We are to simply ask of him and out of the Rock will flow the rivers of living water we need. But Moses broke the significance of that type when, in his anger, he struck the rock twice. Though God, in grace, allowed the water to come flowing out, he said to him, "Because you have disobeyed me and not sanctified me in the eyes of the people, you will not be allowed to lead these people into the land of promise." Later on, when they came to the borders of the land, Moses said to God, in effect, "Lord, allow me to go on in. Forgive this, and let me go on in." And the Lord said to him, "Speak no more to me about this matter," that is, "Do not pray about this, but get up to the mountain and I will let you see the land, but that is as far as you can go." Moses had committed a sin unto death, although in his case it did not occur right away. Nevertheless, he died prematurely, before his work was really completed.

A little further on, in the Book of Joshua you find that Achan commits a sin unto death. As the children of Israel crossed the Jordan and surrounded Jericho, they were told that when the city became theirs they were not to touch anything in it, for it was all cursed of God. But when the walls came tumbling down and they came into the city, one man among them, Achan, saw a beautiful garment and a wedge of gold and he coveted these and buried them in the dirt beneath his tent. As a result, judgment came upon Israel. In their next battle they met with utter and complete defeat. Searching out the camp in obedience to the Word of God, Joshua found that it was Achan who had done this. He was brought out with his whole family, and by command of God they were put to death. That was a sin unto death.

In the New Testament, in Acts 5, Ananias and his wife, Sapphira, pretended to a devotion that they did not really possess, and, wanting a reputation in the eyes of other Christians, they lied about the money they received for certain land. As a result, they were immediately put to death by God when their lie became evident. They were taken out, one by one, and buried. They too had committed a sin unto death.

Also remember what the apostle Paul said to the Corinthians about their conduct, saying, "Some of you are drunken, some are selfish, pushing your way in and eating before others, showing no concern for others, and above all not discerning the meaning of this table, not discerning the Lord's body. For this cause, many are weak and sickly among you, and many have died" (Cor. 11:21,29,30). Certain ones had committed the sin which was unto death.

Willful Presumption

Note that in all these examples the sin was not the same, by any means. It was simply sin which resulted in the judgment of physical death. What, then, is the element that turns ordinary sin into this kind of sin? It is the element of wanton, presumptuous action in the face of clear knowledge that it is wrong. It is willfulness, a willful presumption to pursue something when you know God has said it is wrong. This is sin unto death, and the result is physical judgment. Now it does not always come suddenly. It did with Ananias and Sapphira, it did with Achan, but it did not with Moses, and it did not with the Corinthians. With them it came in stages: first it was weakness, then sickliness, and finally death. Perhaps much of the physical weakness that is apparent among Christians today may arise from this very cause. Not all physical weakness comes from this, not all premature deaths arise from this, but some very likely do. It is persistence in a determined course of action when you know that God has said it is wrong that constitutes sin unto death.

Now let us look again at what John has said. "If any one sees his brother committing sin which is not unto death," sin which arises largely out of ignorance, with no understanding of the implications of it, no awareness of how bad it is, "he will ask, and God will give him life. . . ." Young Christians often stumble into things they are not aware of. They do not understand what they are getting into, and they do not realize the danger. Then, if you see your brother committing that kind of sin, ask of God, and God will give life for those whose sin is not unto death. God will withhold the judgment of physical weakness and grant opportunity for the renewal of life.

You can see that in the Old Testament in the case of King Hezekiah. Remember that in a very unwise moment he allowed the King of Babylon to send visitors into his palace to investigate all that was going on and to see the riches of the palace. The prophet Isaiah warned Hezekiah that these men only wanted to see how much money he had and whether or not it was worth sending an army to take it. He said, "You have sold yourself into the hands of the Babylonians." As a result of that King Hezekiah received a sentence of death from God. God told him to prepare himself, to get everything ready, because he was going to die. Hezekiah turned his face to the wall and prayed, beseeching the Lord. As a result of that prayer of confession and repentance, God stopped the prophet Isaiah as he was going out the door, having delivered the sentence of death, and said, "Go back to the King. I have granted him fifteen more years of life." As a sign that it would happen, the sundial in the garden went backward ten degrees. That is an example of God granting life for those who do not commit a sin which is unto death. Repentance reverses the judgment. Those who willfully determine to go on in a way that is wrong commit sin which is unto death, and when they do God says do not pray for that.

Paul, writing to Titus, says something very similar. In the closing part of that little letter he says, "As for a man who is factious, after admonishing him once or twice, have nothing more to do with him, knowing that such a person is perverted and sinful; he is self-condemned" (Titus 3:10,11). Here is a brother determined to go on his way. Therefore there is no need to pray for him. There is nothing you can do but let God's judgment wake him up. Perhaps God in grace will deal patiently with him, give him a time of sickness or weakness, and that will bring him to his senses. But if not, God will take him home.

Dr. H. A. Ironside used to illustrate this as follows: Sometimes you see children playing outside, and when quarreling breaks out the mother says, "If you don't behave yourself, you will have to come in the house." Her child says, "Don't worry, Mother, I'll be good." But a little while later quarreling breaks out again and the mother comes out and says, "Now that's enough. You've got to come in. I can't trust you outside any more." The child begs his mother to let him stay out some more, "Oh, Mother, I'll be good. I promise I will." But she says, "No, I gave you a chance. Now come on inside. I can't trust you out there any more."

That is what God sometimes says to us. Do we realize, Christian friends, that God's whole reputation is at stake in our behavior? Everything we do and say is reflecting the character and the being of God to the world around. No wonder he watches us so assiduously. No wonder he judges us so precipitously at times. If there be a willful determination to disgrace him in the eyes of others, as Moses had, God will say, "All right, that's enough. I can't trust you out there any more. Come on home." And home we go.

34

Christian Certainty

A colleague of England's great Christian prime minister, William Gladstone, once said of him, "I don't mind that Gladstone always seems to have an ace up his sleeve; what makes me angry is his maddening assurance that it was the Almighty who put it there." Is this not often the reaction of many toward Christians? It is because Christians are relying upon a secret hidden wisdom, imparted by the Spirit of God. John says that true Christianity creates three great certainties and with these he closes this little letter.

The first of these is in verse 18:

> We know that any one born of God does not sin, but He who was born of God keeps him, and the evil one does not touch him.

"We know that any one born of God does not sin. . . ." There is the certainty of righteousness. This is a dogmatic declaration on the part of the apostle that if you are a Christian you will come to a place where you cannot continue in sin. He is not talking about sinlessness. If he were, who of us could possibly measure up? What he means is, "We know that any one born of God cannot continue on in sin."

That means that if there is a Christian profession there must be an accompanying change in the life. There is a basic change in the attitude toward wrongdoing. If that change is not there then the person is only deceiving himself and others about being a Christian. There may be occasional failure in practice, as there is in each of our lives from time to time, but there cannot be a continual, habitual practicing of sin. There must be a deep desire within to be changed which keeps this individual always pushing out against the inhibiting forces and habits of sin. This desire is the proof of the new birth.

An Unbreakable Hold

The apostle tells us why this is true. The reason a Christian cannot go on living in sin, doing what he knows to be wrong, is that "He who was born of God keeps him, and the evil one does not touch him." The RSV is quite right in capitalizing this word, "He"—"*He* who was born of God." This does not refer to the Christian himself, although he is referred to as "one born of God" in the previous phrase. This pronoun refers to the Lord Jesus himself.

Previously in John we saw that anyone born of God cannot sin because "his [God's] seed remaineth in him" (1 John 3:9, KJV). The Lord Jesus Christ is dwelling in that person's heart and life and thus he cannot go on in sin. The One who was born of God, the holy Son of God, is dwelling in him, living in him, and keeping him. The love of Christ has an unbreakable hold on that person's life. He may struggle, he may temporarily fall, he may resist the changes that the Spirit of God is attempting to make, but he cannot continually do so. He will be "kept by the power of God," as the apostle Jude puts it. The One who is dwelling in him will bring him into circumstances and pressures that will make him realize what he is doing and the mess he is making, and make him hunger to give in to God's will and be free. Otherwise he is not a Christian.

The result is, as John says, that the evil one can never repossess him. The evil one, of course, is the devil. John says that the stronger One has now come and the bonds of the strong man (Matt. 12:29) have been broken, and he can never repossess the Christian. That is an encouraging word, is it not? The enemy can frighten us, as he often does. He can harass us, he can threaten us, he can make us believe that we are in his power and that we *have* to do certain things that are wrong. He can create desires and passions within us that are so strong that we think we must yield to them. But that is a lie, because he is a liar. We do not have to yield to them. He can lure us, he can deceive us, as we have seen; he can even temporarily derail us and make us fall. But the great declaration of this Scripture is that once you know Jesus Christ, the devil can never again make you sin. There is never any excuse for giving in because it is all bluster on his part, all a bluff. He is trying to make you believe that you must sin, but you do not have to.

John thus makes the point that if someone goes along blithely living the same way he lived before he claimed to become a Christian, that person has never been born again. You cannot be a Christian without being obedient to the Lord. "If you love me," Jesus said, "you will keep my commandments" (John 14:15). Obedience is the name of the game.

The apostle Paul also put it very plainly when he said, "God's firm foundation stands, bearing this seal: 'The Lord knows those who are his,' and 'Let every one who names the name of the Lord depart from iniquity'" (2 Tim. 2:19). We often quote only the first part of it, saying "Well, I know he's not behaving like a Christian and hasn't for years. There hasn't been a change since he said he came to know Christ, but 'The Lord knows those who are his.'" But that is only part of it: *and*, "'let every one who names the name of the Lord depart from iniquity.'" That is the visible mark, and anything less than that is phony. The truth is that if you are not changed, if you are not living obediently, if you do not have a desire to depart from the things that are wrong, you have never been born again.

Separated and Blessed

Now look at the certainty of relationships:

We know that we are of God, and the whole world is in the power of the evil one (v. 19).

There is the certainty of relationship that any Christian can declare. "We know that we are of God." "Well," someone says, "what smug presumption. Imagine! That's the trouble with you Christians. You think you're so much better than everyone else. You think you're so superior!" No, not superior; just separated! Not better; just blessed—with a blessing that is open to anyone who wants to receive it. This is what makes Christians talk this way. We know, John says, that we are of God; that a fundamental separation has occurred between us and the world system to which we once belonged. The world, on the other hand, "lies in the power of the evil one." The whole world is going in a different direction.

You can see how consistently this touches our relation to the busy, complex world in which we live. We live in this world. We were born in it, we grew up in it. But now that we have become Christians we can no longer be like it, because a fundamental separation has occurred. No longer are we in the same relationship. We now see that the world lies in the power of the evil one. How many scriptures declare this! Remember in Ephesians, Paul says, "And you he made alive, when you were dead through the trespasses and sins in which you once walked, *following the course of this world,* following the prince of the power of the air" (Eph. 2:1,2). The truth about the world is that it is satanically controlled. Jesus called Satan, "The ruler of this world."

This fact is what is called in Scripture, "the offense of the cross." The world does not like to be told this. As long as you leave this truth out of the Christian proclamation, the world will welcome it and say it is wonderful. Worldlings love to hear the great and glorious declarations of the Christian gospel concerning God's love for man and his desire to make him into his image. There is no offense to that aspect of the gospel. When they hear that God loves this world, came into it, and gave himself in order that he might take human nature and mold it, fulfill it, bring it to perfection, and the experience of the full possibilities of its powers, they love that. But what they do not want to hear is the additional word that apart from coming to know Jesus Christ they are all in the grip of and under the control of certain unseen powers of darkness. If you leave this unsaid you will be popular. But if you tell the truth: that every individual is confronted with only two choices—either he is of God, or he is of the devil—you will discover that faces begin to grow cold and hard around you, and there is resistance to the gospel. People say, "I was attracted to it at first, but the more I look into it the less I like it. I think I'll go my own way." And they refuse to believe that what they fondly imagine is their "own" way is only the way of the devil.

The Liar's Work

Yet who can really doubt this statement when they look around them? The marks of the evil one are everywhere. If we believe what Jesus said about Satan, that he is a murderer and a liar, do we not see the signs of murder and lying everywhere? The history of the human race is one unending story of brutality, violence, murder, war, and death. That murderous passion is manifest in other ways as well. Think of the smog that chokes our cities, the filth that pollutes the waters, and the waste that destroys the beauty of the countryside so that, slowly but surely, this world is being turned into one vast garbage pile, threatening human existence. Think of the deceit that is everywhere in public life: the lying, the cheating, the twisting and distorting of truth, in homes and classrooms, in the Congress and our courts, and the highest offices of the land.

Think of the deceit that is prevalent in the thinking of people even in the everyday activities of life. A teenage boy and girl are in the back seat of a car. They have been led to believe that if they love each other, anything they do is all right. Anything is acceptable in the moral realm if they only really love each other. In the passion of the moment they feel as all couples do in these circumstances: no one ever loved like they love, no one is so misunderstood by others as they are, no one ever needed each other more than they do. In the deceitfulness of that feeling, that passion, they go on to give themselves fully to one another. Soon the inevitable results begin to appear in their lives. They begin to reap results in the hurt and damage they have thoughtlessly done to the lives of others. They must face the terrible injury they have done to others whom they profess to love, all because of their selfish overruling of the laws of God. And they reap results in their own personalities. As the apostle Paul put it, they "receive in their own personalities the due penalty of their errors."

Why does this happen? It is the work of the liar, the deceiver, the one who makes sordid things look beautiful. "The whole world lies in the power of the evil one," and that power cannot be broken by merely telling people the pickle they are in. A number of decades ago a prominent Christian lawyer named Philip Mauro wrote a book called *Man's Day* in which he carefully described from the point of view of the Scriptures the civilization of this modern day. Among other things, he said these words:

Among the strong delusions of these times there is none stronger than that Man's Day is a day of glorious achievement, successive triumphs, and continuous progress and that by the forces operating in it mankind is eventually to be brought to the condition of universal blessedness and contentment.

Notice, he called this all a delusion. Then he went on to say,

> The writer knows full well that those who are under the influence of this delusion cannot be freed from it by arguments, however cogent; or by statistics showing the appalling increase of crime, accidents, suicides, and insanity; or by the open and flagrant manifestations of corruption, lawlessness, and profligacy. To all these appeals they resolutely close their ears and eyes, not willing to recognize the real drift and certain end of what is called civilization.

The only answer is the Christian message, the proclamation that a Stronger One has come who binds the strong man and sets his goods free. Here is a message which can actually set men free from the delusions of a world which lies helplessly deceived by the wicked one. By God's grace we Christians can say, "we are of God." It is not superiority that says that, it is gratitude.

> And we know that the Son of God has come and has given us understanding, to know him who is true; and we are in him who is true, in his Son Jesus Christ. This is the true God and eternal life. Little children, keep yourselves from idols (vv. 20,21).

Notice how many times the word "true" occurs. ". . . to know him who is true; and we are in him who is true. . . . This is the true God and eternal life." The word "true" refers to reality. Here is the great rock upon which everything rests. Our faith does not rest upon men's guesses, not upon those erudite explorations of human knowledge called philosophy, not on clever ideas, or untested theories. It rests solidly upon the great events of God's actions in history. It rests on facts.

There is a historical process here. "The Son of God came," John says. We saw him, we felt him, we lived with him. We can testify in every possible way that the Son of God came in the historical process of time. Further, the practical result of that is, "he gave us a new understanding." We began to see life as it really is. He stripped it of its veils, took away its illusions, dispelled the mists and vagueness which cause men to grope through life like blind men. He clarified life, he gave us an understanding, he told us what was true. The glorious result that follows is, "we are in him who is true." We not only know him, we live in him. We are part of his life. We share his thinking, we have the mind of Christ.

What tremendous privileges! How far we have come, how much we have, how tremendous are these great, unshakable, fundamental, foundational truths on which we rest our faith. The glory of Christ's love and his comfort, the warmth of his presence and his peace in our hearts—"this," John says, "is the true God." We are in his Son Jesus Christ, therefore we are "in him." This is the true God and therefore, eternal life—abundant and continual life.

Can you think of anything better than that? What does man aim for but abundant and continual life? That is the goal and purpose of everything that takes place on this planet. It all is an attempt to discover and appropriate abundant and continual life. But this, the apostle John declares, is given to us in Christ. This is the true God and eternal life.

Substitute Gods

No wonder he closes with this final warning. "Little children, keep yourselves from idols." Do not go off to something else. Do not give your attention, your interest, your time, or your energy to anything less than this.

What is an idol, after all? Well, it is a substitute god. A god is whatever you give your time, your energy, and your money to; it is what you live for, what you get excited about, what enthuses you. What is it with you? Is it Jesus Christ—or is it something else?

In various parts of the ancient world there are many temples dedicated to idols. In every place a certain god had been enthroned in the temple and worshiped there— Apollo, Venus, Bacchus, Zeus. It suddenly struck me, after returning from a trip to see these places, that although they have been abandoned, the worship of the god has not ceased. We have changed the names, but the gods, the idols, are exactly the same.

There is the worship of Narcissus, the god who fell in love with himself. Is this not perhaps the supreme god of mankind? The idea constantly set forth is that man is so clever, he can do so many things. Yet we deny the continual evidence of our senses that the world is crumbling to pieces around us. The manifestations of it find expression in such devilish things as the worship of race or country. I am appalled at the number of Christians who worship the United States, who identify Americanism with the gospel of Jesus Christ, and worship it.

We have the worship of Bacchus, the god of pleasure, the god of wine, women, and song. We see the worship of Venus, the goddess of love, enthroned in Hollywood and all that Hollywood stands for. There is Apollo, the god of physical beauty, and Minerva, the goddess of science. Everywhere we have enthroned science. But John says these things will destroy you; they will rob you of what God has for you. "Little children, watch that you do not drift off into the worship that the world around you is constantly engaged in. Do not let these things become important in your life, for God has set you free that you might live as God intended man to live."

What makes you enthusiastic? To what do you give your money? What are you saving up for now? What is it that you regard as supremely important? It is with this question that John closes his Epistle. There has been a fundamental separation between us and the world. We died with Christ and are risen with him. We can no longer go on with the world and its ways. There must be a change. We can mix with worldly people and love them. We must be friends with them, and not separate ourselves from them. But we cannot think as they do. We cannot evalute things as they do any longer. We cannot follow the same urges or seek the same goals. We cannot accept the same standards. There is a difference: we have been separated from the power of darkness; now "we are of God." Therefore let us keep ourselves from idols.

So John ends his letter, emphasizing once again that the only safe place in a troubled, deceiving world is close by the Savior's side, in daily intimate fellowship with him.